A Warrior's Sky

A Warrior's Sky

Two Accounts of Aerial Combat During the First World War in Europe by American Pilots

ILLUSTRATED

High Adventure
James Norman Hall

War Birds
John MacGavock Grider

A Warrior's Sky
Two Accounts of Aerial Combat During the First World War in Europe by American Pilots
ILLUSTRATED
High Adventure
by James Norman Hall
War Birds
by John MacGavock Grider

FIRST EDITION

First published under the titles
High Adventure
and
War Birds

Leonaur is an imprint of Oakpast Ltd

Copyright in this form © 2017 Oakpast Ltd

ISBN: 978-1-78282-606-4 (hardcover)
ISBN: 978-1-78282-607-1 (softcover)

http://www.leonaur.com

Publisher's Notes
The views expressed in this book are not necessarily those of the publisher.

Contents

High Adventure 7

War Birds 159

High Adventure

THE AUTHOR

Contents

Introduction	13
The Franco-American Corps	21
Penguins	33
By the Route of the Air	45
At G. D. E.	63
Our First Patrol	79
A Balloon Attack	104
Brought Down	120
One Hundred Hours	128
"Lonely as a Cloud"	136
"Mais Oui, Mon Vieux!"	141
The Camouflaged Cows	144
Cafard	150

To Sergent-Pilote Douglas MacMonagle
killed in combat near Verdun
September 25, 1917

Captain Guynemer, "The Ace of Aces"

Introduction

When the history of America's participation in the Great War is written, the earliest chapter should be given to a record of the services of the American volunteers who came to France while our country was still neutral. Animated by the finest spirit of patriotism, believing with all their hearts in the justice of the Allied cause, many young men joined the armies of France and England, and among them those who have since become pilots in the Escadrille Lafayette and the Lafayette Flying Corps. I have been associated with this group of volunteer aviators from the very beginning. I have examined every candidate medically and morally. After their acceptance in the corps I have kept their interests at heart, and my feeling toward them is almost a paternal one.

Much has already been written of Chapman, Kiffen Rockwell, Prince, McConnell, McMonagle, Chadwick, Genet, Hoskier, Campbell, to speak only of a few of those who have met glorious deaths; and of those pilots, still living, still taking a splendid part in the aerial battles along the Western Front. To the example set by the American volunteers, perhaps more than to any other cause, was due the awakening of the national soul of America, the realisation that this war is not a local conflict between European nations, but a world-struggle between the forces of Good and Evil.

William Thaw, Kiffen Rockwell, and Victor Chapman joined the Foreign Legion at the beginning of the war. They were infantrymen before they became aviators in the French service. (So, too, were William Dugan, Robert Soubiran, and other men who were later to join the Franco-American Flying Corps). Norman Prince had already flown in America.

After some delay these four men were sent to the French aviation schools, soon joined by Cowdin, Bert Hall, Masson, and our future "ace," Raoul Lufbery. They were distributed in various French *escadrilles*.

Thaw and Prince dreamed of a squadron of American pilots, which would be grouped together at the front, but for some time this suggestion met with no favour on the part of the French military authorities.

In the meantime, the American pilots were being trained in the French schools. The idea came to several of us that this grouping of Americans at the front could and should be accomplished.

M. de Sillac, whose position in the Ministry of Foreign Affairs peculiarly fitted him for approaching the Minister of War, was taking active steps to bring this about, and at the same time, and quite independently of him, whilst I was helping in the organization of the American Ambulance, I was dreaming of a *squadrilla* of American volunteers who would express their sympathy for France in a material form. I believed that these boys were to be but the vanguard of other great hosts that would come from America someday.

In the spring of 1915, Prince, M. de Sillac, and myself met at M. de Sillac's office, Thaw being heartily in accord with us, but obliged to remain on duty at the front. The plans of the future American *squadrilla* were then drawn up.

This grouping together of Americans at the front in a fighting unit, brought up a delicate question of international law, and in the face of America's jealous neutrality, the French Minister of War did not seem inclined to sanction this proposition.

It looked as though we should fail, when M. de Sillac arranged a luncheon at Senator Menier's home, to which were invited: General Hirschauer, then head of French aviation; Colonel Bouttieux, his assistant; Léon Bourgeois, French Minister of State; our ex-Ambassador, Robert Bacon; Dr. William White, of Philadelphia; and M. de Sillac, and myself.

Robert Bacon and General Hirschauer discussed the matter fully, and the conclusion was that there existed no international law which forbade Americans from enlisting individually in a foreign army—as long as the recruiting was not carried out in America.

General Hirschauer promised to give orders immediately that the various American aviators then in the French Army should be grouped together in an *escadrille* commanded by a French captain; it was to be called the "*Escadrille Americaine*" (officially Escadrille N. 124), a name which we shall see later led to a diplomatic incident.

Now that we had succeeded in forming a squadron, it was necessary to appoint a committee and to obtain the necessary funds for monthly allowances, uniforms, distribution of prizes, printing of pamphlets, etc.

The financial question was quickly solved. I called with Robert Bacon on Mr. and Mrs. W. K. Vanderbilt. We spoke with warmth of our plans. Our enthusiasm must have been contagious, for when I appealed for funds, Mrs. Vanderbilt walked to her desk and wrote out a check for five thousand dollars—and turning to her husband said: "Now, K., what will you do?" His check read, fifteen thousand dollars. With this sum in hand, it looked as though our dream was really coming true!

From that day to this, these generous people have never ceased to be the patron saints of the American boys, and have contributed to aviation alone, modestly as is their custom, what would be considered a small fortune.

The composition of the first *Escadrille* (*Escadrille Américaine*) was as follows—authority, letter of Minister of War, March 14, 1916:—

        Captain Thenault } French
        Lieutenant de Laage de Meux }
        Lieutenant William Thaw
        Sergeant Norman Prince
           "   Elliott Cowdin
           "   W. Bert Hall
        Corporal Victor Chapman
           "   Kiffen Rockwell
           "   James McConnell

Raoul Lufbery came very soon after this, followed by Charles C. Johnson and Clyde Balsley, who, for several weeks, were attached to the aerial guard of Paris. Balsley was very severely wounded in an air battle soon after joining the Squadron. By great presence of mind, he succeeded in planing down to the French lines. He was in hospital for more than a year, during which time his life was frequently despaired of. Following the first volunteers came Dudley Hill, Masson, Pavelka, Robert Rockwell, and, as they completed their training, other Americans who have done splendid service for the Allied cause and who have added steadily to the prestige of the Corps.

No sooner had this Squadron been sent to the front than it took a vigorous part in aerial activities, as the following report sets forth:—

> The American pilots who have enlisted in the French Army are already distinguishing themselves by a series of exploits. The

first "*Escadrille*" is composed of only seven Americans, and here are the results of the last seven days:—

Sergeant Elliott Cowdin attacked twelve German planes and brought one down in our lines (Military Medal).

Sergeant Kiffen Rockwell a few days later brought down a L.V.G. enemy plane.

The next day Bert Hall used his machine gun on another airplane which fell in flames.

Finally, two days later, Lieutenant William Thaw destroyed a Fokker.

It is not strange that the pilots of the *Escadrille Américaine* gained renown both in France and in America and were bitterly hated by the Germans.

The following letter of Victor Chapman, written on May 19, 1916, from Luxeuil, gives a vivid picture of the Squadron's activities:—

Dear M. de Sillac:—

The efficiency of the Escadrille has been temporarily reduced by several breakages of the unavoidable variety. Nevertheless, six of us are going to Bar-le-Duc tomorrow, where the unit will join us as soon as possible. On the 17th, two days ago, Thaw played a Boche in the most approved style over the Forest of Carspach. Dodging to the right, then to the left, he ended under the enemy's tail, where he emptied his machine gun. The *bureau de tir* at Souane telephoned and reported that all their observers saw the "*appareil ennemi regagnant ses lignes en paraissant bien touché. Il est piqué à mort.*"

Yesterday, May 18th, Kiffen Rockwell, finding himself above another L.V.G., east of Thann, fell upon him. The *mitrailleur* emptied a multitude of cartridges on Rockwell as he sped down, but when the latter, from a distance of thirty metres, gave one "*rafale*" (four or five shots), the *mitrailleur* threw up his hands and fell over on the pilot who likewise seemed to crumple up. Rockwell made a steep bank to avoid hitting the machine, but saw it fall smoking to the ground, where it continued to burn. The artillery signalled the fight and say the machine fell in the German trenches, vicinity of Uffhulz.

This morning, May 19th, two German machines in revenge came over the field before sunrise (3 o'clock and 3.30). I gave chase to the first, but lost him in the haze (I forgot to say one of

his bombs missed our machines on the ground by ten metres). Thaw gave chase to the second one, overtook him at thirty-two hundred metres near the lines, exchanged several volleys at close range, but, with no extra height to manoeuvre with, was forced to desist on account of his machine gun jamming. Rockwell and myself are proposed for sergeant, he being also proposed for the *Médaille*. Thaw is also to be cited when the reports come in.
    Yours sincerely,
              Victor E. Chapman.

 In the meanwhile, a committee was appointed to handle the affairs of the Franco-American Flying Corps, which later became known as the Lafayette Flying Corps.
 This committee was composed as follows :—

Honorary President, W. K. Vanderbilt.
President, J. de Sillac.
Vice-President, Physician, Dr. Edmund Gros.
Director for America, Frederick Allen.
American representatives, Henry Earle, Geo. F. Tyler,
 Philip Carroll, Frank J. McClure.
Treasurers, Laurence Slade, Colonel Bently Mott.
Assistant treasurer, Arthur G. Evans.
Bankers, Bonbright & Co.
Secretary, Mrs. Georgia Ovington.

 It was decided to give a monthly allowance of one hundred *francs*, later increased to two hundred *francs*, to each American volunteer.
 Prizes were distributed as follows :—

Francs	1500 ($300) for Legion of Honour
"	1000 ($200) for Military Medal
"	500 ($100) for War Cross
"	200 ($ 50) for each citation (palm)

 This last item became a very important financial obligation which we were glad to meet.
 For instance, the members of the Escadrille Lafayette alone have received over forty citations. Lufbery has brought down seventeen German machines—he ranks sixth in the list of living "aces" in the French Army, and wears the Legion of Honour, Military Medal, the War Cross with sixteen palm leaves, and the English Military Cross.
 Thaw has the Legion of Honour, Military Medal, and War Cross

with four palms, etc.

The greatest honour which can come to an individual or to a fighting unit is to be mentioned in the French daily official *communiqué*. The *Escadrille Américaine* has been mentioned several times, this leading early to a diplomatic incident which I learned of as follows :—

On November 16, 1916, I was paying a visit to the *Escadrille* when Colonel Barrès, chief of French aviation, at General Headquarters, walked into the tent. He said that he was sorry, but in the future the *Escadrille* could no longer be known as the *Escadrille Américaine*, but should henceforth be designated by its official military number, N. 124.

He seemed reticent to give me an explanation, but I got this the next day at the Ministry of War. I learned that Bernstorff had protested to Washington that Americans were fighting on the French front—that the French *communiqué* contained the name, "*Escadrille Américaine*," and that these volunteer Americans pushed their brazenness to the point of having the head of a red Sioux Indian in full war paint depicted on their machines!

A few days afterwards I called at the Ministry of War and saw Captain Berthaud, who had always been a loyal friend to Americans. He told me that the name which they thought of applying to the *Escadrille* was "*Escadrille de Volontaires*." "Squadron of Volunteers" seemed to me such a colourless name that I protested, suggesting a name which could not lead to any diplomatic protest, "Lafayette Escadrille." Such is the origin of the title which has become celebrated, and which will be perpetuated through the war by being applied to the first American Squadron of our United States Air Service.

Attracted by the fame of the Lafayette Escadrille even before the United States entered the war, more than two hundred American volunteers have joined the Lafayette Flying Corps. Some have become pilots in the Lafayette Escadrille, to take the place of those who have fallen, others have served and are serving with equal brilliancy in various French *squadrillas*.

Over twenty have lost their lives, the majority having fallen in combat.

The names of Chapman, Rockwell, Prince, McConnell, Genet, Hoskier, Barclay, Chadwick, Biddle, McMonagle, Campbell, Walcott, Trinkard, Spencer, Benney, Tailer, Loughran, who died at the front, and of Dowd, Meeker, Hanford, Fowler, Starrett, Palmer, Grieb, who were killed before they could fight, will not be forgotten.

Walcott, Spencer, Benney, Tailer and Loughran were on the point of being taken over by the Air Service of their country when they died, and were still in the uniform of France which they honoured and glorified.

This brief outline is, in no sense, a history of the Lafayette *Squadrilla* and Lafayette Flying Corps. Much could be written of the wonderful exploits of these heroic pilots. They have paid a heavy toll, and many of them lie within the sound of the guns, side by side with the French soldiers whom they loved, and with whom they served.

They are not dead, their spirits still live, inviting us to higher ideals, nobler aspirations, and unwavering patriotism.

Major Edmund Gros
Air Service, A.E.F.

Paris, February 3, 1918

CHAPTER 1

The Franco-American Corps

It was on a cool, starlit evening, early in September, 1916, that I first met Drew of Massachusetts, and actually began my adventures as a prospective member of the Escadrille Américaine. We had sailed from New York by the same boat, had made our applications for enlistment in the Foreign Legion on the same day, without being aware of each other's existence; and in Paris, while waiting for our papers, we had gone, every evening, for dinner, to the same large and gloomy-looking restaurant in the neighbourhood of the Seine.

As for the restaurant, we frequented it, not assuredly because of the quality of the food. We might have dined better and more cheaply elsewhere. But there was an air of vanished splendour, of faded magnificence, about the place which, in the capital of a warring nation, appealed to both of us. Every evening the tables were laid with spotless linen and shining silver. The wineglasses caught the light from the tarnished chandeliers in little points of colour. At the dinner-hour, a half-dozen ancient serving-men silently took their places about the room. There was not a sound to be heard except the occasional far-off honk of a motor or the subdued clatter of dishes from the kitchens. The serving-men, even the tables and the empty chairs, seemed to be listening, to be waiting for the guests who never came.

Rarely were there more than a dozen diners-out during the course of an evening. There was something mysterious in these elaborate preparations, and something rather fine about them as well; but one thought, not without a touch of sadness, of the old days when there had been laughter and lights and music, sparkling wines and brilliant talk, and how those merrymakers had gone, many of them, long ago to the wars. As it happened on this evening, Drew and I were sitting at adjoining tables. Our common citizenship was our introduction, and after five minutes of talk, we learned of our common purpose in coming to France. I suppose that we must have eaten after making this latter discovery. I vaguely remember seeing our old waiter hobbling down a long *vista* of empty tables on his way to and from the kitchens. But if we thought of our food at all, it must have been in a purely mechanical way.

Drew can talk—by Jove, how the man can talk!—and he has the faculty of throwing the glamour of romance over the most commonplace adventures. Indeed, the difficulty which I am going to have in writing this narrative is largely due to this romantic influence of his. I might have succeeded in writing a plain tale, for I have kept my diary faithfully, from day to day, and can set down our adventures, such as they are, pretty much as they occurred. But Drew has bewitched me. He does not realise it, but he is a weaver of spells, and I am so enmeshed in his moonshine that I doubt if I shall be able to write of our experiences as they must appear to those of our comrades in the Franco-American Corps who remember them only through the medium of the revealing light of day.

Not one of these men, I am sure, would confess to so strange an immediate cause for joining the aviation service, as that related to me by Drew, as we sat over our coffee and cigarettes, on the evening of our first meeting. He had come to France, he said, with the intention of joining the *Légion Étrangère* as an infantryman. But he changed his mind, a few days after his arrival in Paris, upon meeting Jackson of the American Aviation Squadron, who was on leave after a service of six months at the front. It was all because of the manner in which Jackson looked at a Turkish rug. He told him of his adventures in the most matter-of-fact way. No heroics, nothing of that sort. He had not a glimmer of imagination, he said. But he had a way of looking at the floor which was "irresistible," which "fascinated him with the sense of height." He saw towns, villages, networks of trenches, columns of toy troops moving up ribbons of road—all in the patterns of a Turkish rug. And the next day, he was at the headquarters of the Franco-American Corps, in the Champs Élysées, making application for membership.

It is strange that we should both have come to France with so little of accurate knowledge of the corps, of the possibilities for enlistment, and of the nature of the requirements for the service. Our knowledge of it, up to the time of sailing, had been confined to a few brief references in the press. It was perhaps necessary that its existence should not be officially recognised in America, or its furtherance encouraged.

But it seemed to us at that time, that there must have been actual discouragement on the part of the Government at Washington. However, that may be, we wondered if others had followed clues so vague or a call so dimly heard.

This led to a discussion of our individual aptitudes for the service, and we made many comforting discoveries about each other. It is permissible to reveal them now, for the particular encouragement of others who, like ourselves at that time, may be conscious of deficiencies, and who may think that they have none of the qualities essential to the successful aviator. Drew had never been farther from the ground than the top of the Woolworth building. I had once taken a trip in a captive balloon. Drew knew nothing of motors, and had no more knowledge of mechanics than would enable him to wind a watch without breaking the mainspring. My ignorance in this respect was a fair match for his.

We were further handicapped for the French service by our lack of the language. Indeed, this seemed to be the most serious obstacle in the way to success. With a good general knowledge of the language it seemed probable that we might be able to overcome our other deficiencies. Without it, we could see no way to mastering the mechanical knowledge which we supposed must be required as a foundation for the training of a military pilot. In this connection, it may be well to say that we have both been handicapped from the beginning. We have had to learn, through actual experience in the air, and at risk to life and limb, what many of our comrades, both French and American, knew before they had ever climbed into an aeroplane. But it is equally true that scores of men become very excellent pilots with little or no knowledge of the mechanics of the business.

In so far as Drew and I were concerned, these were matters for the future. It was enough for us at the moment that our applications had been approved, our papers signed, and that tomorrow we were leaving for the École d'Aviation Militaire to begin our training. And so, after a long evening of pleasant talk and pleasanter anticipation of coming events, we left our restaurant and walked together through the silent streets to the Place de la Concorde. The great windy square was almost deserted. The monuments to the lost provinces bulked large in the dim lamplight. Two disabled soldiers hobbled across the bridge and disappeared in the deep shade of the avenue. Their service had been rendered, their sacrifices made, months ago. They could look about them now with a peculiar sense of isolation, and with, perhaps, a feeling of the futility of the effort they had made. Our adventures were all before us. Our hearts were light and our hopes high. As we stood by the obelisk, talking over plans for the morrow, we heard, high overhead, the faint hum of motors, and saw two lights, one green, one red, moving rapidly across the sky. A moment later the long, slender finger of a searchlight probed among little heaps of cloud, then, sweeping in a wide arc, revealed in striking outline the shape of a huge biplane circling over the sleeping city. It was one of the night guard of Paris.

On the following morning, we were at the Gare des Invalides with our luggage, a long half-hour before train-time. The luggage was absurdly bulky. Drew had two enormous suitcases and a bag, and I a steamer trunk and a family-size portmanteau. We looked so much the typical American tourists that we felt ashamed of ourselves, not because of our nationality, but because we revealed so plainly, to all the world military, our non-military antecedents. We bore the hallmark of fifty years of neutral aloofness, of fifty years of indifference to the business of national defence. What makes the situation amusing as a retrospect is the fact that we were traveling on third-class military passes, as befitted our rank as *élève-pilotes* and soldiers of the *deuxième classe*.

To our great discomfiture, a couple of *poilus* volunteered their services in putting our belongings aboard the train. Then we crowded into a third-class carriage filled with soldiers—*permissionnaires, blessés, réformés*, men from all corners of France and her colonies. Their uniforms were faded and weather-stained with long service. The stocks of their rifles were worn smooth and bright with constant usage, and their packs fairly stowed themselves upon their backs.

Drew and I felt uncomfortable in our smart civilian clothing. We looked too soft, too clean, too spick-and-span. We did not feel that we belonged there. But in a whispered conversation we comforted ourselves with the assurance that if ever America took her rightful stand with the Allies, in six months after the event, hundreds of thousands of American boys would be lugging packs and rifles with the same familiarity of use as these French *poilus*. They would become equally good soldiers, and soon would have the same community of experience, of dangers and hardships shared in common, which make men comrades and brothers in fact as well as in theory.

By the time we had reached our destination we had persuaded ourselves into a much more comfortable frame of mind. There we piled into a cab, and soon we were rattling over the cobblestones, down a long, sunlit avenue in the direction of B———. It was late of a mild afternoon when we reached the summit of a high plateau and saw before us the barracks and hangars of the *École d'Aviation*. There was not a breath of air stirring. The sun was just sinking behind a bank of crimson cloud. The earth was already in shadow, but high overhead the light was caught and reflected from the wings of scores of *avions* which shone like polished bronze and silver. We saw the long lines of Blériot monoplanes, like huge dragon-flies, and as pretty a sight in the air as heart could wish. Farther to the left, we recognised Farman biplanes, floating battleships in comparison with the Blériots, and twin-motor Caudrons, much more graceful and alert of movement.

But, most wonderful of all to us then, we saw a strange, new *avion,*— a biplane, small, trim, with a body like a fish. To see it in flight was to be convinced for all time that man has mastered the air, and has outdone the birds in their own element. Never was swallow more consciously joyous in swift flight, never eagle so bold to take the heights or so quick to reach them. Drew and I gazed in silent wonder, our bodies jammed tightly into the cab-window, and our heads craned upward. We did not come back to earth until our ancient, earth-creeping conveyance brought up with a jerk, and we found ourselves in front of a gate marked "*École d'Aviation Militaire de B*———."

After we had paid the cabman, we stood in the road, with our mountain of luggage heaped about us, waiting for something to happen. A moment later a window in the administration building was thrown open and we were greeted with a loud and not over-musical chorus of

"Oh, say, can you see by the dawn's early light—"

It all came from one throat, belonging to a chap in leathers, who came down the drive to give us welcome.

"Spotted you *toute suite*" he said. "You can tell Americans at six hundred yards by their hats. How's things in the States? Do you think we're coming in?"

We gave him the latest budget of home news, whereupon he offered to take us over to the barracks. When he saw our luggage he grinned.

"Some equipment, believe me! *Attendez un peu* while I commandeer a battalion of Annamites to help us carry it, and we'll be on our way."

The Annamites, from Indo-China, who are quartered at the camp for guard and fatigue duty, came back with him about twenty strong, and we started in a long procession to the barracks. Later, we took

The Blériot monoplane Division

a vindictive pleasure in witnessing the beluggaged arrival of other Americans, for in nine cases out of ten they came as absurdly over-equipped as did we.

Our barracks, one of many built on the same pattern, was a long, low wooden building, weather-stained without and whitewashed within. It had accommodation for about forty beds. One end of the room was very manifestly American. There was a phonograph on the table, baseball equipment piled in one corner, and the walls were covered with cartoons and pictures clipped from American periodicals. The other end was as evidently French, in the frugality and the neatness of its furnishings. The American end of the room looked more homelike, but the French end more military. Near the centre, where the two nations joined, there was a very harmonious blending of these characteristics.

Drew and I were delighted with all this. We were glad that we were not to live in an exclusively American barracks, for we wanted to learn French; but more than this, we wanted to live with Frenchmen on terms of barrack-room familiarity.

By the time we had given in our papers at the captain's office and had passed the hasty preliminary examination of the medical officer, it was quite dark. Flying for the day was over, and lights gleamed cheerily from the barrack-room windows. As we came down the principal street of the camp, we heard the strains of "Waiting for the Robert E. Lee," to a gramophone accompaniment, issuing from the *chambre des Américains*.

See them shuffle along,
Oh, ma honey babe,
Hear that music and song.

It gave us the home feeling at once. Frenchmen and Americans were singing together, the Frenchmen in very quaint English, but hitting off the syncopated time as though they had been born and brought up to it as we Americans have.

Over in one corner, a very informal class in French-English pronunciation was at work. Apparently, this was tongue-twisters' night. "*Heureux*" was the challenge from the French side, and "*Hooroo*" the nearest approach to a pronunciation on the part of the Americans, with many more or less remote variations on this theme. An American, realising how difficult it is for a Frenchman to get his tongue between his teeth, counter-challenged with "Father, you are withered with age." The result, as might have been expected, was a series of hissing sounds of *z*, whereupon there was an answering howl of derision from all the Americans. Up and down the length of the room there were little groups of two and three, chatting together in combinations of Franco-American which must have caused all deceased professors of modern languages to spin like midges in their graves. And throughout all this before-supper merriment, one could catch the feeling of good-comradeship which, so far as my experience goes, is always prevalent whenever Frenchmen and Americans are gathered together.

At the *ordinaire*, at supper-time, we saw all of the *élevè-pilotes* of the school, with the exception of the non-commissioned officers, who have their own mess. To Drew and me, but newly come from remote America, it was a most interesting gathering. There were about one hundred and twenty-five in all, including eighteen Americans. The large majority of the Frenchmen had already been at the front in other branches of army service. There were artillerymen, infantrymen, marines,—in training for the naval air-service,—cavalrymen, all wearing the uniforms of the arm to which they originally belonged. No one was dressed in a uniform which distinguished him as an aviator; and upon making inquiry, I found that there is no official dress for this branch of the service.

During his period of training in aviation, and even after receiving his military brevet, a pilot continues to wear the dress of his former service, plus the wings on the collar, and the star-and-wings insignia on his right breast. This custom does not make for the fine uniform appearance of the men of the British Royal Flying Corps, but it gives a picturesqueness of effect which is, perhaps, ample recompense. As for the Americans, they follow individual tastes, as we learned later. Some of them, with an eye to colour, salute the sun in the red trousers and black tunic of the artilleryman. Others choose more sober shades, various French blues, with the thin orange aviation stripe running down the seams of the trousers. All this in reference to the dress uniform. At the camp most of the men wear leathers, or a combination of leathers and the grey-blue uniform of the French *poilu*, which is issued to all Americans at the time of their enlistment.

We had a very excellent supper of soup, followed by a savoury roast of meat, with mashed potatoes and lentils. Afterward, cheese and beer. I was slightly discomfited physically on learning that the beef was horse-meat, but Drew convinced me that it was absurd to let old scruples militate against a healthy appetite. In 1870 the citizens of

France ate *ragoût de chat* with relish. Furthermore, the roast was of so delicious a flavour and so closely resembled the finest cuts of beef, that it was easy to persuade one's self that it was beef, after all.

After the meal, to our great surprise, every one cleaned his dishes with huge pieces of bread. Such waste seemed criminal in a country beleaguered by submarines, in its third year of war, and largely dependent for its food-supply on the farm labour of women and children.

We should not have been surprised if it had been only the Americans who indulged in this wasteful dish-cleansing process; but the Frenchmen did it, too. When I remarked upon this to one of my American comrades, a Frenchman, sitting opposite, said :—

Pardon, monsieur, but I must tell you what we Frenchmen are. We are very economical when it is for ourselves, for our own families and purses, that we are saving. But when it is the government which pays the bill, we do not care. We do not have to pay directly and so we waste, we throw away. We are so careful at home, all of our lives, that this is a little pleasure for us.

I have had this same observation made to me by so many Frenchmen since that time, that I believe there must be a good deal of truth in it.

After supper, all of the Americans adjourned for coffee to Ciret's, a little *café* in the village which nestles among the hills not far from the camp. The *café* itself was like any one of thousands of French provincial restaurants. There was a great dingy common room, with a sanded brick floor, and faded streamers of tricolour paper festooned in curious patterns from the smoky ceiling. The kitchen was clean, and filled with the appetizing odour of good cooking. Beyond it was another, inner room, "*toujours réservée à mes Américains*" as M. Ciret, the fat, genial patron continually asserted. Here we gathered around a large circular table, pipes and cigarettes were lighted, and, while the others talked, Drew and I listened and gathered impressions.

For a time, the conversation did not become general, and we gathered up odds and ends of it from all sides. Then it turned to the reasons which had prompted various members of the group to come to France, the topic, above all others, which Drew and I most wanted to hear discussed. It seemed to me, as I listened, that we Americans closely resemble the British in our sensitive fear of any display of fine personal feeling. We will never learn to examine our emotions with anything but suspicion. If we are prompted to a course of action by generous impulses, we are anxious that others shall not be let into the secret. And so it was that of all the reasons given for offering their services to France, the first and most important was the last to be acknowledged, and even then it was admitted by some with a reluctance nearly akin to shame. There was no man there who was not ready and willing to give his life, if necessary, for the Allied cause, because he believed in it; but the admission could hardly have been dragged from him by wild horses.

But the adventure of the life, the peculiar fascination of it—that was a thing which might be discussed without reserve, and the men talked of it with a willingness which was most gratifying to Drew and me, curious as we were about the life we were entering. They were all in the flush of their first enthusiasms. They were daily enlarging their conceptions of distance and height and speed. They talked a new language and were developing a new cast of mind. They were like children who had grown up overnight, whose horizons had been immeasurably broadened in the twinkling of an eye. They were still keenly conscious of the change which was upon them, for they were but fledgling aviators. They were just finding their wings. But as I listened, I thought of the time which must come soon, when the air, as the sea, will be filled with stately ships, and how the air-service will develop its own peculiar type of men, and build up about them its own laws and its own traditions.

As we walked back through the straggling village street to the camp, I tried to convey to Drew something of the new vision which had come to me during the evening. I was aglow with enthusiasm and hoped to strike an answering spark from him. But all that I was thinking and feeling then he had thought and felt long before. I am sure that he had already experienced, in imagination, every thrill, every keen joy, and every sudden sickening fear which the life might have in store for him. For this reason, I forgave him for his rather bored manner of answering to my mood, and the more willingly because he was full of talk about a strange illusion which he had had at the restaurant. During a moment of silence, he had heard a clatter of hoof-beats in the village street. (I had heard them too. Someone rode by furiously.) Well, Drew said that he almost jumped from his seat, expecting M. Ciret to throw open the door and shout, "The British are coming!" He actually believed for a second or two that it was the year 1775, and that he was sitting in one of the old roadside inns of Massachusetts. The illusion was perfect, he said.

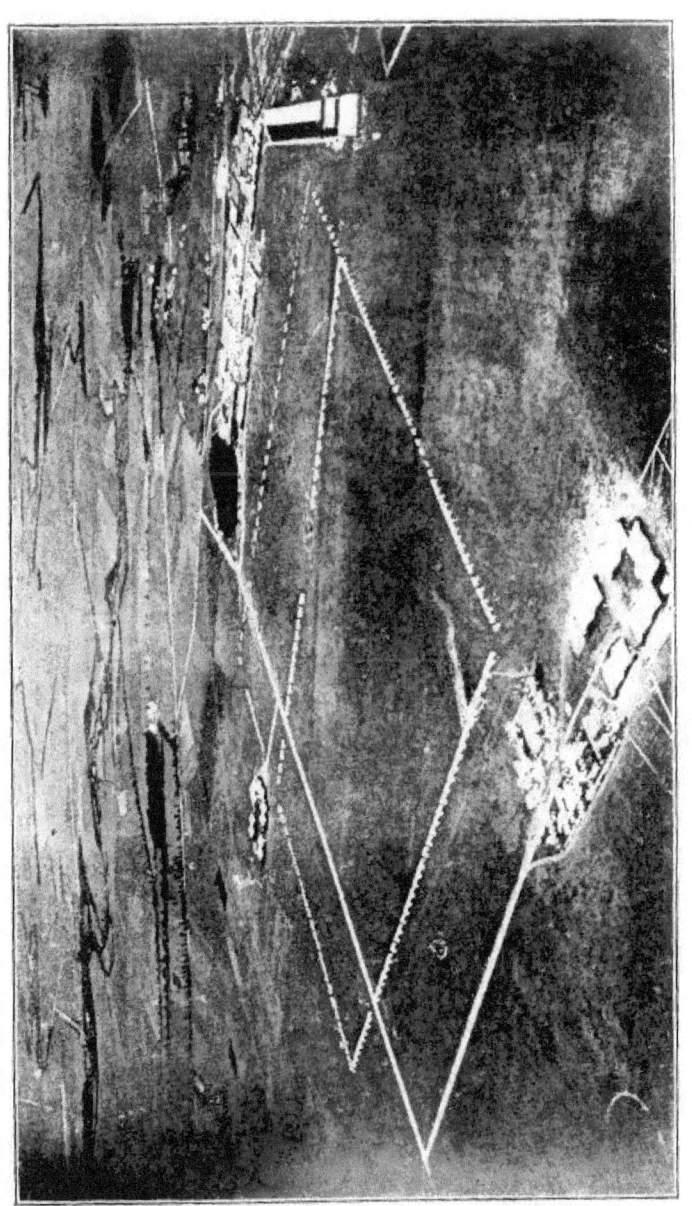

A French Aviation School
The broken lines are aeroplanes on parade

Now, why—etc., etc. At another time I should have been much interested; but in the presence of new and splendid realities I could not summon any enthusiasm for illusions. Nevertheless, I should have had to listen to him indefinitely, had it not been for an event which cut short all conversation and ended our first day at the École *d'Aviation* in a truly spectacular manner.

Suddenly we heard the roar of motors just over the barracks, and, at the same time, the siren sounded the alarm in a series of prolonged, wailing shrieks. Some belated pilot was still in the air. We rushed out to the field just as the flares were being lighted and placed on the ground in the shape of an immense T, with the cross-bar facing in the direction from which the wind was coming. By this time the hum of motors was heard at a great distance, but gradually it increased in volume and soon the light of the flares revealed the machine circling rapidly over the *piste*. I was so much absorbed in watching it manoeuvre for a landing that I did not see the crowd scattering to safe distances. I heard many voices shouting frantic warnings, and so ran for it, but, in my excitement, directly within the line of descent of the machine. I heard the wind screaming through the wires, a terrifying sound to the novice, and glancing hurriedly over my shoulder, I saw what appeared to be a monster of gigantic proportions, almost upon me. It passed within three metres of my head and landed just beyond.

When at last I got to sleep, after a day filled with interesting incidents, Paul Revere pursued me relentlessly through the mazes of a weird and horrible dream. I was on foot, and shod with lead-soled boots. He was in a huge, twin-motor Caudron and flying at a terrific pace, only a few metres from the ground. I can see him now, as he leaned far out over the hood of his machine, an aviator's helmet set atilt over his powdered wig, and his eyes glowing like coals through his goggles. He was waving two lighted torches and shouting, "The British are coming! The British are coming!" in a voice strangely like Drew's.

CHAPTER 2

Penguins

Having simple civilian notions as to the amount of time necessary for dressing, Drew and I rose with the sound of the bugle on the following morning. We had promised each other that we would begin our new life in true soldier style, and so we reluctantly hurried to the wash-house, where we shaved in cold water, washed after a fashion, and then hurried back to the unheated barrack-room. We felt refreshed, morally and physically, but our heroic example seemed to make no impression upon our fellow aviators, whether French or American. Indeed, not one of them stirred until ten minutes before time for the morning *appel*, when there was a sudden upheaval of blankets down the entire length of the room.

It was as though the patients in a hospital ward had been inoculated with some wonderful, instantaneous-health-giving virus. Men were jumping into boots and trousers at the same time, and running to and from the wash-house, buttoning their shirts and drying their faces as they ran. It must have taken months of experiment to perfect the system whereby every one remained in bed until the last possible moment. They professed to be very proud of it, but it was clear that they felt more at ease when Drew and I, after a week of heroic, early-morning resolves, abandoned our daily test of courage. We are all Doctor Johnsons at heart.

It was a crisp, calm morning—an excellent day for flying. Already the mechanicians were bringing out the machines and lining them up in front of the hangars, in preparation for the morning work, which began immediately after *appel*. Drew and I had received notice that we were to begin our training at once. Solicitous fellow countrymen had warned us to take with us all our flying clothes. We were by no means to forget our goggles, and the fur-lined boots which are worn over ordinary boots as a protection against the cold.

Innocently, we obeyed all instructions to the letter. The absurdity of our appearance will be appreciated only by airmen. Novices begin their training, at a Blériot monoplane school, in Penguins—low-powered machines with clipped wings, which are not capable of leaving the ground. We were dressed as we would have no occasion to be dressed until we should be making sustained flights at high altitudes. Everyone, Frenchmen and Americans alike, had a good laugh at our expense, but it was one in which we joined right willingly; and one kind-hearted *adjudant-moniteur*, in order to remove what discomfiture we may have felt, told us, through an interpreter, that he was sure we would become good air-men. The *très bon pilote* could be distinguished, in embryo, by the way he wore his goggles.

The beginners' class did not start work with the others, owing to the fact that the Penguins, driven by unaccustomed hands, covered a vast amount of ground in their rolling sorties back and forth across the field. Therefore, Drew and I had leisure to watch the others, and to see in operation the entire scheme by means of which France trains her combat pilots for the front. Exclusive of the Penguin, there were seven classes, graded according to their degree of advancement. These, in their order, were the rolling class (a second-stage Penguin class, in which one still kept on the ground, but in machines of higher speed); the first flying class—short hops across the field at an altitude of two or three metres; the second flying class, where one learned to mount to from thirty to fifty metres, and to make landings without the use of the motor; *tour de piste (a)*—flights about the aerodrome in a forty-five horse-power Blériot; *tour de piste (b)*—similar flights in a fifty horse-power machine; the spiral class, and the brevet class.

Our reception committee of the day before volunteered his services as guide, and took us from one class to another, making comments upon the nature of the work of each in a bewildering combination of English and Americanized French. I understood but little of his explanation, although later I was able to appreciate his French translation of some of our breezy Americanisms. But explanation was, for the most part, unnecessary. We could see for ourselves how the prospective pilot advanced from one class to another, becoming accustomed to machines of higher and higher power, "growing his wings" very gradually, until at last he reached the spiral class, where he learned to make landings at a given spot and without the use of his motor, from an altitude of from eight hundred to one thousand metres, los-

PENGUIN

BRINGING HOME THE BUS

ing height in volplanes and serpentines. The final tests for the military brevet were two cross-country flights of from two hundred to three hundred kilometres, with landings during each flight, at three points, two short voyages of sixty kilometres each, and an hour flight at a minimum altitude of two thousand metres.

With all the activities of the school taking place at once, we were as excited as two boys seeing their first three-ring circus. We scarcely knew which way to turn in our anxiety to miss nothing. But my chief concern, in anticipation, had been this: how were English-speaking *élèves-pilotes* to overcome the linguistic handicap? My uneasiness was set at rest on this first morning, when I saw how neatly most of the difficulties were overcome. Many of the Americans had no knowledge of French other than that which they had acquired since entering the French service, and this, as I have already hinted, had no great utilitarian value.

An interpreter had been provided for them through the generosity and kindness of the Franco-American Committee in Paris; but it was impossible for him to be everywhere at once, and much was left to their own quickness of understanding and to the ingenuity of the *moniteurs*. The latter, being French, were eloquent with their gestures. With the additional aid of a few English phrases which they had acquired from the Americans, and the simplest kind of French, they had little difficulty in making their instructions clear. Both of us felt much encouraged as we listened, for we could understand them very well.

As for the business of flying, as we watched it from below, it seemed the safest and simplest thing in the world. The machines left the ground so easily, and mounted and descended with such sureness of movement, that I was impatient to begin my training. I believed that I could fly at once, after a few minutes of preliminary instruction, without first going through with all the tedious rolling along the ground in low-powered machines. But before the morning's work was finished, I revised my opinion. Accidents began to happen, the first one when one of the "old family cuckoos," as the rolling machines were disdainfully called, showed a sudden burst of old-time speed and left the ground in an alarming manner.

It was evident that the man who was driving it, taken completely by surprise, had lost his head, and was working the controls erratically. First he swooped upward, then dived, tipping dangerously on one wing. In this sudden emergency he had quite forgotten his newly acquired knowledge. I wondered what I would do in such a strait, when one must think with the quickness and sureness of instinct. My heart was in my mouth, for I felt certain that the man would be killed. As for the others who were watching, no one appeared to be excited. A *moniteur* near me said, "*Oh, là là! Il est perdu!*" in a mild voice. The whole affair happened so quickly that I was not able to think myself into a similar situation before the end had come. At the last, the machine made a quick swoop downward, from a height of about fifty metres, then careened upward, tipped again, and diving sidewise, struck the ground with a sickening rending crash, the motor going at full speed. For a moment it stood, tail in air; then slowly the balance was lost, and it fell, bottom up, and lay silent.

An enterprising moving-picture company would have given a great deal of money to film that accident. It would have provided a splendid dramatic climax to a war drama of high adventure. Civilian audiences would have watched in breathless, awe-struck silence; but at a military school of aviation it was a different matter. "*Oh, là là! Il est perdu!*" adequately gauges the degree of emotional interest taken in the incident. At the time I was surprised at this apparent callousness, but I understood it better when I had seen scores of such accidents occur, and had watched the pilots, as in this case, crawl out from the wreckage, and walk sheepishly, and a little shaken, back to their classes. Although the machines were usually badly wrecked, the pilots were rarely severely hurt. The landing chassis of a Blériot is so strong that it will break the force of a very heavy fall, and the motor, being in front, strikes the ground first instead of pinning the pilot beneath it.

To anticipate a little, in more than four months of training at the Blériot school there was not a single fatality, although as many as eleven machines were wrecked in the course of one working day, and rarely less than two or three. There were so many accidents as to convince me that Blériot training for novices is a mistake from the economic point of view. The upkeep expense is vastly greater than in double-command biplane schools, where the student pilot not only learns to fly in a much more stable machine, but makes all his early flights in company with a *moniteur* who has his own set of controls and may immediately correct any mistakes in handling.

But France is not guided by questions of expense in her training of *pilotes de chasse*, and opinion appears to be that single-command monoplane training is to be preferred for the airman who is to be a combat pilot. Certain it is that men have greater confidence in themselves when they learn to fly alone from the beginning; and the Blériot, which requires the most delicate and sensitive handling, offers excellent preliminary schooling for the Nieuport and Spad, the fast and high-powered biplanes which are the *avions de chasse* above the French lines.

A spice of interest was added to the morning's thrills when an American, not to be outdone by his French compatriot, wrecked a machine so completely that it seemed incredible that he could have escaped without serious injury. But he did, and then we witnessed the amusing spectacle of an American, who had no French at all, explaining through the interpreter just how the accident had happened. I saw his *moniteur*, who knew no English, grin in a relieved kind of way when the American crawled out from under the wreckage. The reception committee whispered to me, "This is Pourquoi, the best bawler-out we've got. '*Pourquoi?*' is always his first broadside. Then he wades in and you can hear him from one end of the field to the other. *Attendez!* this is going to be rich!"

Both of them started talking at once, the *moniteur* in French and the American in English. Then they turned to the interpreter, and anyone witnessing the conversation from a distance would have thought that he was the culprit. The American had left the ground with the wind behind him, a serious fault in an airman, and he knew it very well.

"Look here, Pete," he said; "tell him I know it was my fault. Tell him I took a Steve Brody. I wanted to see if the old cuckoo had any pep in 'er. When I—"

"*Pourquoi? Nom de Dieu! Qu'est-ce que je vous ai dit? Jamais faire comme ca! Jamais monter avec le vent en arri*è*re! Jamais! Jamais!*"

The others listened in hilarious silence while the interpreter turned first to one and then to the other. "Tell him I took a Steve Brody." I wondered if he translated that literally. Steve took a chance, but it is hardly to be expected that a Frenchman would know of that daring gentleman's history. In this connection, I remember a little talk on caution which was given to us, later, by an English-speaking *moniteur*. It was after rather a serious accident, for which the spirit of Steve Brody was again responsible.

"You Americans," he said, "when you go to the front you will get the Boche; but let me tell you, they will kill many of you. Not one or two; very many."

Accidents delayed the work of flying scarcely at all. As soon as a machine was wrecked, Annamites appeared on the spot to clear away the debris and take it to the repair-shops, where the usable portions

You can drive a "Zang" to water but you can't make it drink

Passenger killed; Pilot badly injured

were quickly sorted out. We followed one of these processions in, and spent an hour watching the work of this other department of aviation upon which our own was so entirely dependent. Here machines were being built as well as repaired. The air vibrated with the hum of machinery, with the clang of hammers upon anvils and the roar of motors in process of being tested.

There was a small army of women doing work of many kinds. They were quite apt at it, particularly in the department where the fine strong linen cloth which covers the wings was being sewn together and stretched over the framework. There were great husky peasant women doing the hardest kind of manual labour. In these latter days of the great world-war, women are doing everything, surely, with the one exception of fighting. It is not a pleasant thing to see them, however strong they may be, doing the rough, coarse work of men, bearing great burdens on their backs as though they were oxen. There must be many now whose muscles are as hard and whose hands as horny as those of a stevedore. Several months after this time, when we were transferred to another school of aviation, one of the largest in Europe, we saw women employed on a much larger scale. They lived in barracks which were no better than our own,—not so good, in fact,—and roughed it like common soldiers.

Toward evening the wind freshened and flying was brought to a halt. Then the Penguins were brought from their hangars, and Drew and I, properly dressed this time, and accompanied by some of the Americans, went out to the field for our first sortie. As is usual on such occasions, there was no dearth of advice. Every graduate of the Penguin class had a method of his own for keeping that unmanageable bird traveling in a direct line, and everyone was only too willing to give us the benefit of his experience. Finally, out of the welter of suggestions, one or two points became clear: it was important that one should give the machine full gas, and get the tail off the ground. Then, by skilful handling of the rudder, it might be kept traveling in the same general direction. But if, as usually happened, it showed wilful tendencies, and started to turn within its own length, it was necessary to cut the contact, to prevent it from whirling so rapidly as to overturn.

Never have I seen a stranger sight than that of a swarm of Penguins at work. They looked like a brood of prehistoric birds of enormous size, with wings too short for flight. Most unwieldy birds they were, driven by, or more accurately, driving beginners in the art of flying;

but they ran along the ground at an amazing speed, zigzagged this way and that, and whirled about as if trying to catch their own tails. As we stood watching them, an accident occurred which would have been laughable had we not been too nervous to enjoy it. In a distant part of the field two machines were rushing wildly about. There were acres of room in which they might pass, but after a moment of uncertainty, they rushed headlong for each other as though driven by the hand of fate, and met head-on, with a great rending of propellers.

The onlookers along the side of the field howled and pounded each other in an ecstasy of delight, but Drew and I walked apart for a hasty consultation, for it was our turn next. We kept rehearsing the points which we were to remember in driving a Penguin: full gas and tail up at once. Through the interpreter, our *moniteur* explained very carefully what we were to do, and mounted the step, to show us, in turn, the proper handling of the gas *manet* and of the *coupe-contact* button. Then he stepped down and shouted, "*Allez! en route!*" with a smile meant to be reassuring.

I buckled myself in, fastened my helmet, and nodded to my mechanic.

"*Coupe, plein gaz*," he said.

"*Coupe, plein gaz*," I repeated.

He gave the propeller a few spins to suck in the mixture.

"*Contact, reduisez.*"

"*Contact, reduisez.*"

Again he spun the propeller, and the motor took. I pulled back my *manet*, full gas, and off I went at what seemed to me then breakneck speed. Remembering instructions, I pushed forward on the lever which governs the elevating planes, and up went my tail so quickly and at such an angle that almost instinctively I cut off my contact. Down dropped my tail again, and I whirled round in a circle—my first *cheval de bois*, as this absurd-looking manoeuvre is called. I had forgotten that I had a rudder. I was like a man learning to swim, and could not yet coordinate the movements of my hands and feet. My bird was purring gently, with the propeller turning slowly. It seemed thoroughly domesticated, but I knew that I had but to pull back on that *manet* to transform it into a rampant bird of prey.

Before starting again, I looked about me, and there was Drew racing all over the field. Suddenly he started in my direction as if the whole force of his will was turned to the business of running me down. Luckily he shut off his motor, and by the grace of the law of inertia came to a halt when he was within a dozen paces of me.

We turned our machines tail to tail and started off in opposite directions, but in a moment I was following hard after him. Almost it seemed that those evil birds had wills of their own. Drew's turned as though it were angry at the indignity of being pursued. We missed each other, but it was a near thing, and, not being able to think fast enough, I stalled my motor, and had to await helplessly the assistance of a mechanic. Far away, at our starting-point, I could see the Americans waving their arms and embracing each other in huge delight, and then I realised why they had all been so eager to come with us to the field. They had been through all this. Now they were having their innings. I could hear them shouting, although their voices sounded very thin and faint. "Why don't you come back?" they yelled. "This way! Here we are! Here's your class!" They were having the time of their vindictive lives, and knew very well that we would go back if we could.

Finally, we began to get the hang of it, and we did go back, although by circuitous routes. But we got there, and the *moniteur* explained again what we were to do. We were to anticipate the turn of the machine with the rudder, just as in sailing a boat. Then we understood the difficulty. In my next sortie, I fixed my eye upon the flag at the opposite side of the field, and reached it without a single *cheval de bois*. I could have kissed the Annamite who was stationed there to turn the machines which rarely came. I had mastered the Penguin! I had forced my will upon it, compelled it to do my bidding! Back across the field I went, keeping a direct course, and thinking how they were all watching, the *moniteur*, doubtless, making approving comments. I reduced the gas at the proper time, and taxied triumphantly up to the starting-point.

But no one had seen my splendid sortie. Now that I had arrived, no one paid the least attention to me. All eyes were turned upward, and following them with my own, I saw an airplane outlined against a heaped-up pile of snow-white cloud. It was moving at tremendous speed, when suddenly it darted straight upward, wavered for a second or two, turned slowly on one wing and fell, nose-down, turning round and round as it fell, like a scrap of paper. It was the *vrille*, the prettiest piece of aerial acrobatics that one could wish to see. It was a wonderful, an incredible sight. Only seven years ago Blériot crossed the English Channel, and a year earlier the world was astonished at the exploits of the Wright brothers, who were making flights, straight-line flights, of from fifteen to twenty minutes' duration!

Someone was counting the turns of the *vrille*. Six, seven, eight; then the airman came out of it on an even keel, and, nosing down to gather speed, looped twice in quick succession. Afterward he did the *retournement*, turning completely over in the air and going back in the opposite direction; then spiralled down and passed over our heads at about fifty metres, landing at the opposite side of the field so beautifully that it was impossible to know when the machine touched the ground. The airman taxied back to the hangars and stopped just in front of us, while we gathered round to hear the latest news from the front.

For he had left the front, this birdman, only an hour before! I was incredulous at first, for I still thought of distances in the old way. But I was soon convinced. Mounted on the hood was the competent-looking Vickers machine gun, with a long belt of cartridges in place, and on the side of the *fuselage* were painted the insignia of an *escadrille*.

The pilot was recognised as soon as he removed his helmet and goggles. He had been a *moniteur* at the school in former days, and was well known to some of the older Americans. He greeted us all very cordially, in excellent English, and told us how, on the strength of a hard morning's work over the lines, he had asked his captain for an afternoon off that he might visit his old friends at B———.

As soon as he had climbed down, those of us who had never before seen this latest type of French *avion de chasse*, crowded round, examining and admiring with feelings of awe and reverence. It was a marvellous piece of aero-craftsmanship, the result of more than two years of accumulating experience in military aviation. It was hard to think of it as an inanimate thing, once having seen it in the air. It seemed living, intelligent, almost human. I could readily understand how it is that airmen become attached to their machines and speak of their fine points, their little peculiarities of individuality, with a kind of loving interest, as one might speak of a fine-spirited horse.

While the mechanicians were grooming this one, and replenishing the fuel-tanks, Drew and I examined it line by line, talking in low tones which seemed fitting in so splendid a presence. We climbed the step and looked down into the compact little car, where the pilot sat in a luxuriously upholstered seat. There were his compass, his *altimétre*, his revolution-counter, his map in its roller case, with a course pricked out on it in a red line. Attached to the machine gun, there was an ingenious contrivance by means of which he fired it while still keeping a steady hand on his controls. The gun itself was fired directly through the propeller by means of a device which timed the shots. The necessity for accuracy in this timing device is clear, when one remembers that the propeller turns over at a normal rate of between fifteen hundred and nineteen hundred revolutions per minute.

It was with a chastened spirit that I looked from this splendid fighting 'plane, back to my little three-cylinder Penguin, with its absurd clipped wings and its impudent tail. A moment ago it had seemed a thing of speed, and the mastery of it a glorious achievement. I told Drew what my feeling was as I came racing back to the starting-point, and how brief my moment of triumph had been. He answered me at first in grunts and nods, so that I knew he was not listening. Presently he began to talk about romance again, the "romance of high adventure," as he called it. "All this"—moving his arm in a wide gesture—was but an evidence of man's unconquerable craving for romance. War itself was a manifestation of it, gave it scope, relieved the pent-up longings for it which could not find sufficient outlet in times of peace. Romance would always be one of the minor, and sometimes one of the major causes for war, indirectly of course, but none the less really; for the craving for it was one reason why millions of men so readily accepted war at the hands of the little groups of diplomats who ruled their destinies.

Half an hour later, as we stood watching the little biplane again climbing into the evening sky, I understood, in a way, what he was driving at, and with what keen anticipation he was looking forward to the time when we too would know all that there was to know of the joy of flight. Higher and higher it mounted, now and then catching the sun on its silver wings in a flash of light, growing smaller and smaller, until it vanished in a golden haze, far to the north. It was then four o'clock. In an hour's time the pilot would be circling down over his aerodrome on the Champagne front.

CHAPTER 3

By the Route of the Air

The winter of 1916-17 was the most prolonged and bitter that France has known in many years. It was a trying period to the little group of Americans assembled at the École Militaire d 'Aviation, eager as they were to complete their training, and to be ready, when spring should come, to share in the great offensive, which they knew would then take place on the Western front. Aviation is a waiting game at the best of seasons. In winter it is a series of seemingly endless delays. Day after day, the plain on the high plateau overlooking the old city of V—— was storm-swept, a forlorn and desolate place as we looked at it from our windows, watching the flocks of crows as they beat up against the wind, or as they turned, and were swept with it, over our barracks, crying and calling derisively to us as they passed.

"Birdmen do you call yourselves?" they seemed to say. "Then come on up; the weather's fine!"

Well they knew that we were impostors, fair-weather fliers, who dared not accept their challenge.

It is strange how vague and shadowy my remembrance is of those long weeks of inactivity, when we were dependent for employment and amusement on our own devices. To me there was a quality of unreality about our life at B——. Our environment was, no doubt, partly responsible for this feeling. Although we were not far distant from Paris,—less than an hour by train,—the country round about our camp seemed to be quite cut off from the rest of the world. With the exception of our Sunday afternoons of leave, when we joined the boulevardiers in town, we lived a life as remote and cloistered as that of some brotherhood of monks in an inaccessible monastery. That is how it appeared to me, although here again I am in danger of making it seem that my own impressions were those of all the others. This of

Student pilots at a Blériot School, December, 1916

course was not true. The spirit of the place appealed to us, individually, in widely different ways, and upon some, perhaps, it had no effect at all.

Sometimes we spent our winter afternoons of enforced leisure in long walks through country roads which lay empty to the eye for miles. They gave one a sense of loneliness which coloured thought, not in any sentimental way, but in a manner very natural and real. The war was always in the background of one's musings, and while we were far removed from actual contact with it, every depopulated country village brought to mind the sacrifice which France has made for the cause of all freedom-loving nations. Every roadside *café*, long barren of its old patronage, was an evidence of the completeness of the sacrifice. Americans, for the most part, are of an unconquerably healthy cast of mind; but there were few of us who could frequent these places light-heartedly.

Paris was our emotional storehouse, to use Kipling's term, during the time we were at B——. We spent our Sunday afternoons there, mingling with the crowds on the *boulevards*, or, in pleasant weather, sitting outside the *cafés*, watching the soldiers of the world go by. The streets were filled with *permissionnaires* from all parts of the Western front, and there were many of those despised of all the rest, the *embusqués*, as they are called, who hold the comfortable billets in safe places well back of the lines. It was very easy to distinguish them from the men newly arrived from the trenches, in whose eyes one saw the look of wonder, almost of unbelief, that there was still a goodly world to be enjoyed. It was often beyond the pathetic to see them trying to satisfy their need for all the wholesome things of life in a brief seven days of leave; to see the family parties at the modest restaurants on the side streets, making merry in a kind of forced way, as if everyone were thinking of the brevity of the time for such enjoyment.

Scarcely a week went by without bringing one or two additional recruits to the Franco-American Corps. We wondered why they came so slowly. There must have been thousands of Americans who would have been, not only willing, but glad to join us; and yet the opportunities for doing so had been made widely known. For those who did come this was the legitimate by-product of glorious adventure and a training in aviation not to be surpassed in Europe. This was to be had by any healthy young American, almost for the asking; but our numbers increased very gradually, from fifteen to twenty-five, until by the spring of 1917 there were fifty of us at the various aviation schools of France. Territorially we represented at least a dozen states, from the Atlantic to the Pacific. There were rich men's sons and poor men's sons among our number; the sons of very old families, and those who neither knew nor cared what their antecedents were.

The same was true of our French comrades, for membership in the French air service is not based upon wealth or family position or political influence. The policy of the government is as broad and democratic as may be. Men are chosen because of an aptitude that promises well, or as a reward for distinguished service at the front. A few of the French *élèves-pilotes* had been officers, but most of them N.C.O.'s and private soldiers in infantry or artillery regiments. This very wide latitude in choice at first seemed "laxitude" to some of us Americans. But evidently, experience in training war pilots, and the practical results obtained by these men at the front, have been proof enough to the French authorities of the folly of setting rigid standards, making hard-and-fast rules to be met by prospective aviators. As our own experience increased, we saw the wisdom of a policy which is more concerned with a man's courage, his self-reliance, and his powers of initiative, than with his ability to work out theoretical problems in aerodynamics.

There are many French pilots with excellent records of achievement in war-flying who have but a sketchy knowledge of motor and aircraft construction. Some are college-bred men, but many more have only a common-school education. It is not at all strange that this should be the case, for one may have had no technical training worth mentioning; one may have only a casual speaking acquaintance with motors, and a very imperfect idea of why and how one is able to defy the law of gravity, and yet prove his worth as a pilot in what is, after all, the best possible way—by his record at the front.

A judicious amount of theoretical instruction is, of course, not wanting in the aviation schools of France; but its importance is not exaggerated. We Americans, with our imperfect knowledge of the language, lost the greater part of this. The handicap was not a serious one, and I think I may truthfully say that we kept pace with our French comrades. The most important thing was to gain actual flying experience, and as much of it as possible. Only in this way can one acquire a sensitive ear for motors, and an accurate sense of flying speed: the feel of one's machine in the air. These are of the greatest importance. Once the pilot has developed this airman's sixth sense, he need not, and never does, worry about the scantiness of his knowledge of the theory of flight.

Sometimes the winds would die away and the thick clouds lift, and we would go joyously to work on a morning of crisp, bright winter weather. Then we had moments of glorious revenge upon the crows. They would watch us from afar, holding noisy indignation meetings in a row of weather-beaten trees at the far side of the field. And when some inexperienced pilot lost control of his machine and came crashing to earth, they would take the air in a body, circling over the wreckage, cawing and jeering with the most evident delight. "The Oriental Wrecking Company," as the Annamites were called, were on the scene almost as quickly as our enemies the crows. They were a familiar sight on every working day, chattering together in their high-pitched gutturals, as they hauled away the wrecked machines. They appeared to side with the birds, and must have thought us the most absurd of men, making wings for ourselves, and always coming to grief when we tried to use them.

We made progress regardless of all this scepticism. It was necessarily slow, for beginners at a single-command monoplane school are permitted to fly only under the most favourable weather conditions. Even then, old Mother Earth, who is not kindly disposed toward those of her children who leave her so jauntily, would clutch us back to her bosom, whenever we gave her the slightest opportunity, with an embrace that was anything but tender. We were inclined to think rather highly of our own courage in defying her; and sometimes our vanity was increased by our *moniteurs*. After an exciting misadventure they often gave expression to their relief at finding an amateur pilot still whole, by praising his "presence of mind" in too generous French fashion.

We should not have been so proud, I think, of our own little exploits, had we remembered those of the pioneers in aviation, so many of whom lost their lives in experiment with the first crude types of the heavier-than-air machines. They were pioneers in the fine and splendid meaning of the word—men to be compared in spirit with the old fifteenth-century navigators. We were but followers, adventuring, in comparative safety, along a well-defined trail.

This, at any rate, was Drew's opinion. He would never allow me the pleasure of indulging in any flights of fancy over these trivial adventures of ours. He would never let me set them off against "the heroic background" of Paris. As for Paris, we saw nothing of war there, he would say, except the lighter side, the homecoming, leave-enjoying

A Review at the Aerodrome

side. We needed to know more of the horror and the tragedy of it. We needed to keep that close and intimate to us as a right perspective for our future adventures. He believed it to be our duty as aviators to anticipate every kind of experience which we might have to meet at the front. His imagination was abnormally vivid. Once he discussed the possibility of "falling in flames," which is so often the end of an airman's career. I shall never again be able to take the same wholehearted delight in flying that I did before he was so horribly eloquent upon the subject. He often speculated upon one's emotions in falling in a machine damaged beyond the possibility of control.

"Now try to imagine it," he would say: "your gasoline tanks have been punctured and half of your *fuselage* has been shot away. You believe that there is not the slightest chance for you to save your life. What are you going to do—lose your head and give up the game? No, you've got to attempt the impossible"; and so on, and so forth.

I would accuse him of being morbid. Furthermore, I saw no reason why we should plan for terrible emergencies which might never arrive. His answer was that we were military pilots in training for combat machines. We had no right to ignore the grimness of the business ahead of us. If we did, so much the worse for us when we should go to the front. But beyond this practical interest, he had a great curiosity about the nature of fear, and a great dread of it, too. He was afraid that in some last adventure, in which death came slowly enough for him to recognise it, he might die like a terror-stricken animal, and not bravely, as a man should.

We did not often discuss these gruesome possibilities, although this was not Drew's fault. I would not listen to him; and so he would be silent about them until convinced that the furtherance of our careers as airmen demanded additional unpleasant imaginings. There was something of the Hindoo fanatic in him; or perhaps it was the outcropping of the stern spirit of his New England forbears. But when he talked of the pleasant side of the adventures before us, it was more than compensation for all the rest. Then he would make me restless and impatient, for I did not have his faculty of enjoyment in anticipation. The early period of training, when we were flying only a few metres above the ground, seemed endless.

At last came the event which really marked the beginning of our careers as airmen: the first *tour de piste*, the first flight round the aerodrome. We had talked of this for weeks, but when at last the day for it came, our enthusiasm had waned. We were eager to try our wings and yet afraid to make the start.

This first *tour de piste* was always the occasion for a gathering of the Americans, and there was the usual assembly present. The beginners were there to shiver in anticipation of their own forthcoming trials, and the more advanced pilots, who had already taken the leap, to offer gratuitous advice.

"Now don't try to pull any big league stuff. Not too much rudder on the turns. Remember how that Frenchman piled up on the Farman hangars when he tried to bank the corners."

"You'll find it pretty rotten when you go over the woods. The air currents there are something scandalous!"

"Believe me, it's a lot worse over the fort. Rough? *Oh, là là!*"

"And that's where you have to cut your motor and dive, if you're going to make a landing without hanging up in the telephone wires."

"When you do come down, don't be afraid to stick her nose forward. Scare the life out of you, that drop will, but you may as well get used to it in the beginning."

"But wait till we see them redress! Where's the Oriental Wrecking Gang?"

"Don't let that worry you, Drew: pan-caking isn't too bad. Not in a Blériot. Just like falling through a shingle roof. Can't hurt yourself much."

"If you do spill, make it a good one. There ha n't been a decent smash-up today."

These were the usual comforting assurances. They did not frighten us much, although there was just enough truth in the warnings to make us uneasy. We took our hazing as well as we could inwardly, and of course with imperturbable calm outwardly; but, to make a confession, I was somewhat reluctant to hear the businesslike "*Allez! en route!*" of our *moniteur*.

When it came, I taxied across to the other side of the field, turned into the wind, and came racing back, full motor. It seemed a thing of tremendous power, that little forty-five-horsepower Anzani. The roar of it struck awe into my soul, and I gripped the controls in no very professional manner. Then, when I had gathered full ground speed, I eased her off gently, and up we went, over the class and the assembled visitors, above the hangars, the lake, the forest, until, at the halfway point, my *altimétre* registered three hundred and fifty metres. Out of the corner of my eye I saw all the beautiful countryside spread out beneath me, but I was too busily occupied to take in the prospect. I was

Aerial landing-stages may be practicable

watching my wings, nervously, in order to anticipate and counteract the slightest pitch of the machine. But nothing happened, and I soon realised that this first grand tour was not going to be nearly so bad as we had been led to believe. I began to enjoy it. I even looked down over the side of the fuselage, although it was a very hasty glance.

All the time I was thinking of the rapidly approaching moment when I should have to come down. I knew well enough how the descent was to be made. It was very simple. I had only to shut off my motor, push forward with my "broom-stick,"—the control connected with the elevating planes,—and then wait and redress gradually, beginning at from six to eight metres from the ground. The descent would be exciting, a little more rapid than Shooting the Chutes. Only one could not safely hold on to the sides of the car and await the splash. That sort of thing had sometimes been done in aeroplanes, by over-excited pilots. The results were disastrous, without exception.

The moment for the decision came. I was above the fort, otherwise I should not have known when to dive. At first the sensation was, I imagine, exactly that of falling, feet foremost; but after pulling back slightly on the controls, I felt the machine answer to them, and the uncomfortable feeling passed. I brought up on the ground in the usual bumpy manner of the beginner. Nothing gave way, however, so this did not spoil the fine rapture of a rare moment. It was shared—at least it was pleasant to think so—by my old Annamite friend of the Penguin experience, who stood by his flag nodding his head at me. He said, "*Beaucoup bon,*" showing his polished black teeth in an approving grin. I forgot for the moment that "*beaucoup bon*" was his enigmatical comment upon all occasions, and that he would have grinned just as broadly had he been dragging me out from a mass of wreckage.

Drew came in a few moments later, making an almost perfect landing. In the evening we walked to a neighbouring village, where we had a wonderful dinner to celebrate the end of our apprenticeship. It was a curious feast. We had little to say to one another, or, better, we were both afraid to talk. We were under an enchantment which words would have broken. After a silent meal, we walked all the way home without speaking.

We started off together on our triangles. That was in April, just passed, so that I have now brought this casual diary almost up to date. We were then at the great school of aviation at A in central France, where, for the first time, we were associated with men in training for every branch of aviation service, and became familiar with other types

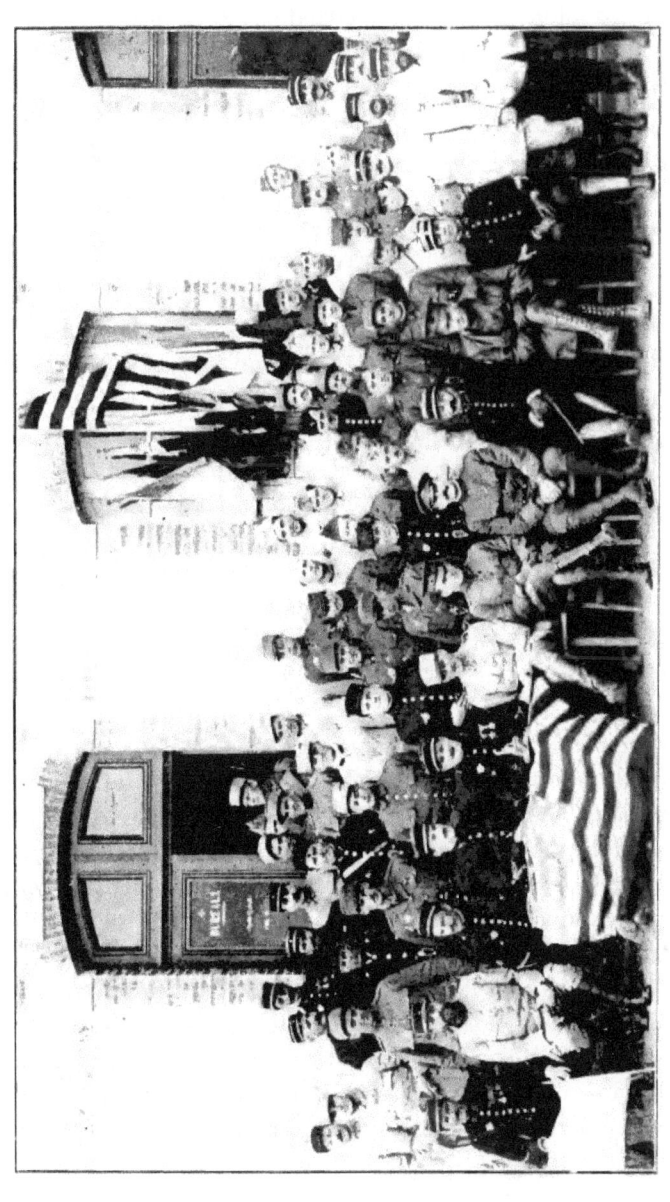

American student pilots and some of their French officers and instructors at an École Militaire d'Aviation, April 2, 1917

of French machines. But the brevet tests, which every pilot must pass before he becomes a military aviator, were the same in every department of the school. The triangles were two cross-country flights of two hundred kilometres each, three landings to be made *en route*, and each flight to be completed within forty-eight hours. In addition, there were two short voyages of sixty kilometres each—these preceded the triangular tests—and an hour of flight at a minimum altitude of sixty-five hundred feet.

The short voyages gave us a delightful foretaste of what was to come. We did them both one afternoon, and were at the hangars at five o'clock on the following morning, ready to make an early start. A fresh wind was blowing from the northeast, but the brevet *moniteur*, who went up for a short flight to try the air, came back with the information that it was quite calm at twenty-five hundred feet. We might start, he said, as soon as we liked.

Drew, in his joy, embraced the old woman who kept a coffee-stall at the hangars, while I danced a one-step with a mechanician. Neither of them was surprised at this procedure. They were accustomed to such emotional outbursts on the part of aviators who, by the very nature of their calling, were always in the depths of despair or on the farthest jutting peak of some mountain of delight. Our departure had been delayed, day after day, for more than a week, because of the weather. We were so eager to start that we would willingly have gone off in a blizzard.

During the week of waiting we had studied our map until we knew the location of every important road and railroad, every forest, river, canal, and creek within a radius of one hundred kilometres. We studied it at close range, on a table, and then on the floor, with the compass-points properly orientated, so that we might see all the important landmarks with the birdman's eye. We knew our course so well, that there seemed no possibility of our losing direction.

Our military papers had been given us several days before. Among these was an official-looking document to be presented to the mayor of any town or village near which we might be compelled to land. It contained an extract from the law concerning aviators, and the duty toward them of the civilian and military authorities. In another was an itemised list of the amounts which might be exacted by farmers for damage to growing crops: so much for an *atterrissage* in a field of sugar-beets, so much for wheat, etc. Besides these, we had a book of detailed instructions as to our duty in case of emergencies of every conceivable kind—among others, the course of action to be followed if we should be compelled to land in an enemy country. At first sight this seemed an unnecessary precaution; but we remembered the experience of one of our French comrades at B——, who started confidently off on his first cross-country flight. He lost his way and did not realise how far astray he had gone until he found himself under fire from German anti-aircraft batteries on the Belgian front.

The most interesting paper of all was our *Ordre de Service*, the text of which was as follows:

> It is commanded that the bearer of this Order report himself at the cities of C—— and R——, by the route of the air, flying an *avion* Caudron, and leaving the École Militaire d'Aviation at A—— on the 21st of April, 1917, without passenger on board.
>
> Signed, Le Capitaine B——
> *Commandant de l'École*

We read this with feelings which must have been nearly akin to those of Columbus on a memorable day in 1492 when he received his clearance papers from Cadiz. "By the route of the air!" How the imagination lingered over that phrase! We had the better of Columbus there, although we had to admit that there was more glamour in the hazard of his adventure and the uncertainty of his destination.

Drew was ready first. I helped him into his fur-lined combination and strapped him to his seat. A moment later he was off. I watched him as he gathered height over the aerodrome. Then, finding that his motor was running satisfactorily, he struck out in an easterly direction, his machine growing smaller and smaller until it vanished in the early morning haze. I followed immediately afterward, and had a busy ten minutes, being buffeted this way and that, until, as the brevet *moniteur* had foretold, I reached quiet air at twenty-five hundred feet.

This was my first experience in passing from one air current to another. It was a unique one, for I was still a little incredulous. I had not entirely lost my old boyhood belief that the wind went all the way up.

I passed over the old cathedral town of B—— at fifteen hundred metres. Many a pleasant afternoon had we spent there, walking through its narrow, crooked streets, or lounging on the banks of the canal. The cathedral too was a favourite haunt. I loved the fine spaciousness of it. Looking down on it now, it seemed no larger than a toy cathedral in a toy town, such as one sees in the shops of Paris. The streets were empty, for it was not yet seven o'clock. Strips of shadow crossed them where taller roofs cut off the sunshine. A toy train, which I could have put nicely into my fountain-pen case, was pulling into a station no larger than a wren's house. The Greeks called their gods "derisive." No doubt they realised how small they looked to them, and how insignificant this little world of affairs must have appeared from high Olympus.

There was a road, a fine straight thoroughfare converging from the left. It led almost due southwest. This was my route to C——. I followed it, climbing steadily until I was at two thousand metres. I had never flown so high before. "Over a mile!" I thought. It seemed a tremendous altitude. I could see scores of villages and fine old *chateaux*, and great stretches of forest, and miles upon miles of open country in checkered patterns, just beginning to show the first fresh green of the early spring crops. It looked like a world planned and laid out by the best of Santa Clauses for the eternal delight of all good children. And for untold generations only the birds have had the privilege of seeing and enjoying it from the wing. Small wonder that they sing. As for non-musical birds—well, they all sing after a fashion, and there is no doubt that crows, at least, are extremely jealous of their prerogative of flight.

My biplane was flying itself. I had nothing to do other than to give occasional attention to the revolution counter, *altimétre*, and speed-dial. The motor was running with perfect regularity. The propeller was turning over at twelve hundred revolutions per minute without the slightest fluctuation. Flying is the simplest thing in the world, I thought. Why doesn't everyone travel by route of the air? If people knew the joy of it, the exhilaration of it, aviation schools would be overwhelmed with applicants. Biplanes of the Farman and Voisin type would make excellent family cars, quite safe for women to drive. Mothers, busy with household affairs, could tell their children to "run out and fly" a Caudron such as I was driving, and feel not the slightest anxiety about them. I remembered an imaginative drawing I had once seen of aerial activity in 1950. Even house pets were granted the privilege of traveling by the air route. The artist was not far wrong except in his date. He should have put it at 1925. On a fine April morning there seemed no limit to the realisation of such interesting possibilities.

I had no more than started on my southwest course, as it seemed to me, when I saw the spires and the red-roofed houses of C ——, and, a kilometre or so from the outskirts, the barracks and hangars of the aviation school where I was to make the first landing. I reduced the gas, and, with the motor purring gently, began a long, gradual descent. It was interesting to watch the change in the appearance of the country beneath me as I lost height. Checkerboard patterns of brown and green grew larger and larger. Shining threads of silver became rivers and canals, tiny green shrubs became trees, individual aspects of houses emerged. Soon I could see people going about the streets and laundry-maids hanging out the family washing in the back gardens. I even came low enough to witness a minor household tragedy—a mother vigorously spanking a small boy. Hearing the whir of my motor, she stopped in the midst of the process, whereupon the youngster very naturally took advantage of his opportunity to cut and run for it.

Drew doubted my veracity when I told him about this. He called me an aerial eavesdropper and said that I ought to be ashamed to go buzzing over towns at such low altitudes, frightening housemaid,, disorganizing domestic penal institutions, and generally disturbing the privacy of respectable French citizens. But I was unrepentant, for I knew that one small boy in France was thinking of me with joy. To have escaped maternal justice with the assistance of an aviator would be an event of glorious memory to him. How vastly more worthwhile such a method of escape, and how jubilant Tom Sawyer would have been over such an opportunity when his horrified warning, "Look behind you, aunt!" had lost efficacy.

Drew had been waiting a quarter of an hour, and came rushing out to meet me as I taxied across the field. We shook hands as though we had not seen each other for years. We could not have been more surprised and delighted if we had met on another planet after long and hopeless wanderings in space.

While I superintended the replenishing of my fuel and oil tanks he walked excitedly up and down in front of the hangars. He was an odd-looking sight in his flying clothes, with a pair of Meyrowitz goggles set back on his head, like another set of eyes, gazing at the sky with an air of wide astonishment. He paid no attention to my critical comments, but started thinking aloud as soon as I rejoined him.

"It was lonely! Yes, by Jove! that was it. A glorious thing, one's isolation up there; but it was too profound to be pleasant. A relief to get down again, to hear people talk, to feel the solid earth under one's feet. How did it impress you?"

This was like Drew. I felt ashamed of the lightness of my own thoughts, but I had to tell him of my speculations upon after-the-war developments in aviation: nurses flying Voisins, with the cars filled with babies; old men having after-dinner naps in twenty-three-metre Nieuports, fitted, for safety, with Sperry gyroscopes; family parties taking comfortable outings in gigantic biplanes of the R-6 type; mothers, as of old, gazing apprehensively at speed-dials, cautioning fathers about "driving too fast," and all of the rest.

Drew looked at me reprovingly, to be sure, but he felt the need, just as I did, of an outlet to his feelings, and so he turned to this kind of comic relief with the most delightful reluctance. He quickly lost his reserve, and in the imaginative spree which followed we went far beyond the last outposts of absurdity. We laughed over our own wit until our faces were tired. However, I will not be explicit about our folly. It might not be so amusing from a critical point of view.

After our papers had been *viséed* at the office of the *commandant*, we hurried back to our machines, eager to be away again. We were to make our second landing at R———. It was about seventy kilometres distant and almost due north. The mere name of the town was an invitation. Somewhere, in one of the novels of William J. Locke, may be found this bit of dialogue:—

"But, master," said I, "there is, after all, colour in words. Don't you remember how delighted you were with the name of a little town we passed through on the way to Orleans? R———? You were haunted by it and said it was like the purple note of an organ."

We were haunted by it, too, for we were going to that very town. We would see it long before our arrival—a cluster of quaint old houses lying in the midst of pleasant fields, with roads curving toward it from the north and south, as though they were glad to pass through so delightful a place. Drew was for taking a leisurely route to the eastward, so that we might look at some villages which lay some distance off our course. I wanted to fly by compass in a direct line, without following my map very closely. We had planned to fly together, and were the more eager to do this because of an argument we had had about the relative speed of our machines. He was certain that his was the faster. I knew that, with mine, I could fly circles around him. As we were not able to agree on the course, we decided to postpone the race until we started on the homeward journey. Therefore, after we had passed over the town, he waved his hand, bent off to the northeast, and was soon out of sight.

I kept straight on, climbing steadily, until I was again at five thousand feet. As before, my motor was running perfectly and I had plenty of leisure to enjoy the always new sensation of flight and to watch the wide expanse of magnificent country as it moved slowly past. I let my mind lie fallow, and every now and then I would find it hauling out fragments of old memories which I had forgotten that I possessed.

I recalled, for the first time in many years, my earliest interpretations of the meanings of all the phenomena of the heavens. Two old janitor saints had charge of the floor of the skies. One of them was a jolly old man who liked boys, and always kept the sky swept clean and blue. The other took a sour delight in shirking his duties, so that it might rain and spoil all our fun. Perhaps it was Drew's sense of loneliness and helplessness so far from earth, which made me think of winds and clouds in friendly human terms. However, that may be, these reveries, hardly worthy of a military airman, were abruptly broken into.

All at once, I realised that, while my biplane was headed due north, I was drifting north and west. This seemed strange. I puzzled over it for some time, and then, brilliantly, in the manner of the novice, deduced the reason: wind. I was being blown off my course, all the while comfortably certain that I was flying in a direct line toward R——. Our *moniteurs* had often cautioned us against being comfortably certain about anything while in the air. It was our duty to be uncomfortably alert. Wind! I wonder how many times we had been told to keep it in mind at all times, whether on the ground or in the air? And here was I forgetting the existence of wind on the very first occasion. The speed of my machine and the current of air from the propeller had deceived me into thinking that I was driving dead into whatever breeze there was at that altitude. I discovered that it was blowing out of the east, therefore I headed a quarter into it, to overcome the drift, and looked for landmarks.

I had not long to search. Wisps of mist obstructed the view, and within ten minutes a bank of solid cloud cut it off completely. I had only a vague notion of my location with reference to my course, but I could not persuade myself to come down just then. To be flying in the full splendour of bright April sunshine, knowing that all the earth was in shadow, gave me a feeling of exhilaration. For there is no sensation like that of flight, no isolation so complete as that of the airman who has above him only the blue sky, and below, a level floor of pure white cloud, stretching in an unbroken expanse toward every horizon. And so I kept my machine headed northeast, that I might regain the ground lost before I discovered the drift northwest. I had made a rough calculation of the time required to cover the seventy kilometres to R—— at the speed at which I was traveling. The rest I left to Chance, the godfather of all adventurers.

He took the initiative, as he so frequently does with aviators who, in moments of calm weather, are inclined to forget that they are still children of earth. The floor of dazzling white cloud was broken and tumbled into heaped-up masses which came drifting by at various altitudes. They were scattered at first and offered splendid opportunities for aerial steeplechasing. Then, almost before I was aware of it, they surrounded me on all sides. For a few minutes I avoided them by flying in curves and circles in rapidly vanishing pools of blue sky. I feared to take my first plunge into a cloud, for I knew, by report, what an alarming experience it is to the new pilot.

The wind was no longer blowing steadily out of the east. It came in gusts from all points of the compass. I made a hasty revision of my opinion as to the calm and tranquil joys of aviation, thinking what fools men are who willingly leave the good green earth and trust themselves to all the winds of heaven in a frail box of cloth-covered sticks.

The last clear space grew smaller and smaller. I searched for an outlet, but the clouds closed in and in a moment I was hopelessly lost in a blanket of cold drenching mist.

I could hardly see the outlines of my machine and had no idea of my position with reference to the earth. In the excitement of this new adventure I forgot the speed-dial, and it was not until I heard the air screaming through the wires that I remembered it. The indicator had leaped up fifty kilometres an hour above safety speed, and I realised that I must be traveling earthward at a terrific pace. The manner of the descent became clear at the same moment. As I rolled out of the cloud-bank, I saw the earth jauntily tilted up on one rim, looking like a gigantic enlargement of a page out of Peter Newell's *Slant Book*. I expected to see dogs and dishpans, baby carriages and ash-barrels roll out of every house in France, and go clattering off into space.

CHAPTER 4

At G. D. E.

Somewhere to the north of Paris, in the *zone des armées*, there is a village, known to all aviators in the French service as G. D. E. It is the village through which pilots who have completed their training at the aviation schools pass on their way to the front; and it is here that I again take up this journal of aerial adventure.

We are in lodgings, Drew and I, at the *Hôtel de la Bonne Rencontre*, which belies its name in the most villainous fashion. An inn at Rochester in the days of Henry the Fourth must have been a fair match for it, and yet there is something to commend it other than its convenience to the flying field. Since the early days of the Escadrille Lafayette, many Americans have lodged here while awaiting their orders for active service. As I write, J. B. is asleep in a bed which has done service for a long line of them. It is for this reason that he chose it, in preference to one in a much better state of repair which he might have had. And he has made plans for its purchase after the war. Madame Rodel is to keep careful record of all its American occupants, just as she has done in the past. She is pledged not to repair it beyond the bare necessity which its uses as a bed may require, an injunction which it was hardly necessary to lay upon her, judging by the other furniture in our apartment. Drew is not sentimental, but he sometimes carries sentiment to extremities which appear to me absurd.

When I attempt to define, even to myself, the charm of our adventures thus far, I find it impossible. How, then, make it real to others? To tell of aerial adventure one needs a new language, or, at least, a parcel of new adjectives, sparkling with bright and vivid meaning, as crisp and fresh as just-minted bank-notes. They should have no taint of flatness or insipidity. They should show not the faintest trace of wear. With them, one might hope, now and then, to startle the imagination, to set it running in channels which are strange and delightful to it. For there is something new under the sun: aerial adventure; and the most lively and unjaded fancy may, at first, need direction toward the realisation of this fact. Soon it will have a literature of its own, of prose and poetry, of fiction, biography, memoirs, of history which will read like the romance it really is. The essayists will turn to it with joy. And the poets will discover new aspects of beauty which have been hidden from them through the ages; and as men's experience "in the wide fields of air" increases, epic material which will tax their most splendid powers.

    This brings me sadly back to my own purpose, which is, despite many wistful longings of a more ambitious nature, to write a plain tale of the adventures of two members—prospective up to this point—of the Escadrille Lafayette. To go back to some of those earlier ones, when we were making our first cross-country flights, I remember them now with a delight which, at the time, was not unmixed with other emotions. Indeed, an aviator, and a fledgling aviator in particular, often runs the whole gamut of human feeling during a single flight. I did in the course of half an hour, reaching the high C of acute panic as I came tumbling out of the first cloud of my aerial experience. Fortunately, in the air the sense of equilibrium usually compels one to do the right thing, and so, after some desperate handling of my "broomstick," as the control is called which governs ailerons and elevating planes, I soon had the horizons nicely adjusted again.

    What a relief it was! I shut down my motor and commenced a more gradual descent, for I was lost, of course, and it seemed wiser to land and make inquiries than to go cruising over half of France looking for one among hundreds of picturesque old towns. There were at least a dozen within view. Some of them were at least a three hours' walk distant from each other. But in the air! I was free to go whither I would, and swiftly. After leisurely deliberation I selected one surrounded by wide fields which appeared to be as level as a floor. But as I descended the landscape widened, billowing into hills and folding into valleys. By sheer good luck, nothing more, I made a landing without accident. My Caudron barely missed colliding with a hedge of fruit trees, rolled down a long incline, and stopped not ten feet short of a small stream.

    The experience taught me the folly of choosing landing-ground from high altitudes. I needn't have landed, of course, but I was then so much an amateur that the buffeting of cross-currents of air near

AIRMEN PREFER A TREELESS COUNTRY

the ground awed me into it, come what might. The village was out of sight over the crest of the hill. However, thinking that someone must have seen me, I decided to await developments where I was.

Very soon I heard a shrill, jubilant shout. A boy of eight or ten years was running along the ridge as fast as he could go. Outlined against the sky, he reminded me of silhouettes I had seen in Paris shops, of children dancing, the very embodiment of joy in movement. He turned and waved to some one behind, whom I could not see, then came on again, stopping a short distance away, and looking at me with an air of awe, which, having been a small boy myself, I was able to understand and appreciate. I said, "*Bonjour, mon petit*," as cordially as I could, but he just stood there and gazed without saying a word.

Then the others began to appear: scores of children, and old men as well, and women of all ages, some with babies in their arms, and young girls. The whole village came, I am sure. I was mightily impressed by the haleness of the old men and women, which one rarely sees in America. Some of them were evidently well over seventy, and yet, with one or two exceptions, they had sound limbs, clear eyes, and healthy complexions. As for the young girls, many of them were exceptionally pretty; and the children were sturdy youngsters, not the wan, thin-legged little creatures one sees in Paris. In fact, all of these people appeared to belong to a different race from that of the Parisians, to come from finer, more vigorous stock.

They were very curious, but equally courteous, and stood in a large circle around my machine, waiting for me to make my wishes known. For several minutes I pretended to be busy attending to dials and valves inside the car. While trying to screw my courage up to the point of making a verbless explanation of my difficulty, someone pushed through the crowd, and to my great relief began speaking to me. It was *Monsieur the Mayor*. As best I could, I explained that I had lost my way and had found it necessary to come down for the purpose of making inquiries. I knew that it was awful French, but hoped that it would be intelligible, in part at least. However, the Mayor understood not a word, and I knew by the curious expression in his eyes that he must be wondering from what weird province I hailed.

After a moment's thought he said, "*Vous êtes Anglais, monsieur?*" with a smile of very real pleasure. I said, "*Non, monsieur, Américain.*" That magic word! What potency it has in France, the more so at that time, perhaps, for America had placed herself definitely upon the side of the Allies only a short time before. I enjoyed that moment. I might have had the village for the asking. I willingly accepted the role of ambassador of the American people. Had it not been for the language barrier, I think I would have made a speech, for I felt the generous spirit of Uncle Sam prompting me to give those fathers and mothers, whose husbands and sons were at the front, the promise of our unqualified support. I wanted to tell them that we were with them now, not only in sympathy, but with all our resources in men and guns and ships and aircraft. I wanted to convince them of our new understanding of the significance of the war. Alas! this was impossible. Instead I gave each one of an army of small boys the privilege of sitting in the pilot's seat, and showed them how to manage the controls.

The astonishing thing to me was, that while this village was not twenty kilometres off the much-frequented air route between C—— and R——, mine was the first aeroplane which most of them had seen. During long months at various aviation schools pilots grow accustomed to thinking that aircraft are as familiar a sight to others as to them. But here was a village, not far distant from several aviation schools, where an aviator was looked upon with wonder. To have an American aviator drop down upon them was an event even in the history of that ancient village. To have been that aviator,—well, it was an unforgettable experience, coming as it did so opportunely with America's entry into the war. I shall always have it in the background of memory, and one day it will be among the pleasantest of many pleasant tales which I shall have in store for my grandchildren.

However, it is not their potentialities as memories which endear these adventures now, but rather it is because they are in such contrast to any that we had known before. We are always comparing this new life with the old, so different in every respect as to seem a separate existence, almost a previous incarnation.

Having been set right about my course, I pushed my biplane to more level ground, with the willing help of all the boys, started my motor, and was away again. Their shrill cheers reached me even above the roar of the motor. As a lad in a small, Middle-Western town, I have known the rapture of holding to a balloon guy-rope at a county fair, until "the world's most famous aeronaut" shouted, "Let 'er go, boys!" and swung off into space. I kept his memory green until I had passed the first age of hero worship. I know that every youngster in a small village in central France will so keep mine. Such fame is the only kind worth having.

A flight of fifteen minutes brought me within sight of the large white circle which marks the landing-field at R . J. B. had not yet arrived. This was a great disappointment, for we had planned a race home. I was anxious about him, too, knowing that the godfather of all adventurers can be very stern at times, particularly with his aerial godchildren. I waited for an hour and then decided to go on alone. The weather having cleared, the opportunity was too favourable to be lost. The cloud formations were the most remarkable that I had ever seen. I flew around and over and under them, watching at close hand the play of light and shade over their great, billowing folds.

Sometimes I skirted them so closely that the current of air from my propeller ravelled out fragments of shining vapour, which streamed into the clear spaces like wisps of filmy silk. I knew that I ought to be savouring this experience, but for some reason I couldn't. One usually pays for a fine mood by a sudden and unaccountable change of feeling which shades off into a kind of dull, colourless depression.

I passed a twin-motor Caudron going in the opposite direction. It was fantastically painted, the wings a bright yellow and the circular hoods, over the two motors, a fiery red. As it approached, it looked like some prehistoric bird with great ravenous eyes. The thing startled me, not so much because of its weird appearance as by the mere fact of its being there. Strangely enough, for a moment it seemed impossible that I should meet another *avion*. Despite a long apprenticeship in aviation, in these days when one's mind has only begun to grasp the fact that the mastery of the air has been accomplished, the sudden presentation of a bit of evidence sometimes shocks it into a moment of amazement bordering upon incredulity.

As I watched the big biplane pass, I was conscious of a feeling of loneliness. I remembered what J. B. had said that morning. There *was* something unpleasant in the isolation; it made us look longingly down to earth, wondering whether we shall ever feel really at home in the air. I, too, longed for the sound of human voices, and all that I heard was the roar of the motor and the swish of the wind through wires and struts, sounds which have no human quality in them, and are no more companionable than the lapping of the waves to a man adrift on a raft in mid-ocean.

Underlying this feeling, and no doubt in part responsible for it, was the knowledge of the fallibility of that seemingly perfect mechanism which rode so steadily through the air; of the quick response that ingenious arrangement of inanimate matter would make to an eternal and inexorable law if a few frail wires should part; of the equally quick,

French Sopwith two-seater

Caudron three-passenger Avion type R4

but less phlegmatic response of another fallible mechanism, capable of registering horror, capable—it is said—of passing its past life in review in the space of a few seconds, and then—capable of becoming equally inanimate matter.

Luckily nothing of this sort happened, and the feeling of loneliness passed the moment I came in sight of the long rows of barracks, the hangars and machine shops of the aviation school. My joy when I saw them can only be appreciated in full by fellow aviators who remember the end of their own first long flight. I had been away for years. I would not have been surprised to find great changes. If the brevet monitor had come hobbling out to meet me holding an ear trumpet in his withered hand, the sight would have been quite in keeping with my own sense of the lapse of time. However, he approached with his ancient springy, businesslike step, as I climbed down from my machine. I swallowed to clear the passage to my ears, and heard him say, "*Alors ça va?*" in a most disappointingly perfunctory tone of voice.

I nodded.

"Where's your biograph?"

My biograph! It is the altitude-registering instrument which also marks, on a cross-lined chart, the time consumed on each lap of an aerial voyage. My card should have shown four neat outlines in ink, something like this—

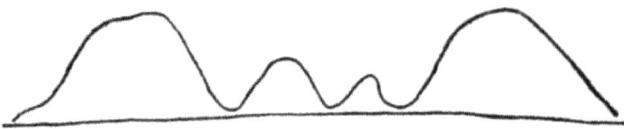

. . . . .one for each stage of my journey, including the forced landing when I had lost my way. But having started the mechanism going upon leaving A——, I had then forgotten all. about it, so that it had gone on running while my machine was on the ground as well as during the time it was in the air. The result was a sketch of a magnificent mountain range which might have been drawn by the futurist son, aged five, of a futurist artist. Silently I handed over the instrument. The monitor looked at it, and then at me without comment. But there is an international language of facial expression, and his said, unmistakably, "You poor, simple prune! You choice sample of mouldy American cheese!"

J. B. didn't return until the following afternoon. After leaving me over C——, he had blown out two spark-plugs. For a while he limped along on six cylinders, and then landed in a field three kilometres from the nearest town. His French, which is worse, if that is possible, than mine, aroused the suspicions of a patriot farmer, who collared him as a possible German spy. Under a bodyguard of two peasants, armed with hoes, he was marched to a neighbouring *chateau*. And then, I should have thought, he would have had another historical illusion,—this time with a French Revolutionary setting. He says not, however. All his faculties were concentrated in enjoying this unusual adventure; and he was wondering what the outcome of it would be.

At the *château* he met a fine old gentleman who spoke English with that nicety of utterance which only a cultivated Frenchman can achieve. He had no difficulty in clearing himself. Then he had dinner in a hall hung with armour and hunting trophies, was shown to a chamber half as large as the lounge at the Harvard Club, and slept in a bed which he got into by means of a ladder of carved oak. This is a mere outline. Out of regard for J. B.'s opinions about the sanctities of his own personal adventures, I refrain from giving further details.

These were the usual experiences which every American pilot has had while on his brevet flights. As I write I think of scores of others, for they were of almost daily occurrence.

Jackson landed—unintentionally, of course—in a town square and was banqueted by the Mayor, although he had nearly run him down a few hours earlier, and had ruined forever his reputation as a man of dignified bearing. But the Mayor was not alone in his forced display of unseemly haste. Many other townspeople, long past the nimbleness of youth, rushed for shelter; and pride goeth before a collision with a wayward aeroplane. Jackson said the sky rained hats, market baskets, and wooden shoes for five minutes after his Blériot had come to rest on the steps of the *bureau de poste*. And no one was hurt.

Murphy's defective motor provided him with the names and addresses of every possible and impossible *marraine* in the town of Y——, near which he was compelled to land. While waiting for the arrival of his mechanician with a new supply of spark-plugs, he left his monoplane in a field close by. A path to the place was worn by the feet of the young women of the town, whose dearest wish appeared to be to have an aviator as a *filleul*. They covered the wings of his *avion* with messages in pencil. The least pointed of these hints were, "Écrivez *le plus tôt possible*"; and, "*Je voudrais bien un filleul américain, très gentil, comme vous.*"

Matthews' biplane crashed through the roof of a camp bakery. If he had practiced this unusual *atterrissage* a thousand times he could not have done it so neatly as at the first attempt. He followed the motor through to the kitchen and finally hung suspended a few feet from the ceiling. The army bread-bakers stared up at him with faces as white as fear and flour could make them. The commandant of the camp rushed in. He asked, "What have you done with the corps?" The bread-bakers pointed to Matthews, who apologised for his bad choice of landing-ground. He was hardly scratched.

Mac lost his way in the clouds and landed near a small village for gasoline and information. The information he had easily, but gasoline was scarce. After laborious search through several neighbouring villages he found a supply and had it carried to the field where his machine was waiting. Some farmer lads agreed to hold on to the tail while Mac started the engine. At the first roar of the rotary motor they all let loose. The Blériot pushed Mac contemptuously aside, lifted its tail and rushed away. He followed it over a level tract of country miles in extent, and found it at last in a ditch, nose down, tail in air, like a duck hunting bugs in the mud. This story loses nine tenths of its interest for want of Mac's pungent method of telling it.

One of the *bona-fide* godchildren of Chance was Millard. The circumstances leading to his engagement in the French service as a member of the Franco-American Corps proves this. Millard was a real human being,—he had no grammar, no polish, no razor, safety or otherwise, but likewise no pretence, no "swank." He was *persona non grata* to a few, but the great majority liked him very much, although they wondered how in the name of all that is curious he had ever decided to join the French Air Service. Once he told us his history at great length. He had been a scout in the Philippine service of the American Army. He had been a roustabout on cattle boats. He had boiled his coffee down by the stockyards in every sizable town on every transcontinental railroad in America. In the spring of 1916 he had employment with a roofing company which had contracted for a job in Richmond, Virginia, I think it was. But Richmond went "dry" in the State elections; the roofing job fell through, owing, so Millard insisted, to the natural and inevitable depression which follows a dry election. Having lost his prospective employment as a roofer, what more natural than that he should turn to this other high calling?

He was game. He tried hard and at last reached his brevet tests. Three times he started off on triangles. No one expected to see him return, but he surprised them every time. He could never find the

AN AMERICAN PILOT'S INVESTIGATION OF A CAMP BAKERY.

towns where he was supposed to land, so he would keep on going till his gas gave out. Then his machine would come down of itself, and Millard would crawl out from under the wreckage and come back by train.

"I don't know," he would say doubtfully, rubbing his eight-days' growth of beard; "I'm seeing a lot of France, but this coming-down business ain't what it's cracked up to be. I can swing in on the rods of a box car with the train going hell bent for election, but I guess I 'm too old to learn to fly."

The War Office came to this opinion after Millard had smashed three machines in three tries. Wherever he may be now, I am sure that Chance is still ruling his destiny, and I hope, with all my heart, benevolently.

Our final triangle was completed uneventfully. J. B.'s motor behaved splendidly; I remembered my biograph at every stage of the journey, and we were at home again within three hours. We did our altitude tests and were then no longer élèves pilotes, but pilotes aviateurs. By reason of this distinction we passed from the rank of soldier of the second class to that of corporal. At the tailor's shop the wings and star insignia were sewn upon our collars and our corporal's stripes upon our sleeves. For we were proud, as every aviator is proud, who reaches the end of his apprenticeship and enters into the dignity of a brevetted military pilot.

Six months have passed since I made the last entry in my journal. J. B. was asleep in his historic bed, and I was sitting at a rickety table writing by candle-light, stopping now and then to listen to the mutter of guns on the Aisne front. It was only at night that we could hear them, and then not often, the very ghost of sound, as faint as the beating of the pulses in one's ears. That was a May evening, and this, one late in November. I arrived at the Gare du Nord only a few hours ago. Never before have I come to Paris with a finer sense of the joy of living. I walked down the *rue* Lafayette, through the rue de Provence, the *rue* du Havre, to a little hotel in the vicinity of the Gare Saint-Lazare. Under ordinary circumstances none of these streets, nor the people in them, would have appeared particularly interesting. But on this occasion—it was the finest walk of my life. I saw everything with the eyes of the *permissionnaire*, and sniffed the odours of roasting chestnuts, of restaurants, of shops, of people, never so keenly aware of their numberless variety.

After dinner I walked out on the boulevards from the Madeleine to the Place de la Republique, through the maze of narrow streets to the river, and over the Pont Neuf to Notre Dame. I was surprised that the spell which Hugo gives it should have lost none of its old potency for me after coming direct from the realities of modern warfare. If he were writing this journal, what a story it would be!

It will be necessary to pass rapidly over the period between the day when we received our *brevets militaires* and that upon which we started for the front. The event which bulked largest to us was, of course, the departure on active service. Preceding it, and next in importance, was the last phase of our training and the culmination of it all, at the School of Acrobacy. Preliminary to our work there, we had a six weeks' course of instruction, first on the twin-motor Caudron and then on various types of the Nieuport biplane. We thought the Caudron a magnificent machine. We liked the steady throb of its powerful motors, the enormous spread of its wings, the slow, ponderous way it had of answering to the controls. It was our business to take officer observers for long trips about the country while they made photographs, spotted dummy batteries, and perfected themselves in the wireless code. At that time the Caudron had almost passed its period of usefulness at the front, and there was a prospect of our being transferred to the yet larger and more powerful Léotard, a three-passenger biplane carrying two machine gunners besides the pilot, and from three to five machine guns.

This appealed to us mightily. J. B. was always talking of the time when he would command not only a machine, but also a "gang of men." However, being Americans, and recruited for a particular combat corps which flies only single-seater *avions de chasse*, we eventually followed the usual course of training for such pilots. We passed in turn to the Nieuport biplane, which compares in speed and grace with these larger craft as the flight of a swallow with the movements of a great lazy buzzard. And now the Nieuport has been surpassed, and almost entirely supplanted, by the Spad of 140, 180, 200, and 230 horsepower, and we have transferred our allegiance to each in turn, marvelling at the genius of the French in motor and aircraft construction.

At last we were ready for acrobacy. I will not give an account of the trials by means of which one's ability as a combat pilot is most severely tested. This belongs among the pages of a textbook rather than in those of a journal of this kind. But to us who were to undergo the ordeal,—for it is an ordeal for the untried pilot,—our typewritten notes on acrobacy read like the pages of a fascinating romance. A year

THE NIEUPORT BIPLANE OF LIEUTENANT NUNGESSER THE FRENCH ACE

SPAD BIPLANES OF CAPTAIN GUYNEMERS *ESCADRILLE*

or two ago these aerial manoeuvres would have been thought impossible. Now we were all to do them as a matter of routine training. The worst of it was, that our civilian pursuits offered no criterion upon which to base forecasts of our ability as acrobats. There was J. B., for example. He knew a mixed metaphor when he saw one, for he had had wide experience with them as an English instructor at a New England "prep" school. But he had never done a barrel turn, or anything resembling it. How was he to know what his reaction would be to this bewildering manoeuvre, a series of rapid, horizontal, corkscrew turns? And to what use could I put my hazy knowledge of Massachusetts statutes dealing with neglect and non-support of family, in that exciting moment when, for the first time, I should be whirling earthward in a spinning nose-dive? Accidents and fatalities were most frequent at the school of acrobacy, for the reason that one could not know, beforehand, whether he would be able to keep his head, with the earth gone mad, spinning like a top, standing on one rim, turning upside down.

In the end we all mastered it after a fashion, for the tests are by no means so difficult of accomplishment as they appear to be. Up to this time, November 28, 1917, there has been but one American killed at it in French schools. We were not all good acrobats. One must have a knack for it which many of us will never be able to acquire. The French have it in larger proportion than do we Americans. I can think of no sight more pleasing than that of a Spad in the air, under the control of a skilful French pilot. Swallows perch in envious silence on the chimney pots, and the crows caw in sullen despair from the hedgerows.

At G. D. E., while awaiting our call to the front, we perfected ourselves in these manoeuvres, and practiced them in combat and group flying. There, the restraints of the schools were removed, for we were supposed to be accomplished pilots. We flew when and in what manner we liked. Sometimes we went out in large formations, for a long flight; sometimes, in groups of two or three, we made sham attacks on villages, or trains, or motor convoys on the roads. It was forbidden to fly over Paris, and for this reason we took all the more delight in doing it. J. B. and I saw it in all its moods: in the haze of early morning, at midday when the air had been washed clean by spring rains, in the soft light of afternoon,—domes, theatres, temples, spires, streets, parks, the river, bridges, all of it spread out in magnificent panorama.

We would circle over Montmartre, Neuilly, the Bois, Saint-Cloud, the Latin Quarter, and then full speed homeward, listening anxiously to the sound of our motors until we spiralled safely down over our aerodrome. Our monitor never asked questions. He is one of many Frenchmen whom we shall always remember with gratitude.

We learned the songs of all motors, the peculiarities and uses of all types of French *avions*, pushers and tractors, single motor and bimotor, monoplace, biplace, and triplace, monoplane and biplane. And we mingled with the pilots of all these many kinds of aircraft. They were arriving and departing by every train, for G. D. E. is the depot for old pilots from the front, transferring from one branch of aviation to another, as well as for new ones fresh from the schools. In our talks with them, we became convinced that the air service is forming its traditions and developing a new type of mind. It even has an odour, as peculiar to itself as the smell of the sea to a ship. There are those who say that it is only a compound of burnt castor oil and gasoline. One might, with no more truth, call the odour of a ship a mixture of tar and stale cooking. But let it pass. It will be all things to all men; I can sense it as I write, for it gets into one's clothing, one's hair, one's very blood.

We were as happy during those days at G. D. E. as any one has the right to be. Our whole duty was to fly, and never was the voice of Duty heard more gladly. It was hard to keep in mind the stern purpose behind this seeming indulgence. At times I remembered Drew's warning that we were military pilots and had no right to forget the seriousness of the work before us. But he himself often forgot it for days together. War on the earth may be reasonable and natural, but in the air it seems the most senseless folly. How is an airman, who has just learned a new meaning for the joy of life, to reconcile himself to the insane business of killing a fellow aviator who may have just learned it too? This was a question which we sometimes put to ourselves in purely Arcadian moments. We answered it, of course.

I was sitting at our two-legged table, writing up my *carnet de vol*. Suzanne, the maid of all work at the Bonne Rencontre, was sweeping a passageway along the centre of the room, telling me, as she worked, about her family. She was ticking off the names of her brothers and sisters, when Drew put his head through the doorway.

"*Il y a Pierre*," said Suzanne.

"We're posted," said J. B.

"*Et Hélène*," she continued.

I shall never know the names of the others.

CHAPTER 5

Our First Patrol

We got down from the train late in the afternoon at a village which reminded us, at first glance, of a boom town in the Far West. Crude shelters of corrugated iron and rough pine boards faced each other down the length of one long street. They looked sadly out of place in that landscape. They did not have the cheery, buoyant ugliness of pioneer homes in an unsettled country, for behind them were the ruins of the old village, fragments of blackened wall, stone chimneys filled with accumulations of rubbish, garden-plots choked with weeds, reminding us that here was no outpost of a new civilization, but the desolation of an old one, fallen upon evil days.

A large crowd of *permissionnaires* had left the train with us. We were not at ease among these men, many of them well along in middle life, bent and streaming with perspiration under their heavy packs. We were much better able than most of them to carry our belongings, to endure the fatigue of a long night march to billets or trenches; and we were waiting for the motor in which we should ride comfortably to our aerodrome. There we should sleep in beds, well housed from the weather, and far out of the range of shell fire.

"It isn't fair," said J. B. "It is going to war *de luxe*. These old *poilus* ought to be the aviators. But, hang it all! of course, they couldn't be. Aviation is a young man's business. It has to be that way. And you can't have aerodromes along the front-line trenches."

Nevertheless, it did seem very unfair, and we were uncomfortable among all those infantrymen. The feeling increased when attention was called to our branch of the service by the distant booming of anti-aircraft guns. There were shouts in the street, "A Boche!" We hurried to the door of the *café* where we had been hiding. Officers were ordering the crowds off the street. "Hurry along there! Under cover!

THE VALLE

Desolation

Oh, I know that you're brave enough, *mon enfant*. It is n't that. He's not to see all these soldiers here. That's the reason. *Allez! Vite!*"

Soldiers were going into dugouts and cellars among the ruined houses. Some of them, seeing us at the door of the *café*, made pointed remarks as they passed, grumbling loudly at the laxity of the air service.

"It's up there you ought to be, *mon vieux*, not here," one of them said, pointing to the white *éclatements*.

"You see that?" said another. "He's a Boche, not French, I can tell you that. Where are your comrades?"

There was much good-natured chaffing as well, but through it all I could detect a note of resentment. I sympathized with their point of view then as I do now, although I know that there is no ground for the complaint of laxity. Here is a German over French territory. Where are the French aviators? Soldiers forget that aerial frontiers must be guarded in two dimensions, and that it is always possible for an airman to penetrate far into enemy country. They do not see their own pilots on their long raids into German territory. Furthermore, while the outward journey is often accomplished easily enough, the return home is a different matter. Telephones are busy from the moment the lines are crossed, and a hostile patrol, to say nothing of a lone *avion*, will be fortunate if it returns safely.

But infantrymen are to be forgiven readily for their outbursts against the aviation service. They have far more than their share of danger and death while in the trenches. To have their brief periods of rest behind the lines broken into by enemy aircraft—who would blame them for complaining? And they are often generous enough with their praise.

On this occasion there was no bombing. The German remained at a great height and quickly turned northward again.

Dunham and Miller came to meet us. We had all four been in the schools together, they preceding us on active service only a couple of months. Seeing them after this lapse of time, I was conscious of a change. They were keen about life at the front, but they talked of their experiences in a way which gave one a feeling of tension, a tautness of muscles, a kind of ache in the throat. It set me to thinking of a conversation I had had with an old French pilot, several months before. It came *apropos* of nothing. Perhaps he thought that I was sizing him up, wondering how he could be content with an instructor's job while the war is in progress. He said: "I've had five hundred hours over the lines. You don't know what that means, not yet. I'm no good any more. It's strain. Let me give you some advice. Save your nervous energy. You will need all you have and more. Above everything else, don't think at the front. The best pilot is the best machine."

Dunham was talking about patrols.

"Two a day of two hours each. Occasionally you will have six hours' flying, but almost never more than that."

"What about voluntary patrols?" Drew asked. "I don't suppose there is any objection, is there?"

Miller pounded Dunham on the back, singing, "*Hi-doo-dedoo-dum-di*. What did I tell you! Do I win?" Then he explained. "We asked the same question when we came out, and every other new pilot before us. This voluntary patrol business is a kind of standing joke. You think, now, that four hours a day over the lines is a light programme. For the first month or so you will go out on your own between times. After that, no. Of course, when they call for a voluntary patrol for some necessary piece of work, you will volunteer out of a sense of duty. As I say, you may do as much flying as you like. But wait. After a month, or we'll give you six weeks, that will be no more than you have to do."

We were not at all convinced.

"What do you do with the rest of your time?"

"Sleep," said Dunham. "Read a good deal. Play some poker or bridge. Walk. But sleep is the chief amusement. Eight hours used to be enough for me. Now I can do with ten or twelve."

Drew said: "That's all rot. You fellows are having it too soft. They ought to put you on the school regime again."

"Let 'em talk, Dunham. They know. J. B. says it's laziness. Let it go at that. Well, take it from me, it's contagious. You'll soon be victims."

I dropped out of the conversation in order to look around me. Drew did all of the questioning, and thanks to his interest, I got many hints about our work which came back opportunely, afterward.

"Think down to the gunners. That will help a lot. It's a game after that: your skill against theirs. I couldn't do it at first, and shell fire seemed absolutely damnable."

"And you want to remember that a chasse machine is almost never brought down by anti-aircraft fire. You are too fast for them. You can fool 'em in a thousand ways."

"I had been flying for two weeks before I saw a Boche. They are not scarce on this sector, don't worry. I simply couldn't see them. The others would have scraps. I spent most of my time trying to keep track of them."

"Take my tip, J. B., don't be too anxious to mix it with the first German you see, because very likely he will be a Frenchman, and if he isn't, if he is a good Hun pilot, you'll simply be meat for him—at first, I mean."

"They say that all the Boche aviators on this front have had several months' experience in Russia or the Balkans. They train them there before they send them to the Western Front."

"Your best chance of being brought down will come in the first two weeks."

"That's comforting."

"No, *sans blague*. Honestly, you'll be almost helpless. You don't see anything, and you don't know what it is that you do see. Here's an example. On one of my first sorties I happened to look over my shoulder and I saw five or six Germans in the most beautiful alignment. And they were all slanting up to dive on me. I was scared out of my life: went down full motor, then cut and fell into a *vrille*. Came out of that and had another look. There they were in the same position, only farther away. I didn't tumble even then, except farther down. Next time I looked, the five Boches, or six, whichever it was, had all been ravelled out by the wind. Éclats *d'obus*."

"You may have heard about Franklin's Boche. He got it during his first combat. He didn't know that there was a German in the sky, until he saw the tracer bullets. Then the machine passed him about thirty metres away. And he kept going down: may have had motor trouble. Franklin said that he had never had such a shock in his life. He dived after him, spraying all space with his Vickers, and he got him!"

"That all depends on the man. In chasse, unless you are sent out on a definite mission, protecting photographic machines or *avions de bombardement*, you are absolutely on your own. Your job is to patrol the lines. If a man is built that way, he can loaf on the job. He need never have a fight. At two hundred kilometres an hour, it won't take him very long to get out of danger. He stays out his two hours and comes in with some framed-up tale to account for his disappearance: 'Got lost. Went off by himself into Germany. Had motor trouble; gun jammed, and went back to arm it.' He may even spray a few bullets toward Germany and call it a combat. Oh, he can find plenty of excuses, and he can get away with them."

"That's spreading it, Dunham. What about Huston? is he getting away with it?"

"Now, don't let's get personal. Very likely Huston can't help it. Anyway, it is a matter of temperament mostly."

"Temperament, hell! There's Van, for example. I happen to know that he has to take himself by his bootlaces every time he crosses into Germany. But he sticks it. He has never played a yellow trick. I hand it to him for pluck above every other man in the squadron."

"What about Talbott and Barry?"

"Lord! They haven't any nerves. It's no job for them to do their work well."

This conversation continued during the rest of the journey. The life of a military pilot offers exceptional opportunities for research in the matter of personal bravery. Dunham and Miller agreed that it is a varying quality. Sometimes one is really without fear; at others only a sense of shame prevents one from making a very sad display.

"Huston is no worse than some of the rest of us, only he hasn't a sense of shame."

"Well, he has the courage to be a coward, and that is more than you have, son, or I either."

Our fellow pilots of the Lafayette Corps were lounging outside the barracks on our arrival. They gave us a welcome which did much to remove our feelings of strangeness; but we knew that they were only mildly interested in the news from the schools and were glad when they let us drop into the background of conversation. By a happy chance mention was made of a recent newspaper article of some of the exploits of the *Escadrille*, written evidently by a very imaginative journalist; and from this the talk passed to the reputation of the Squadron in America, and the almost fabulous deeds credited to it by some newspaper correspondents.

One pilot said that he had kept record of the number of German machines actually reported as having been brought down by members of the corps. I don't remember the number he gave, but it was an astonishing total. The daily average was so high, that, granting it to be correct, America might safely have abandoned her far-reaching aerial programme. Long before her first pursuit squadron could be ready for service, the last of the imperial German air-fleet would, to quote from the article, have "crashed in smouldering ruin on the war-devastated plains of northern France."

In this connection I can't forbear quoting from another, one of the brightest pages in the journalistic history of the legendary Escadrille Lafayette. It is an account of a sortie said to have taken place on the receipt of news of America's declaration of war.

"Uncle Sam is with us, boys! Come on! Let's get those fellows!" These were the stirring words of Captain Georges Thenault, the valiant leader of the Escadrille Lafayette, upon the morning when news was received that the United States of America had declared war upon the rulers of Potsdam. For the first time in history, the Stars and Stripes of Old Glory were flung to the breeze over the camp, in France, of American fighting men. Inspired by the sight, and spurred to instant action by the ringing call of their French captain, this band of aviators from the U.S.A. sprang into their trim little biplanes. There was a deafening roar of motors, and soon the last airman had disappeared in the smoky haze which hung over the distant battle-lines.

We cannot follow them on that journey. We cannot see them as they mount higher and higher into the morning sky, on their way to meet their prey. But we may await their return. We may watch them as they descend to their flying-field, dropping down to earth, one by one. We may learn, then, of their adventures on that flight of death: how, far back of the German lines, they encountered a formidable battle-squadron of the enemy, vastly superior to their own in numbers. Heedless of the risk they swooped down upon their foe.

Lieutenant A—— was attacked by four enemy planes at the same time. One he sent hurtling to the ground fifteen thousand feet below. He caused a second to retire disabled. Sergeant B—— accounted for another in a running fight which lasted for more than a quarter of an hour. Adjutant C——, although his biplane was riddled with bullets, succeeded, by a clever ruse, in decoying two pursuers, bent on his destruction, to the vicinity of a cloud where several of his comrades were lying in wait for further victims. A moment later both Germans were seen to fall earthward, spinning like leaves in that last terrible dive of death. "These boys are Yankee aviators. They form the vanguard of America's aerial forces. We need thousands of others just like them," etc.

Stories of this kind have, without doubt, a certain imaginative appeal. J. B. and I had often read them, never wholly credulous, of course, but with feelings of uneasiness. Discounting them by more than half, we still had serious doubts of our ability to measure up to the standard set by our fellow Americans who had preceded us on active service. We were in part reassured during our first afternoon at the front. If these men were the demons on wings of the newspapers, they took great pains to give us a different impression.

Many of the questions which had long been accumulating in our minds got themselves answered during the next few days, while we were waiting for machines. We knew, in a general way, what the nature of our work would be. We knew that the Escadrille Lafayette was one of four pursuit squadrons occupying hangars on the same field, and that, together, these formed what is called a *groupe de combat*, with a definite sector of front to cover. We had been told that combat pilots are "the police of the air," whose duty it is to patrol the lines, harass the enemy, attacking whenever possible, thus giving protection to their own *corps-d'armée* aircraft—which are only incidentally fighting machines—in their work of reconnaissance, photography, artillery direction, and the like. But we did not know how this general theory of combat is given practical application.

When I think of the depths of our ignorance, to be filled in, day by day, with a little additional experience; of our self-confidence, despite warnings; of our willingness to leave so much for our "godfather" Chance to decide, it is with feelings nearly akin to awe. We awaited our first patrol almost ready to believe that it would be our first victorious combat. We had no realisation of the conditions under which aerial battles are fought. Given goodwill, average ability, and the opportunity, we believed that the results must be decisive, one way or the other.

Much of our enforced leisure was spent at the bureau of the group, where the pilots gathered after each sortie to make out their reports. There we heard accounts of exciting combats, of victories and narrow escapes, which sounded like impossible fictions. A few of them may have been, but not many. They were told simply, briefly, as a part of the day's work, by men who no longer thought of their adventures as being either very remarkable or very interesting. What, I thought, will seem interesting or remarkable to them after the war, after such a life as this? Once an American gave me a hint: "I'm going to apply for a job as attendant in a natural-history museum."

Only a few minutes before, these men had been taking part in aerial battles, attacking infantry in trenches, or enemy transport on roads fifteen or twenty kilometres away. And while they were talking of these things the drone of motors overhead announced the departure of other patrols to battle-lines which were only five minutes distant by the route of the air. For when weather permitted there was an interlapping series of patrols flying over the sector from daylight till dark. The number of these, and the number of *avions* in each patrol, varied as circumstances demanded.

On one wall of the bureau hung a large-scale map of the sector, which we examined square by square with that delight which only the study of maps can give. Trench-systems, both French and German, were outlined upon it in minute detail. It contained other features of a very interesting nature. On another wall there was a yet larger map, made of aeroplane photographs taken at a uniform altitude and so pieced together that the whole was a complete picture of our sector of front. We spent hours over this one. Every trench, every shell hole, every splintered tree or fragment of farmhouse wall stood out clearly. We could identify machine-gun posts and battery positions. We could see at a glance the result of months of fighting; how terribly men had suffered under a rain of high explosives at this point, how lightly they had escaped at another; and so we could follow, with a certain degree of accuracy, what must have been the infantry actions at various parts of the line.

The history of these trench campaigns will have a forbidding interest to the student of the future; for, as he reads of the battles on the Aisne, the Somme, of Verdun and Flanders, he will have spread out before him photographs of the battlefields themselves, just as they were at different phases of the struggle. With a series of these pictorial records, men will be able to find the trenches from which their fathers or grandfathers scrambled with their regiments to the attack, the wire entanglements which held up the advance at one point, the shell holes where they lay under machine-gun fire. And often they will see the men themselves as they advanced through the barrage fire, the sun glinting on their helmets. It will be a fascinating study, in a ghastly way; and while such records exist, the outward meanings, at least, of modern warfare will not be forgotten.

Tiffin, the messroom steward, was standing by my cot with a lighted candle in his hand. The furrows in his kindly old face were outlined in shadow. His bald head gleamed like the bottom of a yellow bowl. He said, "*Beau temps, monsieur,*" put the candle on my table, and went out, closing the door softly. I looked at the window square, which was covered with oiled cloth for want of glass. It was a black patch showing not a glimmer of light.

The other pilots were gathering in the messroom, where a fire was going. Someone started the phonograph. Fritz Kreisler was playing the "*Chansons sans Paroles.*" This was followed by a song, "Oh, movin' man, don't take ma baby grand." It was a strange combination, and to hear them, at that hour of the morning, before going out for a first sortie over the lines, gave me a "mixed-up" feeling, which it was impossible to analyse.

Two patrols were to leave the field at the same time, one to cover the sector at an altitude of from two thousand to three thousand metres, the other, thirty-five hundred to five thousand metres. J. B. and I were on high patrol. Owing to our inexperience, it was to be a purely defensive one between our observation balloons and the lines. We had still many questions to ask, but having been so persistently inquisitive for three days running, we thought it best to wait for Talbott, who was leading our patrol, to volunteer his instructions.

He went to the door to look at the weather. There were clouds at about three thousand metres, but the stars were shining through gaps in them. On the horizon, in the direction of the lines, there was a broad belt of blue sky. The wind was blowing into Germany. He came back yawning. "We'll go up—ho, hum!"— tremendous yawn— "through a hole before we reach the river. It's going to be clear presently, so the higher we go the better."

The others yawned sympathetically.

"I don't feel very pugnastic this morning."

"It's a crime to send men out at this time of day—night, rather."

More yawns of assent, of protest. J. B. and I were the only ones fully awake. We had finished our chocolate and were watching the clock uneasily, afraid that we should be late getting started. Ten minutes before patrol time we went out to the field. The canvas hangars billowed and flapped, and the wooden supports creaked with the quiet sound made by ships at sea. And there was almost the peace of the sea there, intensified, if anything, by the distant rumble of heavy cannonading.

Our Spad biplanes were drawn up in two long rows, outside the hangars. They were in exact alignment, wing to wing. Some of them were clean and new, others discoloured with smoke and oil; among these latter were the ones which J. B. and I were to fly. Being new pilots we were given used machines to begin with, and ours had already seen much service. Fuselage and wings had many patches over the scars of old battles, but new motors had been installed, the bodies overhauled, and they were ready for further adventures.

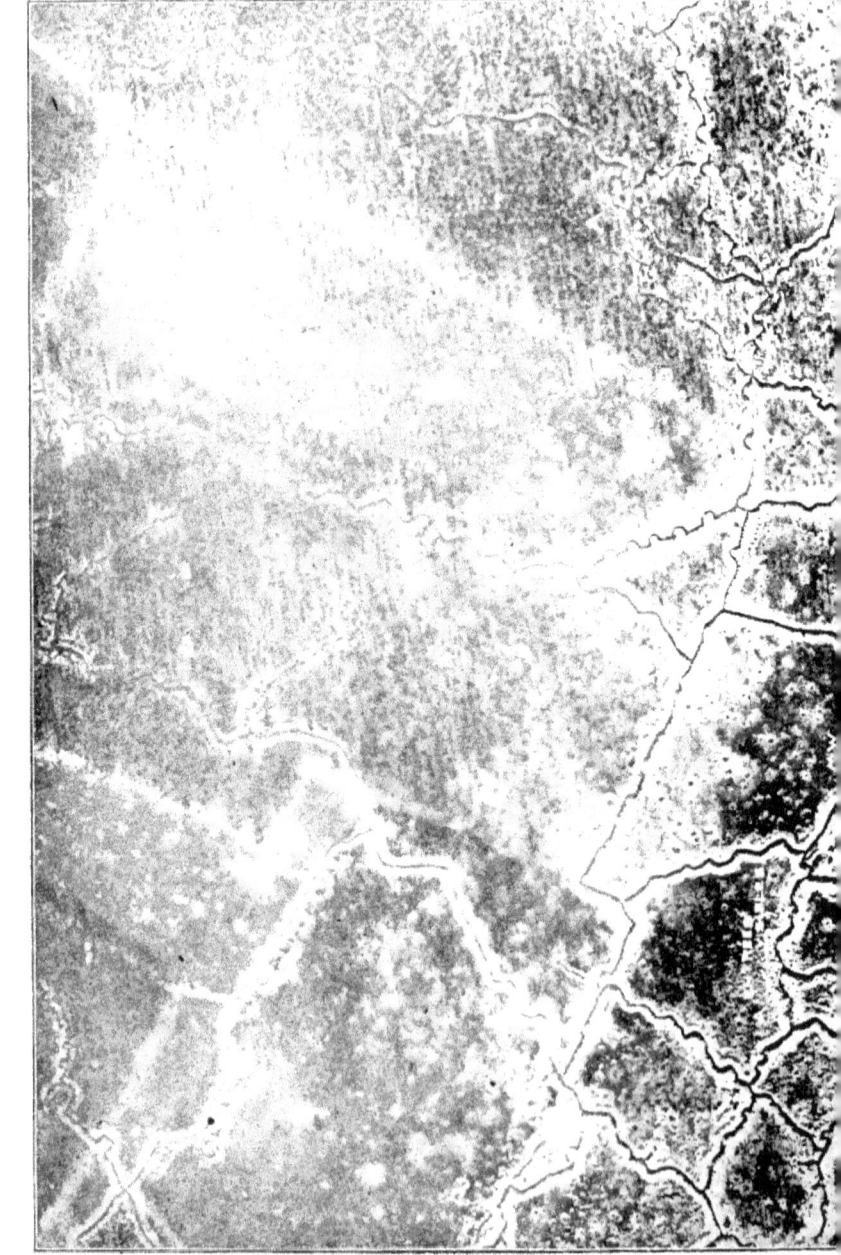

Segment of Trench Line, showing No Man's Land

It mattered little to us that they were old. They were to carry us out to our first air battles; they were the first *avions* which we could call our own, and we loved them in an almost personal way. Each machine had an Indian head, the symbol of the Lafayette Corps, painted on the sides of the *fuselage*. In addition, it bore the personal mark of its pilot,—a triangle, a diamond, a straight band, or an initial,—painted large so that it could be easily seen and recognised in the air.

The mechanicians were getting the motors *en route*, arming the machine guns, and giving a final polish to the glass of the windshields. In a moment every machine was turning over *ralenti*, with the purring sound of powerful engines which gives a voice to one's feeling of excitement just before patrol time. There was no more yawning, no languid movement.

Rodman was buttoning himself into a combination suit which appeared to add another six inches to his six feet two. Barry, who was leading the low patrol, wore a woollen helmet which left only his eyes uncovered. I had not before noticed how they blazed and snapped. All his energy seemed to be concentrated in them. Porter wore a leather face-mask, with a lozenge-shaped breathing-hole, and slanted openings covered with yellow glass for eyes. He was the most fiendish-looking demon of them all. I was glad to turn from him to the Duke, who wore a *passe-montagne* of white silk which fitted him like a bonnet. As he sat in his machine, adjusting his goggles, he might have passed for a dear old lady preparing to read a chapter from the Book of Daniel. The fur of Dunham's helmet had frayed out, so that it fitted around the sides of his face and under the chin like a beard, the kind worn by old-fashioned sailors.

The strain of waiting patiently for the start was trying. The sudden transformation of a group of typical-looking Americans into monsters and devotional old ladies gave a moment of diversion which helped to relieve it.

I heard Talbott shouting his parting instructions and remembered that I did not know the rendezvous. I was already strapped in my machine and was about to loosen the fastenings, when he came over and climbed on the step of the car.

"Rendezvous two thousand over field!" he yelled.

I nodded.

"Know me—Big T—wings—fuselage. I'll—turning right. You and others left. When—see me start—lines, fall in behind—left. Remember stick close—patrol. If—get lost, better—home. Compass southwest. Look carefully—landmarks going out. Got—straight?"

I nodded again to show that I understood. Machines of both patrols were rolling across the field, a mechanician running along beside each one. I joined the long line, and taxied over to the starting-point, where the captain was superintending the send-off, and turned into the wind in my turn. As though conscious of his critical eye, my old veteran Spad lifted its tail and gathered flying speed with all the vigour of its youth, and we were soon high above the hangars, climbing to the rendezvous.

When we had all assembled, Talbott headed northeast, the rest of us falling into our places behind him. Then I found that, despite the new motor, my machine was not a rapid climber. Talbott noticed this and kept me well in the group, he and the others losing height in *renversements* and *retournements*, diving under me and climbing up again. It was fascinating to watch them doing stunts, to observe the constant changing of positions. Sometimes we seemed, all of us, to be hanging motionless, then rising and falling like small boats riding a heavy swell. Another glance would show one of them suspended bottom up, falling sidewise, tipped vertically on a wing, standing on its tail, as though being blown about by the wind, out of all control. It is only in the air, when moving with them, that one can really appreciate the variety and grace of movement of a flock of high-powered *avions de chasse*.

I was close to Talbott as we reached the cloudbank. I saw him in dim silhouette as the mist, sunlight-filtered, closed around us. Emerging into the clear, fine air above it, we might have been looking at early morning from the casement

> *opening on the foam*
> *Of perilous seas, in faery lands forlorn.*

The sun was just rising, and the floor of cloud glowed with delicate shades of rose and amethyst and gold. I saw the others rising through it at widely scattered points. It was a glorious sight.

Then, forming up and turning northward again, just as we passed over the receding edge of the cloud-bank, I saw the lines. It was still dusk on the ground and my first view was that of thousands of winking lights, the flashes of guns and of bursting shells. At that time the Germans were making trials of the French positions along the Chemin des Dames, and the artillery fire was unusually heavy.

The lights soon faded and the long, winding battle-front emerged from the shadow, a broad strip of desert land through a fair, green

THE EFFECT OF DESTRUCTIVE
A village before, during

SHELL-FIRE AS SEEN FROM THE AIR
and after a bombardment

country. We turned westward along the sector, several kilometres within the French lines, for J. B. and I were to have a general view of it all before we crossed to the other side. The fort of Malmaison was a minute square, not as large as a postage-stamp. With thumb and forefinger, I could have spanned the distance between Soissons and Laon. Clouds of smoke were rising from Allemant to Craonne, and these were constantly added to by infinitesimal puffs in black and white. I knew that shells of enormous calibre were wrecking trenches, blasting out huge craters; and yet not a sound, not the faintest reverberation of a gun. Here was a sight almost to make one laugh at man's idea of the importance of his pygmy wars.

But the Olympian mood is a fleeting one. I think of Paradis rising on one elbow out of the slime where he and his comrades were lying, waving his hand toward the wide, unspeakable landscape.

What are we, we chaps? And what's all this here? Nothing at all. All we can see is only a speck. When one speaks of the whole war, it's as if you said nothing at all—the words are strangled. We're here, and we look at it like blind men.

To look down from a height of more than two miles, on an endless panorama of suffering and horror, is to have the sense of one's littleness even more painfully quickened. The best that the airman can do is to repeat, "*We're here, and we look at it like blind men.*"

We passed on to the point where the line bends northward, then turned back. I tried to concentrate my attention on the work of identifying landmarks. It was useless. One might as well attempt to study Latin grammar at his first visit to the Grand Cañon. My thoughts went wool-gathering. Looking up suddenly, I found that I was alone.

To the new pilot the sudden appearance or disappearance of other *avions* is a weird thing. He turns his head for a moment. When he looks again, his patrol has vanished. Combats are matters of a few seconds' duration, rarely of more than two or three minutes. The opportunity for attack comes almost with the swiftness of thought and has passed as quickly. Looking behind me, I was in time to see one machine tip and dive. Then it, too, vanished as though it had melted into the air. Shutting my motor, I started down, swiftly, I thought; but I had not yet learned to fall vertically, and the others—I can say almost with truth—were miles below me.

I passed long streamers of white smoke, crossing and recrossing in the air. I knew the meaning of these, machine-gun tracer bullets. The delicately pencilled lines had not yet frayed out in the wind. I went on down in a steep spiral, guiding myself by them, and seeing nothing. At the point where they ended, I re-dressed and put on my motor. My altimeter registered two thousand metres. By a curious chance, while searching the empty sky, I saw a live shell passing through the air. It was just at the second when it reached the top of its trajectory and started to fall. "Lord!" I thought, "I have seen a shell, and yet I can't find my patrol!"

While coming down I had given no attention to my direction. I had lost twenty-five hundred metres in height. The trenches were now plainly visible, and the brown strip of sterile country where they lay was vastly broader. Several times I felt the concussion of shell explosions, my machine being lifted and then dropped gently with an uneasy motion. Constantly searching the air, I gave no thought to my position with reference to the lines, nor to the possibility of anti-aircraft lire. Talbott had said: "Never fly in a straight line for more than fifteen seconds. Keep changing your direction constantly, but be careful not to fly in a regularly irregular fashion. The German gunners may let you alone at first, hoping that you will become careless, or they may be plotting out your style of flight. Then they make their calculations and they let you have it. If you have been careless, they'll put 'em so close, there'll be no question about the kind of a scare you will have."

There wasn't in my case. I was looking for my patrol to the exclusion of thought of anything else. The first shell burst so close that I lost control of my machine for a moment. Three others followed, two in front, and one behind, which I believed had wrecked my tail. They burst with a terrific rending sound in clouds of coal-black smoke. A few days before I had been watching without emotion the bombardment of a German plane. I had seen it twisting and turning through the *éclatements*, and had heard the shells popping faintly, with a sound like the bursting of seed-pods in the sun.

My feeling was not that of fear, exactly. It was more like despair. Every airman must have known it at one time or another, a sudden overwhelming realisation of the pitilessness of the forces which men let loose in war. In that moment one doesn't remember that men have loosed them. He is alone, and he sees the face of an utterly evil thing. Miller's advice was, "Think down to the gunners"; but this is impossible at first. Once a French captain told me that he talked to the shells. "I say, '*Bonjour, mon vieux! Tiens! Comment ça va, toi! Ah, non! je suis*

THE MAZE OF TRAFFIC ROUT
The first, second, and third positio

... THE REAR OF THE TRENCHES
...overing line for artillery are indicated

*press*é*!'* or something like that. It amuses one."

This need of some means of humanizing shell fire is common. Aviators know little of modern warfare as it touches the infantryman; but in one respect, at least, they are less fortunate. They miss the human companionship which helps a little to mask its ugliness.

However, it is seldom that one is quite alone, without the sight of friendly planes near at hand, and there is a language of signs which, in a way, fills this need. One may "waggle his flippers," or "flap his wings," to use the common expressions, and thus communicate with his comrades. Unfortunately for my ease of mind, there were no comrades present with whom I could have conversed in this way. Miller was within five hundred metres and saw me all the time, although I didn't know this until later.

Talbott's instructions were, "If you get lost, go home"—somewhat ambiguous. I knew that my course to the aerodrome was southwest. At any rate, by flying in that direction I was certain to land in France. But with German gunners so keen on the baptism-of-fire business, I had been turning in every direction, and the floating disk of my compass was revolving first to the right, then to the left. In order to let it settle, I should have to fly straight for some fixed point for at least half a minute. Under the circumstances I was not willing to do this. A compass which would point north immediately and always would be a heaven-sent blessing to the inexperienced pilot during his first few weeks at the front. Mine was saying North—northwest—west—southwest—south—southeast—east—and after a moment of hesitation reading off the points in the reverse order. The wind was blowing into Germany, and unconsciously, in trying to find a way out of the *éclatements*, I was getting farther and farther away from home and coming within range of additional batteries of hostile anti-aircraft guns.

I might have landed at Karlsruhe or Cologne, had it not been for Miller. My love for concentric circles of red, white, and blue dates from the moment when I saw the French *cocarde* on his Spad.

"And if I had been a Hun !" he said, when we landed at the aerodrome. "Oh, man! you were fruit salad! Fruit salad, I tell you! I could have speared you with my eyes shut."

I resented the implication of defencelessness. I said that I was keeping my eyes open, and if he had been a Hun, the fruit salad might not have been so palatable as it looked.

"Tell me this: Did you see me?"

I thought for a moment, and then said, "Yes."

"When?"

"When you passed over my head."

"And twenty seconds before that you would have been a sieve, if either of us had been a Boche."

I yielded the point to save further argument.

He had come swooping down fairly suddenly. When I saw him making his way so saucily among the *éclatements* I felt my confidence returning in increasing waves. I began to use my head, and found that it was possible to make the German gunners guess badly. There was no menace in the sound of shells barking at a distance, and we were soon clear of all of them.

J. B. took me aside the moment I landed. He had one of his fur boots in his hand and was wearing the other. He had also lighted the cork end of his cigarette. To one acquainted with his magisterial orderliness of mind and habit, these signs were eloquent.

"Now, keep this quiet!" he said. "I don't want the others to know it, but I've just had the adventure of my life. I attacked a German. Great Scott! what an opportunity! and I bungled it through being too eager!"

"When was this?"

"Just after the others dove. You remember—"

I told him, briefly, of my experience, adding, "And I didn't know there was a German in sight until I saw the smoke of the tracer bullets."

"Neither did I, only I didn't see even the smoke."

This cheered me immensely. "What! you didn't—"

"No. I saw nothing but sky where the others had disappeared. I was looking for them when I saw the German. He was about four hundred metres below me. He couldn't have seen me, I think, because he kept straight on. I dove, but didn't open fire until I could have a nearer view of his black crosses. I wanted to be sure. I had no idea that I was going so much faster. The first thing I knew I was right on him. Had to pull back on my stick to keep from crashing into him. Up I went and fell into a nose-dive. When I came out of it there was no sign of the German, and I hadn't fired a shot!"

"Did you come home alone?"

"No; I had the luck to meet the others just afterward. Now, not a word of this to anyone!"

But there was no need for secrecy. The near combat had been seen by both Talbott and Porter. At luncheon we both came in for our share of ragging.

"You should have seen them following us down!" said Porter; "like two old rheumatics going into the subway. We saw them both when we were taking height again. The scrap was all over hours before, and they were still a thousand metres away."

"You want to dive vertically. Needn't worry about your old 'bus. She'll stand it."

"Well, the Lord has certainly protected the innocent today!"

"One of them was wandering off into Germany. Bill had to waggle Miller to page him."

"And there was Drew, going down on that biplane we were chasing. I've been trying to think of one wrong thing he might have done which he didn't do. First he dove with the sun in his face, when he might have had it at his back. Then he came all the way in full view, instead of getting under his tail. Good thing the *mitrailleur* was firing at us. After that, when he had the chance of a lifetime, he fell into a *vrille* and scared the life out of the rest of us. I thought the gunner had turned on him. And while we were following him down to see where he was going to splash, the Boche got away."

★★★★★★

All this happened months ago, but every trifling incident connected with our first patrol is still fresh in mind. And twenty years from now, if I chance to hear the "*Chansons sans Paroles,*" or if I hum to myself a few bars of a ballad, then sure to be long forgotten by the world at large, "Oh, movin' man, don't take ma baby grand!" I shall have only to close my eyes, and wait passively. First Tiffin will come with the lighted candle: "*Beau temps, monsieur.*" I shall hear Talbott shouting, "Rendezvous two thousand over field. If—get lost—better—home." J. B. will rush up smoking the cork end of a cigarette. "I've just had the adventure of my life!" And Miller, sitting on an essence-case, will have lost none of his old conviction. "Oh, man! you were fruit salad! Fruit salad, I tell you! I could have speared you with my eyes shut!"

And in those days, happily still far off, there will be many another old grey-beard with such memories; unless they are all to wear out their days uselessly regretting that they are no longer young, there must be clubs where they may exchange reminiscences. These need not be pretentious affairs. Let there be a strong odour of burnt castor oil and gasoline as you enter the door; a wide view from the verandas of earth and sky; maps on the walls; arid on the roof a canvas "pantaloon-leg" to catch the wind. Nothing else matters very much. There they will be as happy as any old airman can expect to be, arguing about the winds and disputing one another's judgment about the height of the clouds.

If you say to one of them, "Tell us something about the Great War," as likely as not he will tell you a pleasant story enough. And the pity of it will be that, hearing the tale, a young man will long for another war. Then you must say to him, "But what about the shell fire? Tell us something of machines falling in flames." Then, if he is an honest old airman whose memory is still unimpaired, the young one who has been listening will have sober second thoughts.

CHAPTER 6

A Balloon Attack

"I'm looking for two balloonatics," said Talbott, as he came into the messroom; "and I think I've found them."

Percy, Talbott's orderly, Tiffin the steward, Drew, and I were the only occupants of the room. Percy is an old *légionnaire*, crippled with rheumatism. His active service days are over. Tiffin's working hours are filled with numberless duties. He makes the beds, and serves food from three to five times daily to members of the Escadrille Lafayette. These two being eliminated, the identity of the balloonatics was plain.

"The orders have just come," Talbott added, "and I decided that the first men I met after leaving the bureau would be balloonatics. Virtue has gone into both of you. Now, if you can make fire come out of a Boche sausage, you will have done all that is required. Listen. This is interesting. The orders are in French, but I will translate as I read:"—

> On the umteenth day of June, the *escadrilles* of Groupe de Combat Blank (that's ours) will cooperate in an attack on the German observation balloons along the sector extending from X to Y. The patrols to be furnished are: (1) two patrols of protection, of five *avions* each, by the *escadrilles* Spa. 87 and Spa. 12; (2) four patrols of attack, of three *avions* each, by the *escadrilles* Spa. 124 (that's us), Spa. 93, Spa. 10, and Spa. 12.
>
> The attack will be organised as follows: on the day set, weather permitting, the two patrols of protection will leave the field at 10.30 a.m. The patrol of Spa. 87 will rendezvous over the village of N———. The patrol of protection of Spa. 12 will rendezvous over the village of C———. At 10.45, precisely, they will start for the lines, crossing at an altitude of thirty-five hundred metres. The patrol furnished by Spa. 87 will guard the sector

from X to T, between the town of O—— and the two enemy balloons on that sector. The patrol furnished by Spa. 12 will guard the sector from T to Y, between the railway line and the two enemy balloons on that sector. Immediately after the attack has been made, these formations will return to the aerodrome. At 10.40 a.m. the four patrols of attack will leave the field, and will rendezvous as follows. (Here followed the directions.) At 10.55, Precisely, they will start for the lines, crossing at an approximate altitude of sixteen hundred metres, each patrol making in a direct line for the balloon assigned to it. Numbers 1 and 2 of each of these patrols will carry rockets. Number 3 will fly immediately above them, offering further protection in case of attack by enemy aircraft. Number 1 of each patrol will first attack the balloon. If he fails, number 2 will attack. If number 1 is successful, number 2 will then attack the observers in their parachutes. If number 1 fails, and number 2 is successful, number 3 will attack the observers. The patrol will then proceed to the aerodrome by the shortest route.

Squadron commanders will make a return before noon today, of the names of pilots designated by them for their respective patrols.

In case of unfavourable weather, squadron commanders will be informed of the date to which the attack has been postponed. Pilots designated as numbers 1 and 2 of the patrols of attack will be relieved from the usual patrol duty from this date. They will employ their time at rocket shooting. A target will be in place on the east side of the field from 1.30 p.m. today.

"Are there any remarks?" said Talbott, as if he had been reading the minutes at a debating-club meeting.

"Yes," said J. B. "When is the umteenth of June?"

"Ah, *mon vieux*! that's the question. The *commandant* knows, and he isn't telling. Any other little thing?"

I suggested that we would like to know which of us was to be number 1.

"That's right. Drew, how would you like to be the first rocketeer?"

"I've no objection," said J. B., grinning as if the frenzy of balloon-aticking had already got into his blood.

"Right! that's settled. I'll see your mechanicians about fitting your machines for rockets. You can begin practice this afternoon."

Percy had been listening with interest to the conversation.

"You got some nice job, you boys. But if you bring him down, there will be a lot of chuckling in the trenches. You won't hear it, but they will all be saying, '*Bravo! Épatant!*' I've been there. I've seen it and I know. Does 'em all good to see a sausage brought down. 'There's another one of their eyes knocked out,' they say."

"Percy is right," said J. B. as we were walking down the road. "Destroying a balloon is not a great achievement in itself. Of course, it's so much equipment gone, so much expense added to the German war-budget. That is something. But the effect on the infantrymen is the important thing. Boche soldiers, thousands of them, will see one of their balloons coming down in flame. They will be saying, 'Where are our airmen?' like those old *poilus* we met at the station when we first came out. It's bound to influence morale. Now let's see. The balloon, we will say, is at sixteen hundred metres. At that height it can be seen by men on the ground within a radius of—" and so forth and so on.

We figured it out approximately, estimating the numbers of soldiers, of all branches of service, who would witness the sight. Multiplying this number by four, our conclusion was that, as a result of the expedition, the length of the war and its outcome might very possibly be affected. At any rate, there would be such an ebbing of German morale, and such a flooding of French, that the way would be opened to a decisive victory on that front.

But supposing we should miss our sausage? J. B. grew thoughtful.

"Have another look at the orders. I don't remember what the instructions were in case we both fail."

I read, "If number 1 fails and number 2 is successful, number 3 will attack the observers. The patrol will then proceed to the aerodrome by the shortest route."

This was plain enough. Allowance could be made for one failure, but two—the possibility had not even been considered.

"By the shortest route." There was a piece of sly humour for you. It may have been unconscious, but we preferred to believe that the *commandant* had chuckled as he dictated it. A sort of afterthought, as much as to say to his pilots, "Well, you young bucks, you would-be airmen: thought it would be all sport, eh? You might have known. It's your own fault. Now go out and attack those balloons. It's possible that you may have a scrap or two on your hands while you are at it. Oh, yes, by the way, coming home, you'll be down pretty low. Every Boche machine in the air will have you at a disadvantage. Better re-

Farman Reconnaissance Avion

Farman Biplanes armed with rockets for balloon attack
(Early days of the war)

turn by the shortest route."

One feature of the programme did not appeal to us greatly, and this was the attack to be made on the observers when they had jumped with their parachutes. It seemed as near the border line between legitimate warfare and coldblooded murder as anything could well be.

"You are armed with a machine-gun. He may have an automatic pistol. It will require from five to ten minutes for him to reach the ground after he has jumped. You can come down on him like a stone. Well, it's your job, thank the Lord! not mine," said Drew.

It was my job, but I insisted that he would be an accomplice. In destroying the balloon, he would force me to attack the observers. When I asked Talbott if this feature of the attack could be eliminated he said:—

"Certainly. I have instructions from the commandant touching on this point. In case any pilot objects to attacking the observers with machine-gun fire, he is to strew their parachutes with autumn leaves and such field-flowers as the season affords. Now, listen! What difference, ethically, is there, between attacking one observation officer in a parachute, and dropping a ton of bombs on a train-load of soldiers? And to kill the observers is really more important than to destroy the balloon. If you are going to be a military pilot, for the love of Pete and Alf be one!"

He was right, of course, but that didn't make the prospect any the more pleasant.

The large map at the bureau now had greater interest for us than ever. The German balloons along the sector were marked in pictorially, with an ink line, representing the cable, running from the basket of each one down to the exact spot on the map from which they were launched. Under one of these, "Spa. 124" was printed, neatly, in red ink. It was the farthest distant from our lines of the four to be attacked, and about ten kilometres within German-held territory. The cable ran to the outskirts of a village situated on a railroad and a small stream. The location of enemy aviation fields was also shown pictorially, each one represented by a minute sketch, very carefully made, of an Albatross biplane. We noticed that there were several aerodromes not far distant from our balloon.

After a survey of the map, the commandant's afterthought, "by the shortest route," was not so needless as it appeared at first. The German positions were in a salient, a large corner, the line turning almost at right angles. We could cross them from the south, attack our balloon, and then, if we wished, return to French territory on the west side of the salient.

"We may miss some heavy shelling. If we double on our tracks going home, they will be expecting us, of course; whereas, if we go out on the west side, we will pass over batteries which didn't see us come in. If there should happen to be an east wind, there will be another reason in favour of the plan. The commandant is a shrewd soldier. It may have been his way of saying that the longest way round is the shortest way home."

Our Spads were ready after luncheon. A large square of tin had been fastened over the fabric of each lower wing, under the rocket fittings, to prevent danger of fire from sparks. Racks for six rockets, three on a side, had been fastened to the struts. The rockets were tipped with sharp steel points to insure their pricking the silk balloon envelope. The batteries for igniting them were connected with a button inside the car, within easy reach of the pilot. Lieutenant Verdane, our French second-in-command, was to supervise our practice on the field.

We were glad of this. If we failed to "spear our sausage," it would not be through lack of efficient instruction. He explained to Drew how the thing was to be done. He was to come on the balloon into the wind, and preferably not more than four hundred metres above it. He was to let it pass from view under the wing; then, when he judged that he was directly over it, to reduce his motor and dive vertically, placing the bag within the line of his two circular sights, holding it there until the bag just filled the circle. At that second he would be about 250 metres distant from it, and it was then that the rockets should be fired.

The instructions were simple enough, but in practicing on the target we found that they were not so easy to carry out. It was hard to judge accurately the moment for diving. Sometimes we overshot the target, but more often we were short of it. Owing to the angle at which the rockets were mounted on the struts, it was very important that the dive should be vertical.

One morning, the attack could have been made with every chance of success. Drew and I left the aerodrome a few minutes before sunrise for a trial flight, that we might give our motors a thorough testing. We climbed through a heavy mist which lay along the ground like water, filling every fold and hollow, flowing up the hillsides, submerging everything but the crests of the highest hills. The tops of the twin spires of S—— cathedral were all that could be seen of the town. Beyond, the

long chain of heights where the first-line trenches were rose just clear of the mist, which glowed blood-red as the sun came up.

The balloons were already up, hanging above the dense cloud of vapour, elongated planets drifting in space. The observers were directing the fire of their batteries to those positions which stood revealed. Shells were also exploding on lower ground, for we saw the mist billow upward time after time with the force of mighty concussions, and slowly settle again. It was an awe-inspiring sight. We might have been watching the last battle of the last war that could ever be, with the world still fighting on, bitterly, blindly, gradually sinking from sight in a sea of blood. I have never seen anything to equal that spectacle of an artillery battle in the mists.

Conditions were ideal for the attack. We could have gone to the objective, fired our rockets, and made our return, without once having been seen from the ground. It was an opportunity made in heaven, an Allied heaven. "But the infantry would not have seen it," said J. B.; which was true. Not that we cared to do the thing in a spectacular fashion. We were thinking of that decisive effect upon morale.

Two hours later we were pitching pennies in one of the hangars, when Talbott came across the field, followed solemnly by Whiskey and Soda, the lion mascots of the Escadrille Lafayette.

"What's the date, anybody know?" he asked, very casually.

J. B. is an agile-minded youth.

"It isn't the umteenth by any chance?"

"Right the first time." He looked at his watch. "It is now ten past ten. You have half an hour. Better get your rockets attached. How are your motors—all right?"

This was one way of breaking the news, and the best one, I think. If we had been told the night before, we should have slept badly.

The two patrols of protection left the field exactly on schedule time. At 10.35, Irving, Drew, and I were strapped in our machines, waiting, with our motors turning *ralenti*, for Talbott's signal to start.

He was romping with Whiskey. "Atta boy, Whiskey! Eat 'em up! Atta ole lion!"

As a squadron leader Talbott has many virtues, but the most important of them all is his casualness. And he is so sincere and natural in it. He has no conception of the dramatic possibilities of a situation—something to be profoundly thankful for in the commander of an *escadrille de chasse*. Situations are dramatic enough, tense enough, without one's taking thought of the fact. He might have stood there,

SODA

WHISKEY

watch in hand, counting off the seconds. He might have said, "Remember, we're all counting on you. Don't let us down. You've got to get that balloon!" Instead of that, he glanced at his watch as if he had just remembered us.

"All right; run along, you sausage-spearers. We're having lunch at twelve. That will give you time to wash up after you get back."

Miller, of course, had to have a parting shot. He had been in hiding somewhere until the last moment. Then he came rushing up with a toothbrush and a safety-razor case. He stood waving them as I taxied around into the wind. His purpose was to remind me of the possibility of landing with a *panne de moteur* in Germany, and the need I would then have of my toilet articles.

At 10.54, J. B. came slanting down over me, then pulled up in *ligne de vol*, and went straight for the lines. I fell in behind him at about one hundred metres distance. Irving was two hundred metres higher. Before we left the field he said: "You are not to think about Germans. That's my job. I'll warn you if I see that we are going to be attacked. Go straight for the balloon. If you don't see me come down and signal, you will know that there is no danger."

The French artillery were giving splendid cooperation. I saw clusters of shell-explosions on the ground. The gunners were carrying out their part of the programme, which was to register on enemy anti-aircraft batteries as we passed over them. They must have made good practice. Anti-aircraft fire was feeble, and, such of it as there was, very wild.

We came within view of the railway line which runs from the German lines to a large town, their most important distributing centre on the sector. Following it along with my eyes to the halfway point, I saw the red roofs of the village which we had so often looked at from a distance. Our balloon was in its usual place. It looked like a yellow plum, and no larger than one; but ripe, ready to be plucked.

A burst of flame far to the left attracted my attention, and almost at the same moment, one to the right. Ribbons of fire flapped upward in clouds of black oily smoke. Drew signalled with his joy-stick, and I knew what he meant: "Hooray! two down! It's our turn next!"

But we were still three or four minutes away. That was unfortunate, for a balloon can be drawn down with amazing speed.

A rocket sailed into the air and burst in a point of greenish white light, dazzling in its brilliancy, even in the full light of day. Immediately after this two white objects, so small as to be hardly visible,

The Escadrille Lafayette in July, 1917

floated earthward: the parachutes of the observers. They had jumped. The balloon disappeared from view behind Drew's machine. It was being drawn down, of course, as fast as the motor could wind up the cable. It was an exciting moment for us. We were coming on at two hundred kilometres an hour, racing against time and very little time at that. "Sheridan, only five miles away," could not have been more eager for his journey's end. Our throttles were wide open, the engines developing their highest capacity for power.

I swerved out to one side for another glimpse of the target: it was almost on the ground, and directly under us. Drew made a steep virage and dived. I started after him in a tight spiral, to look for the observers; but they had both disappeared. The balloon was swaying from side to side under the tension of the cable. It was hard to keep it in view. I lost it under my wing. Tipping up on the other side, I saw Drew release his rockets. They spurted out in long wavering lines of smoke. He missed. The balloon lay close to the ground, looking larger, riper than ever. The sight of its smooth, sleek surface was the most tantalizing of invitations. Letting it pass under me again, I waited for a second or two, then shut down the motor, and pushed forward on the control-stick until I was falling vertically. Standing upright on the rudder-bar, I felt the tugging of the shoulder-straps. Getting the bag well within the sights, I held it there until it just filled the circle. Then I pushed the button.

Although it was only eight o'clock, both Drew and I were in bed; for we were both very tired, it was a chilly evening, and we had no fire. An oil lamp was on the table between the two cots. Drew was sitting propped up, his fur coat rolled into a bundle for a back-rest. He had a sweater, tied by the sleeves, around his shoulders. His hands were clasped around his blanketed knees, and his breath, rising in a cloud of luminous steam,—

Like pious incense from a censer old,
Seemed taking flight for heaven without a death.

And yet, "pious" is hardly the word. J. B. was swearing, drawing from a choice reserve of picturesque epithets which I did not know that he possessed. I regret the necessity of omitting some of them.

"I don't see how I could have missed it! Why, I didn't turn to look for at least thirty seconds. I was that sure that I had brought it down. Then I banked and nearly fell out of my seat when I saw it there. I redressed at four hundred metres. I couldn't have been more than one

Spad Single-Seater Combat Avion

Letord Three-Passenger Biplane

hundred metres away when I fired the rockets."

"What did you do then?"

"Circled around, waiting for you. I had the balloon in sight all the while you were diving. It was a great sight to watch from below, particularly when you let go your rockets. I'll never forget it, never. But, Lord! Without the climax! Artistically, it was an awful fizzle."

There was no denying this. A balloon bonfire was the only possible conclusion to the adventure, and we both failed at lighting it. I, too, redressed when very close to the bag, and made a steep bank in order to escape the burst of flame from the ignited gas. The rockets leaped out, with a fine, blood-stirring roar. The mere sound ought to have been enough to make any balloon collapse. But when I turned, there it was, intact, a super-Brobdingnagian pumpkin, seen at close view, and still ripe, still ready for plucking. If I live to one hundred years, I shall never have a greater surprise or a more bitter disappointment.

There was no leisure for brooding over it then. My altimeter registered only two hundred and fifty metres, and the French lines were far distant. If the motor failed I should have to land in German territory. Any fate but that. Nevertheless, I felt in the pocket of my combination, to be sure that my box of matches was safely in place. We were cautioned always to carry them where they could be quickly got at in case of a forced landing in enemy country. An airman must destroy his machine in such an event. But my Spad did not mean to end its career so ingloriously. The motor ran beautifully, hitting on every cylinder. We climbed from two hundred and fifty metres to three hundred and fifty, four hundred and fifty, and on steadily upward. In the vicinity of the balloon, machine-gun fire from the ground had been fairly heavy; but I was soon out of range, and saw the tracer bullets, like swarms of blue bubbles, curving downward again at the end of their trajectory.

No machines, either French or German, were in sight. Irving had disappeared some time before we reached the balloon. I had not seen Drew from the moment when he fired his rockets. He waited until he made sure that I was following, then started for the west side of the salient. I did not see him, because of my interest in those clouds of blue bubbles which were rising with anything but bubble-like tranquillity. When I was clear of them, I set my course westward and parallel with the enemy lines to the south.

I had never flown so low, so far in German territory. The temptation to forget precaution and to make a leisurely survey of the ground beneath was hard to resist. It was not wholly resisted, in fact. Anti-aircraft fire was again feeble and badly ranged. The shells burst far behind and above, for I was much too low to offer an easy target. This gave me a dangerous sense of safety, and so I tipped up on one side, then on the other, examining the roads, searching the ruins of villages, the trenches, the shell-marked ground. I saw no living thing, brute or human; nothing but endless, inconceivable desolation.

The foolishness of that close scrutiny alone, without the protection of other *avions*, I realise now much better than I did then. Unless flying at six thousand metres or above,—when he is comparatively safe from attack,—a pilot may never relax his vigilance for thirty seconds together. He must look behind him, below, above, constantly. All aviators learn this eventually, but in the case of many new pilots the knowledge comes too late to be of service. I thought this was to be my experience, when, looking up, I saw five combat machines bearing down upon me. Had they been enemy planes my chances would have been very small, for they were close at hand before I saw them.

The old French aviator, worn out by his five hundred hours of flight over the trenches, said, "Save your nervous energy." I exhausted a three-months reserve in as many seconds. The suspense, luckily, was hardly longer than that. It passed when the patrol leader, followed by the others, pulled up in *ligne de vol*, about one hundred metres above me, showing their French *cocardes*. It was the group of protection of Spa. 87. At the time I saw Drew, a quarter of a mile away. As he turned, the sunlight glinted along his rocket-tubes.

A crowded hour of glorious life it seems now, although I was not of this opinion at the time. In reality, we were absent barely forty minutes. Climbing out of my machine at the aerodrome, I looked at my watch. A quarter to twelve. Laignier, the sergeant mechanician, was sitting in a sunny corner of the hangar, reading the *Matin*, just as I had left him.

Lieutenant Talbott's only comment was:

"Don't let it worry you. Better luck next time. The group bagged two out of four, and Irving knocked down a Boche who was trying to get at you. That isn't bad for half an hour's work."

But the decisive effect on morale which was to result from our wholesale destruction of balloons was diminished by half. We had forced ours down, but it bobbed up again very soon afterward. The one-o'clock patrol saw it, higher, Miller said, than it had ever been. It was Miller, by the way, who looked in on us at nine o'clock the same evening. The lamp was out.

"Asleep?"

Neither of us was, but we didn't answer. He closed the door, then reopened it.

"It's laziness, that's what it is. They ought to put you on school regime again."

He had one more afterthought. Looking in a third time, he said,—

"How about it, you little old human dynamos; are you getting rusty?"

CHAPTER 7

Brought Down

The preceding chapters of this journal have been written to little purpose if it has not been made clear that Drew and I, like most pilots during the first weeks of service at the front, were worth little to the Allied cause. We were warned often enough that the road to efficiency in military aviation is a long and dangerous one. We were given much excellent advice by aviators who knew what they were talking about. Much of this we solicited, in fact, and then proceeded to disregard it item by item. Eager to get results, we plunged into our work with the valour of ignorance, the result being that Drew was shot down in one of his first encounters, escaping with his life by one of those more than miracles for which there is no explanation. That I did not fare as badly or worse is due solely to the indulgence of that godfather of ours, already mentioned, who watched over my first flights while in a mood beneficently pro-Ally.

Drew's adventure followed soon after our first patrol, when he had the near combat with the two-seater. Luckily, on that occasion, both the German pilot and his machine-gunner were taken completely off their guard. Not only did he attack with the sun squarely in his face, but he went down in a long, gradual dive, in full view of the gunner, who could not have asked for a better target. But the man was asleep, and this gave J. B. a dangerous contempt for all gunners of enemy nationality.

Lieutenant Talbott cautioned him. "You have been lucky, but don't get it into your head that this sort of thing happens often. Now, I'm going to give you a standing order. You are not to attack again, neither of you are to think of attacking, during your first month here. As likely as not it would be your luck the next time to meet an old pilot. If you did, I wouldn't give much for your chances. He would outmanoeuvre you in a minute. You will go out on patrol with the others, of course; it's the only way to learn to fight. But if you get lost, go back to our balloons and stay there until it is time to go home."

Neither of us obeyed this order, and, as it happened, Drew was the one to suffer. A group of American officers visited the squadron one afternoon. In courtesy to our guests, it was decided to send out all the pilots for an additional patrol, to show them how the thing was done. Twelve machines were in readiness for the sortie, which was set for seven o'clock, the last one of the day. We were to meet at three thousand metres, and then to divide forces, one patrol to cover the east half of the sector and one the west.

We got away beautifully, with the exception of Drew, who had motor-trouble and was five minutes late in starting. With his permission I insert here his own account of the adventure—a letter written while he was in hospital.

> No doubt you are wondering what happened, listening, meanwhile, to many I-told-you-so explanations from the others. This will be hard on you, but bear up, son. It might not be a bad plan to listen, with the understanding as well as with the ear, to some expert advice on how to bag the Hun. To quote the prophetic Miller, "I'm telling you this for your own good." I gave my name and the number of the *escadrille* to the medical officer at the *poste de secours*. He said he would 'phone the captain at once, so that you must know before this, that I have been amazingly lucky. I fell the greater part of two miles—count 'em, two!—before I actually regained control, only to lose it again. I fainted while still several hundred feet from the ground; but more of this later. Couldn't sleep last night. Had a fever and my brain went on a spree, taking advantage of my helplessness. I just lay in bed and watched it function. Besides, there was a great artillery racket all night long. It appeared to be coming from our sector, so you must have heard it as well. This hospital is not very far back and we get the full orchestral effect of heavy firing. The result is that I am dead tired today. I believe I can sleep for a week.
>
> They have given me a bed in the officers' ward—me, a corporal. It is because I am an American, of course. Wish there was some way of showing one's appreciation for so much kindness. My neighbour. on the left is a *chasseur* captain. A hand-grenade

exploded in his face. He will go through life horribly disfigured. An old *padre*, with two machine-gun bullets in his hip, is on the other side. He is very patient, but sometimes the pain is a little too much for him. To a Frenchman, "*Oh, la, la!*" is an expression for every conceivable kind of emotion. In the future it will mean unbearable physical pain to me. Our orderlies are two *poilus*, long past military age. They are as gentle and thoughtful as the nurses themselves. One of them brought me lemonade all night long. Worthwhile getting wounded just to have something taste so good.

******

I meant to finish this letter a week ago, but haven't felt up to it. Quite perky this morning, so I'll go on with the tale of my "heroic combat." Only, first, tell me how that absurd account of it got into the *Herald?* I hope Talbott knows that I was not foolish enough to attack six Germans single-handed. If he doesn't, please enlighten him. His opinion of my common sense must be low enough, as it is.

We were to meet over S—— at three thousand metres, you remember, and to cover the sector at five thousand until dusk. I was late in getting away, and by the time I reached the rendezvous you had all gone. There wasn't a *chasse* machine in sight. I ought to have gone back to the balloons as Talbott advised, but thought it would be easy to pick you up later, so went on alone after I had got some height. Crossed the lines at thirty-five hundred metres, and finally got up to four thousand, which was the best I could do with my rebuilt engine. The Huns started shelling, but there were only a few of them that barked. I went down the lines for a quarter of an hour, meeting two Sepwiths and a Letord, but no Spads.

You were almost certain to be higher than I, but my old packet was doing its best at four thousand, and getting overheated with the exertion. Had to throttle down and *pique* several times to cool off. Then I saw you—at least I thought it was you—about four kilometres inside the German lines. I counted six machines, well grouped, one a good deal higher than the others and one several hundred metres below them. The pilot on top was doing beautiful *renversements* and an occasional barrel-turn, in Barry's manner. I was so certain it was our patrol that I started over at once, to join you. It was getting dusk and I lost sight of the machine lowest down for a few seconds. Without my knowing it, he was approaching at exactly my altitude. You know how difficult it is to see a machine in that position. Suddenly he loomed up in front of me like an express train, as you have seen them approach from the depths of a moving-picture screen, only ten times faster; and he was firing as he came. I realised my awful mistake, of course.

His tracer bullets were going by on the left side, but he corrected his aim, and my motor seemed to be eating them up. I banked to the right, and was about to cut my motor and dive, when I felt a smashing blow in the left shoulder. A sickening sensation and a very peculiar one, not at all what I thought it might feel like to be hit with a bullet. I believed that it came from the German in front of me. But it couldn't have, for he was still approaching when I was hit, and I have learned here that the bullet entered from behind.

This is the history of less than a minute I'm giving you. It seemed much longer than that, but I don't suppose it was. I tried to shut down the motor, but couldn't manage it because my left arm was gone. I really believed that it had been blown off into space until I glanced down and saw that it was still there. But for any service it was to me, I might just as well have lost it. There was a vacant period of ten or fifteen seconds which I can't fill in. After that I knew that I was falling, with my motor going full speed. It was a helpless realisation. My brain refused to act. I could do nothing. Finally, I did have one clear thought, "Am I on fire?" This cut right through the fog, brought me up broad awake. I was falling almost vertically, in a sort of half *vrille*. No machine but a Spad could have stood the strain.

The Huns were following me and were not far away, judging by the sound of their guns. I fully expected to feel another bullet or two boring its way through. One did cut the skin of my right leg, although I didn't know this until I reached the hospital. Perhaps it was well that I did fall out of control, for the firing soon stopped, the Germans thinking, and with reason, that they had bagged me. Some proud Boche airman is wearing an iron cross on my account. Perhaps the whole crew of dare-devils has been decorated. However, no unseemly sarcasm. We would pounce on a lonely Hun just as quickly. There is no chivalry in war in these modern days.

I pulled out of the spin, got the broomstick between my knees, reached over, and shut down the motor with my right hand. The propeller stopped dead. I didn't much care, being very drowsy and tired. The worst of it was that I couldn't get my breath. I was gasping as though I had been hit in the pit of the stomach. Then I lost control again and started falling. It was awful! I was almost ready to give up. I believe that I said, out loud, "I'm going to be killed. This is my last sortie." At any rate, I thought it. Made one last effort and came out in *ligne de vol,* as nearly as I could judge, about one hundred and fifty metres from the ground. It was an ugly-looking place for landing, trenches and shell-holes everywhere. I was wondering in a vague way whether they were French or German, when I fell into the most restful sleep I've ever had in my life.

I have no recollection of the crash, not the slightest. I might have fallen as gently as a leaf. That is one thing to be thankful for among a good many others. When I came to, it was at once, completely. I knew that I was on a stretcher and remembered immediately exactly what had happened. My heart was going pit-a-pat, pit-a-pat, and I could hardly breathe, but I had no sensation of pain except in my chest. This made me think that I had broken every bone in my body. I tried moving first one leg, then the other, then my arms, my head, my body. No trouble at all, except with my left arm and side.

I accepted the miracle without attempting to explain it, for I had something more important to wonder about: who had the handles of my stretcher? The first thing I did was to open my eyes, but I was bleeding from a scratch on the forehead and saw only a red blur. I wiped them dry with my sleeve and looked again. The broad back in front of me was covered with mud. Impossible to distinguish the colour of the tunic. But the shrapnel helmet above it was—French! I was in French hands. If ever I live long enough in one place, so that I may gather a few possessions and make a home for myself, on one wall of my living-room I will have a bust-length portrait, rear view, of a French *brancardier,* mud-covered back and battered tin hat.

Do you remember our walk with Ménault in the rain, and the *déjeuner* at the restaurant where they made such wonderful omelettes? I am sure that you will recall the occasion, although you may have forgotten the conversation. I have not forgotten one remark of Menault's apropos of talk about risks. If a man were willing, he said, to stake everything for it, he would accumulate an experience of fifteen or twenty minutes which would compensate him, a thousand times over, for all the hazard. "And if you live to be old," he said quaintly, "you can never be bored with life. You will have something, always, very pleasant to think about." I mention this in connection with my discovery that I was not in German hands. I have had five minutes of perfect happiness without any background—no thought of yesterday or tomorrow—to spoil it.

I said, "*Bonjour, messieurs,*" in a gurgling voice. The man in front turned his head sidewise and said,—

"*Tiens! Ça va, monsieur l'aviateur?*"

The other one said, "*Ah, mon vieux!*" You know the inflection they give this expression, particularly when it means, "This is something wonderful!" He added that they had seen the combat and my fall, and little expected to find the pilot living, to say nothing of speaking. I hoped that they would go on talking, but I was being carried along a trench; they had to lift me shoulder-high at every turn, and needed all their energy. The Germans were shelling the lines. Several fell fairly close, and they brought me down a long flight of wooden steps into a dugout to wait until the worst of it should be over. While waiting, they told me that I had fallen just within the first-line trenches, at a spot where a slight rise in ground hid me from sight of the enemy. Otherwise, they might have had a bad time rescuing me. My Spad was completely wrecked. It fell squarely into a trench, the wings breaking the force of the fall. Before reaching the ground, I turned, they said, and was making straight for Germany. Fifty metres higher, and I would have come down in No Man's Land.

For a long time, we listened in silence to the subdued *crr-ump, crr-ump*, of the shells. Sometimes showers of earth pattered down the stairway, and we would hear the high-pitched, droning *V-z-z-z* of pieces of shell-casing as they whizzed over the opening. One of them would say, "Not far, that one"; or, "He's looking for someone, that fellow," in a voice without a hint of emotion. Then, long silences and other deep, earth-shaking rumbles.

They asked me, several times, if I was suffering, and offered to go on to the *poste de secours* if I wanted them to. It was not heavy bombardment, but it would be safer to wait for a little while. I told them that I was ready to go on at any time, but not to hurry on my account; I was quite comfortable.

The light glimmering down the stairway faded out and we were in complete darkness. My brain was amazingly clear. It registered every trifling impression. I wish it might always be so intensely awake and active. There seemed to be four of us in the dugout; the two *brancardiers*, and this second self of mine, as curious as an eavesdropper at a keyhole, listening intently to everything, and then turning to whisper to me. The *brancardiers* repeated the same comments after every explosion. I thought: "They have been saying this to each other for over three years. It has become automatic. They will never be able to stop." I was feverish, perhaps. If it was fever, it burned away any illusions I may have had of modern warfare from the infantryman's viewpoint. I know that there is no glamour in it for them; that it has long since become a deadly-monotony, an endless repetition of the same kinds of horror and suffering, a boredom more terrible than death itself, which is repeating itself in the same ways, day after day and month after month. It isn't often that an aviator has the chance I've had. It would be a good thing if they were to send us into the trenches for twenty-four hours, every few months. It would make us keener fighters, more eager to do our utmost to bring the war to an end for the sake of those *poilus*.

The dressing-station was in a very deep dugout, lighted by candles. At a table in the centre of the room the medical officer was working over a man with a terribly crushed leg. Several others were sitting or lying along the wall, awaiting their turn. They watched every movement he made in an apprehensive, animal way, and so did I. They put me on the table next, although it was not my turn. I protested, but the doctor paid no attention. "*Aviateur américain*," again. It's a pity that Frenchmen can't treat us Americans as though we belong here.

As soon as the doctor had finished with me, my stretcher was fastened to a two-wheeled carrier and we started down a cobbled road to the ambulance station. I was light-headed and don't remember much of that part of the journey. Had to take refuge in another dugout when the Huns dropped a shell on an ammunition-dump in a village through which we were to pass. There was a deafening banging and booming for a long time, and when we did go through the town it was on the run. The whole place was in flames and small-arms ammunition still exploding. I remember seeing a long column of soldiers going at the double in the opposite direction, and they were in full marching order.

Well, this is the end of the tale; all of it, at any rate, in which you would be interested. It was one o'clock in the morning before I got between cool, clean sheets, and I was wounded about a quarter past eight. I have been tired ever since.

There is another aviator here, a Frenchman, who broke his jaw and both legs in a fall while returning from a night bombardment. His bed is across the aisle from mine; he has a formidable-looking apparatus fastened on his head and under his chin, to hold his jaw firm until the bones knit. He is forbidden to talk, but breaks the rule whenever the nurse leaves the ward. He speaks a little English and has told me a delightful story about the origin of aerial combat. A French pilot, a friend of his, he says, attached to a certain army group during August and September, 1914, often met a German aviator during his reconnaissance patrols. In those Arcadian days, fighting in the air was a development for the future, and these two pilots exchanged greetings, not cordially, perhaps, but courteously: a wave of the hand, as much as to say, "We are enemies, but we need not forget the civilities."

Then they both went about their work of spotting batteries, watching for movements of troops, etc. One morning the German failed to return the salute. The Frenchman thought little of this, and greeted him in the customary manner at their next meeting. To his surprise, the Boche shook his fist at him in the most blustering and caddish way. There was no mistaking the insult. They had passed not fifty metres from each other, and the Frenchman distinctly saw the closed fist. He was saddened by the incident, for he had hoped that some of the ancient courtesies of war would survive in the aerial branch of the service, at least. It angered him too; therefore, on his next reconnaissance, he ignored the German.

Evidently the Boche air-squadrons were being Prussianised. The enemy pilot approached very closely and threw a missile at him. He could not be sure what it was, as the object went wide of the mark; but he was so incensed that he made a *virage*, and drawing a small flask from his pocket, hurled it at his boorish antagonist. The flask contained some excellent port, he said, but he was repaid for the loss in seeing it crash on the exhaust-pipe of the enemy machine.

This marked the end of courtesy and the beginning of active hostilities in the air. They were soon shooting at each other with rifles, automatic pistols, and at last with machine guns. Later developments we know about. The night bombarder has been telling me this yarn in serial form. When the nurse is present, he illustrates the last chapter by means of gestures. I am ready to believe everything but the incident about the port. That doesn't sound plausible. A Frenchman would have thrown his watch before making such a sacrifice!

CHAPTER 8

One Hundred Hours

A little more than a year after our first meeting in the Paris restaurant which has so many pleasant memories for us, Drew completed his first one hundred hours of flight over the lines, an event in the life of an airman which calls for a celebration of some sort. Therefore, having been granted leave for the afternoon, the two of us came into the old French town of Bar-le-Duc, by the toy train which wanders down from the Verdun sector. We had dinner in one of those homelike little places where the food is served by the proprietor himself. On this occasion it was served hurriedly, and the bill presented promptly at eight o'clock. Our host was very sorry, but "*les sales Boches, vous savez, messieurs?*" They had come the night before: a dozen houses destroyed, women and children killed and maimed. With a full moon to guide them, they would be sure to return tonight. "*Ah, cette guerre! Quand sera-t-elle finie?*" He offered us a refuge until our train should leave. Usually, he said, he played solitaire while waiting for the Germans, but with houses tumbling about one's ears, he much preferred company. "And my wife and I are old people. She is very deaf, *heureusement*. She hears nothing."

J. B. declined the invitation. "A brave way that would be to finish our evening!" he said as we walked down the silent street. "I wanted to say, '*Monsieur*, I have just finished my first one hundred hours of flight at the front.' But he wouldn't have known what that means."

I said, "No, he wouldn't have known." Then we had no further talk for about two hours. A few soldiers, late arrivals, were prowling about in the shadow of the houses, searching for food and a warm kitchen where they might eat it. Some insistent ones pounded on the door of a restaurant far in the distance.

"*Dites done, patron! Nous avons faim, nom de Dieu ! Est-ce-que tout le monde est mort ici?"*

> *Only a host of phantom listeners,*
> *That dwelt in the lone house then,*
> *Stood listening in the quiet of the moonlight*
> *To that voice from the world of men.*

It was that kind of silence, profound, tense, ghostlike. We walked through street after street, from one end of the town to the other, and saw only one light, a faint glimmer which came from a slit of a cellar window almost on the level of the pavement. We were curious, no doubt. At any rate, we looked in. A woman was sitting on a cot bed with her arms around two little children. They were snuggled up against her and both fast asleep; but she was sitting very erect, in a strained, listening attitude, staring straight before her. Since that night we have believed, both of us, that if wars can be won only by haphazard night bombardments of towns where there are women and children, then they had far better be lost.

But I am writing a journal of high adventure of a cleaner kind, in which all the resources in skill and cleverness of one set of men are pitted against those of another set. We have no bomb-dropping to do, and there are but few women and children living in the territory over which we fly. One hundred hours is not a great while as time is measured on the ground, but in terms of combat patrols, the one hundredth part of it has held more of adventure in the true meaning of the word than we have had during the whole of our lives previously.

At first we were far too busy learning the rudiments of combat to keep an accurate record of flying time. We thought our aeroplane clocks convenient pieces of equipment rather than necessary ones. I remember coming down from my first air battle and the breathless account I gave of it at the bureau, breathless and vague. Lieutenant Talbott listened quietly, making out the *compte rendu* as I talked. When I had finished, he emphasized the haziness of my answers to his questions by quoting them: "Region: 'You know, that big wood!' Time: 'This morning, of course!' Rounds fired: 'Oh, a lot!'" etc.

Not until we had been flying for a month or more did we learn how to make the right use of our clocks and of our eyes while in the air. We listened with amazement to after-patrol talk at the mess. We learned more of what actually happened on our sorties, after they were over than while they were in progress. All of the older pilots missed seeing nothing which there was to see. They reported the numbers of the enemy planes encountered, the types, where seen and when. They spotted batteries, trains in stations back of the enemy lines, gave the hour precisely, reported any activity on the roads. In moments of exasperation Drew would say, "I think they are stringing us! This is all a put-up job!" Certainly this did appear to be the case at first. For we were air-blind. We saw little of the activity all around us, and details on the ground had no significance. How were we to take thought of time and place and altitude, note the peculiarities of enemy machines, count their numbers, and store all this information away in memory at the moment of combat? This was a great problem.

"What I need," J. B. used to say, "is a traveling private secretary. I'll do the fighting and he can keep the diary."

I needed one, too, a man air-wise and battle-wise, who could calmly take note of my clock, altimeter, temperature and pressure dials, identify exactly the locality on my map, count the numbers of the enemy, estimate their approximate altitude,—all this when the air was criss-crossed with streamers of smoke from machine-gun tracer bullets, and opposing aircraft were manoeuvring for position, diving and firing at each other, spiralling, nose-spinning, wing-slipping, climbing, in a confusing intermingling of tricolour *cocards* and black crosses.

We made gradual progress, the result being that our patrols became a hundred-fold more fascinating, sometimes, in fact, too much so. It was important that we should be able to read the ground, but more important still to remember that what was happening there was only of secondary concern to us. Often we became absorbed in watching what was taking place below us, to the exclusion of any thought of aerial activity, our chances for attack or of being attacked. The view, from the air, of a heavy bombardment, or of an infantry attack under cover of barrage fires, is a truly terrible spectacle, and in the air one has a feeling of detachment which is not easily overcome.

Yet it must be overcome, as I have said, and cannot say too many times for the benefit of any young airman who may read this journal. During an offensive the air swarms with planes. They are at all altitudes, from the lowest artillery *réglage* machines at a few hundreds of metres, to the highest *avions de chasse* at six thousand meters and above. *Réglage*, photographic, and reconnaissance planes have their particular work to do. They defend themselves as best they can, but almost never attack. Combat *avions*, on the other hand; are always looking for victims. They are the ones chiefly dangerous to the unwary pursuit pilot.

Drew's first official victory came as the result of a one-sided battle with an Albatross single-seater, whose pilot evidently did not know there was an enemy within miles of him. No more did J. B. for that matter. "It was pure accident," he told me afterward. He had gone from Rheims to the Argonne forest without meeting a single German. "And I didn't want to meet one; for it was Thanksgiving Day. It has associations for me, you know. I'm a New Englander." It is not possible to convince him that it has any real significance for men who were not born on the North Atlantic seaboard. Well, all the way he had been humming

> *Over the river and through the wood*
> *To grandfather's house we go,*

...to himself. It is easy to understand why he didn't want to meet a German. He must have been in a curiously mixed frame of mind. He covered the sector again and passed over Rheims, going northeast. Then he saw the Albatross; "and if you had been standing on one of the towers of the cathedral you would have seen a very unequal battle." The German was about two kilometres inside his own lines, and at least a thousand metres below. Drew had every advantage.

"He didn't see me until I opened fire, and then, as it happened, it was too late. My gun didn't jam!"

The German started falling out of control, Drew following him down until he lost sight of him in making a *virage*.

I leaned against the canvas wall of a hangar, registering incredulity. Three times out of seven, to make a conservative estimate, we fight inconclusive battles because of faulty machine guns or defective ammunition. The ammunition, most of it that is bad, comes from America.

While Drew was giving me the details, an orderly from the bureau brought word that an enemy machine had just been reported shot down on our sector. It was Drew's Albatross, but he nearly lost official credit for having destroyed it, because he did not know exactly the hour when the combat occurred. His watch was broken and he had neglected asking for another before starting. He judged the time of the attack, approximately, as two-thirty, and the infantry observers, reporting the result, gave it as twenty minutes to three. The region in both cases coincided exactly, however, and, fortunately, Drew's was the only combat which had taken place in that vicinity during the afternoon.

For an hour after his return he was very happy. He had won his first victory, always the hardest to gain, and had been complimented by the commandant, by Lieutenant Nungesser, the *Roi des Aces*, and by other French and American pilots. There is no petty jealousy among airmen, and in our group the *esprit de corps* is unusually fine. Rivalry is keen, but each squadron takes almost as much pride in the work of the other squadrons as it does in its own.

The details of the result were horrible. The Albatross broke up two thousand metres from the ground, one wing falling within the French lines. Drew knew what it meant to be wounded and falling out of control. But his Spad held together. He had a chance for his life. Supposing the German to have been merely wounded—An airman's joy in victory is a short-lived one.

Nevertheless, a curious change takes place in his attitude toward his work, as the months pass. I can best describe it in terms of Drew's experience and my own. We came to the front feeling deeply sorry for ourselves, and for all airmen of whatever nationality, whose lives were to be snuffed out in their promising beginnings. I used to play "The Minstrel Boy to the War Has Gone" on a tin flute, and Drew wrote poetry. While we were waiting for our first machine, he composed *The Airman's Rendezvous*, written in the manner of Alan Seeger's poem.

> *And I in the wide fields of air*
> *Must keep with him my rendezvous.*
> *It may be I shall meet him there*
> *When clouds, like sheep, move slowly through*
> *The pathless meadows of the sky*
> *And their cool shadows go beneath,—*
> *I have a rendezvous with Death*
> *Some summer noon of white and blue.*

There is more of it, in the same manner, all of which he read me in a husky voice. I, too, was ready to weep at our untimely fate. The strange thing is that his prophecy came so very near being true. He had the first draft of the poem in his breast-pocket when wounded, and has kept the gory relic to remind him—not that he needs reminding—of the airy manner in which he cancelled what ought to have been a *bona-fide* appointment.

I do not mean to reflect in any way upon Alan Seeger's beautiful poem. Who can doubt that it is a sincere, as well as a perfect, expression of a mood common to all young soldiers? Drew was just as sincere in writing his verses, and I put all the feeling I could into my tin whistle interpretation of *The Minstrel Boy*. What I want to make clear is, that a soldier's moods of self-pity are fleeting ones, and if he lives, he outgrows them.

Imagination is an especial curse to an airman, particularly if it takes a gloomy or morbid turn. We used to write "To whom it may concern" letters before going out on patrol, in which we left directions for the notification of our relatives and the disposal of our personal effects in case of death. Then we would climb into our machines thinking, "This may be our last sortie. We may be dead in an hour, in half an hour, in twenty minutes." We planned splendidly spectacular ways in which we were to be brought down, always omitting one, however, the most horrible as well as the most common,—in flames. Thank Fortune, we have outgrown this second and belated period of adolescence and can now take a healthy interest in our work.

Now, an inevitable part of the daily routine is to be shelled, persistently, methodically, and often accurately shelled. Our interest in this may, I suppose, be called healthy, inasmuch as it would be decidedly unhealthy to become indifferent to the activities of the German antiaircraft gunners. It would be far-fetched to say that any airman ever looks forward zestfully to the business of being shot at with one hundred and fives; and seventy-fives, if they are well placed, are unpleasant enough. After one hundred hours of it, we have learned to assume that attitude of contemptuous toleration which is the manner common to all *pilotes de chasse*. We know that the chances of a direct hit are almost negligible, and that we have all the blue dome of the heavens in which to manoeuvre.

Furthermore, we have learned many little tricks by means of which we can keep the gunners guessing. By way of illustration, we are patrolling, let us say, at thirty-five hundred metres, crossing and recrossing the lines, following the patrol leader, who has his motor throttled down so that we may keep well in formation. The guns may be silent for the moment, but we know well enough what the gunners are doing. We know exactly where some of the batteries are, and the approximate location of all of them along the sector; and we know, from earlier experience, when we come within range of each individual battery. Presently one of them begins firing in bursts of four shells.

If their first estimate of our range has been an accurate one, if they place them uncomfortably close, so that we can hear, all too well, above the roar of our motors, the rending *Gr-r-rOW, Gr-r-rOW*, of the shells as they explode, we sail calmly—to all outward appearances—on, manoeuvring very little. The gunners, seeing that we are not disturbed, will alter their ranges, four times out of five, which is exactly what we want them to do.

The next bursts will be hundreds of metres below or above us, whereupon we show signs of great uneasiness, and the gunners, thinking they have our altitude, begin to fire like demons. We employ our well-earned immunity in preparing for the next series of batteries, or in thinking of the cost to Germany, at one hundred *francs* a shot, of all this futile shelling. Drew, in particular, loves this cost-accounting business, and I must admit that much pleasure may be had in it, after patrol. They rarely fire less than fifty shells at us during a two-hour patrol. Making a low general average, the number is nearer one hundred and fifty. On our present front, where aerial activity is fairly brisk and the sector is a large one, three or four hundred shells are wasted upon us often before we have been out an hour.

We have memories of all the good batteries from Flanders to the Vosges Mountains. Battery after battery, we make their acquaintance along the entire sector, wherever we go. Many of them, of course, are mobile, so that we never lose the sport of searching for them. Only a few days ago we located one of this kind which came into action in the open by the side of a road. First we saw the flashes and then the shell-bursts in the same cadence. We tipped up and fired at him in bursts of twenty to thirty rounds, which is the only way airmen have of passing the time of day with their friends, the enemy anti-aircraft gunners, who ignore the art of *camouflage*.

But we can converse with them, after a fashion, even though we do not know their exact position. It will be long before this chapter of my journal is in print. Having given no indication of the date of writing, I may say, without indiscretion, that we are again on the Champagne front. We have a wholesome respect for one battery here, a respect it has justly earned by shooting which is really remarkable. We talk of this battery, which is east of Rheims and not far distant from Nogent l'Abbesse, and take professional pride in keeping its gunners in ignorance of their fine marksmanship. We signal them their bad shots—which are better than the good ones of most of the batteries on the sector—by doing stunts, a barrel turn, a loop, two or three turns of a *vrille*.

As for their good shots, they are often so very good that we are forced into acrobacy of a wholly individual kind. Our *avions* have received many scars from their shells. Between forty-five hundred and five thousand metres, their bursts have been so close under us that we have been lifted by the concussions and set down violently again at the bottom of the vacuum; and this on a clear day when a *chasse* machine is almost invisible at that height, and despite its speed of two hundred kilometres an hour. On a gray day, when we are flying between twenty-five hundred and three thousand metres beneath a film of cloud, they repay the honour we do them by our acrobatic turns. They bracket us, put barrages between us and our own lines, give us more trouble than all the other batteries on the sector combined. For this reason, it is all the more humiliating to be forced to land with motor trouble, just at the moment when they are paying off some old scores.

This happened to Drew while I have been writing up my journal. Coming out of a *tonneau* in answer to three *coups* from the battery, his propeller stopped dead. By planing flatly (the wind was dead ahead, and the area back of the first lines there is a wide one, crossed by many intersecting lines of trenches) he got well over them and chose a field as level as a billiard table for landing-ground. In the very centre of it, however, there was one post, a small worm-eaten thing, of the colour of the dead grass around it. He hit it, just as he was setting his Spad on the ground, the only post in a field acres wide, and it tore a piece of fabric from one of his lower wings. No doubt the crack battery has been given credit for disabling an enemy plane. The honour, such as it is, belongs to our aerial godfather, among whose lesser vices may be included that of practical joking.

The remnants of the post were immediately confiscated for firewood by some *poilus* who were living in a dugout nearby.

Chapter 9

"Lonely as a Cloud"

The French attack which has been in preparation for the past month is to begin at dawn tomorrow. It has been hard, waiting, but it must have been a great deal worse for the infantrymen who are billeted in all of the surrounding villages. They are moving up tonight to the first lines, for these are the shock troops who are to lead the attack. They are chiefly regiments of *Chasseurs*—small men in stature, but clean, hard, well-knit—splendid types. They talk of the attack confidently. It is an inspiration to listen to them. Hundreds of them have visited our aerodrome during the past week, mainly, I think, for a glimpse of Whiskey and Soda, our lions, who are known to French soldiers from one end of the line to the other. Whiskey is almost full-grown, and Soda about the size of a wild cat. They have the freedom of the camp and run about everywhere.

The guns are thundering at a terrific rate, 'the concussions shaking our barracks and rattling the dishes on the table. In the messroom the gramophone is playing, "I'm going 'way back home and have a wonderful time." Music at the front is sometimes a doubtful blessing.

We are keyed up, some of us, rather nervous in anticipation of tomorrow. Porter is trying to give Irving a light from his own cigarette. Irving, who doesn't know the meaning of nerves, asks him who in hell he is waving at. Poor old Porter! His usefulness as a combat pilot has long past, but he hangs on, doing the best he can. He should have been sent to the rear months ago.

The first phase of the battle is over. The French have taken eleven thousand prisoners, and have driven the enemy from all the hills, down to the low ground along the canal. For the most part, we have been too high above them to see the infantry actions; but knowing the plans and the objectives beforehand, we have been able to follow, quite closely, the progress of the battle.

It opened on a wet morning with the clouds very low. We were to have gone on patrol immediately the attack commenced, but this was impossible. About nine o'clock the rain stopped, and Rodman and Davis were sent out to learn weather conditions over the lines. They came back with the report that flying was possible at two hundred metres. This was too low an altitude to serve any useful purpose, and the *commandant* gave us orders to stand by.

About noon the clouds began to break up, and both high and low patrols prepared to leave the ground. Drew, Dunham, and I were on high patrol, with Lieutenant Barry leading. Our orders were to go up through the clouds, using them as cover for making surprise attacks upon enemy *réglage* machines. We were also to attack any enemy formations sighted within three kilometres of their old first lines. The clouds soon disappeared and so we climbed to forty-five hundred metres and lay in wait for combat patrols.

Barry sighted one and signalled. Before I had placed it, he dived, almost full motor, I believe, for he dropped like a stone. We went down on his tail and saw him attack the topmost of three Albatross single-seaters. The other two dived at once, far into their own lines. Dunham, Drew, and I took long shots at them, but they were far outside effective range. The topmost German made a feeble effort to manoeuvre for position. Barry made a *renversement* with the utmost nicety of judgment and came out of it about thirty metres behind and above the Albatross. He fired about twenty shots, when the German began falling out of control, spinning round and round, then diving straight, then past the vertical, so that we could see the silver under-surface of his wings and tail, spinning again until we lost sight of him. (This combat was seen from the ground, and Barry's victory was confirmed before we returned to the field).

Lieutenant Talbott joined us as we were taking our height again. He took command of the patrol and Barry went off hunting by himself, as he likes best to do. There were planes everywhere, of both nationalities. Mounting to four thousand metres within our own lines, we crossed over again, and at that moment I saw a Letord, a three-passenger *réglage* machine, burst into flames and fall. There was no time either to watch or to think of this horrible sight. We encountered a patrol of five Albatross planes almost on our level. Talbott dived at once. I was behind him and picked a German who was spiralling either upward or downward, for a few seconds I was not sure which. It

VICTORS AND VANQUISHED

was upward. He was climbing to offer combat. This was disconcerting. It always is to a green pilot. If your foe is running, you may be sure he is at least as badly rattled as you are. If he is a single-seater and climbing, you may be equally certain that he is not a novice, and that he has plenty of sand. Otherwise he would not accept battle at a disadvantage in the hope of having his inning next.

I was foolish enough to begin firing while still about three hundred metres distant. My opponent ungraciously offered the poorest kind of a target, getting out of the range of my sights by some very skilful manoeuvring. I didn't want him to think that he had an inexperienced pilot to deal with. Therefore, judging my distance very carefully, I did a *renversement* in the Lieutenant Barry fashion. But it was not so well done. Instead of coming out of it above and behind the German, when I pulled up in *ligne de vol* I was under him!

I don't know exactly what happened then, but the next moment I was falling in a *vrille* (spinning nose dive) and heard the well-known crackling sound of machine-gun fire. I kept on falling in a *vrille*, thinking this would give the German the poorest possible target. (A mistake which many new pilots make. In a *vrille*, the machine spins pretty nearly on its own axis, and although it is turning, a skilful pilot above it can keep it fairly well within the line of his sights.)

Pulling up in *ligne de vol* I looked over my shoulder again. The German had lost sight of me for a moment in the swiftness of his dive, but evidently he saw me just before I pulled out of the *vrille*. He was turning up for another shot, in exactly the same position in which I had last seen him. And he was very close, not more than fifty metres distant.

I believed, of course, that I was lost; and why that German didn't bag me remains a mystery. Heaven knows I gave him opportunity enough! In the end, by the merciful intervention of Chance, our godfather, I escaped. I have said that the sky had cleared. But there was one strand of cloud left, not very broad, not very long; but a refuge,—oh! what a welcome refuge! It was right in my path and I tumbled into it, literally, head over heels. I came skidding out, but pulled up, put on my motor, and climbed back at once; and I kept turning round and round in it for several minutes. If the German had waited, he must have seen me ravelling it out like a cat tangled in a ball of cotton. I thought that he was waiting. I even expected him to come nosing into it, in search of me. In that case there would have been a glorious smash, for there wasn't room for two of us.

I almost hoped that he would try this. If I couldn't bag a German with my gun, the next best thing was to run into him and so be gathered to my fathers while he was being gathered to his. There was no crash, and taking sudden resolution, I dived vertically out of the cloud, head over shoulder, expecting to see my relentless foe. He was nowhere in sight.

In that wild tumble, and while chasing my tail in the cloud, I lost my bearings. The compass, which was mounted on a swinging holder, had been tilted upside down. It stuck in that position. I could not get it loose. I had fallen to six hundred metres, so that I could not get a large view of the landscape. Under the continuous bombardment the air was filled with smoke, and through it nothing looked familiar. I knew the direction of our lines by the position of the sun, but I was in a suspicious mood. My motor, which I had praised to the heavens to the other pilots, had let me down at a critical moment. The sun might be ready to play some fantastic trick. I had to steer by it, although I was uneasy until I came within sight of our observation balloons. I identified them as French by sailing close to one of them so that I could see the tricolour pennant floating out from a cord on the bag.

Then, being safe, I put my old Spad through every antic we two had ever done together. The observers in the balloons must have thought me crazy, a pilot running amuck from aerial shell shock. I had discovered a new meaning for that "grand and glorious feeling" which is so often the subject of Briggs's cartoons.

Looking at my watch I received the same old start of surprise upon learning how much of wisdom one may accumulate in a half-hour of aerial adventure. I had still an hour and a half to get through with before I could go home with a clear conscience. Therefore, taking height again, I went cautiously, gingerly, watchfully, toward the lines.

CHAPTER 10

"Mais Oui, Mon Vieux!"

The "grand and glorious feeling" is one of the finest compensations for this uncertain life in the air. One has it every time he turns from the lines toward—home! It comes in richer glow, if hazardous work has been done, after moments of strain, uncertainty, when the result of a combat sways back and forth; and it gushes up like a fountain, when, after making a forced landing in what appears to be enemy territory, you find yourself among friends.

Late this afternoon we started, four of us, with Davis as leader, to make the usual two-hour sortie over the lines. No Germans were sighted, and after an uneventful half-hour, Davis, who is always springing these surprises, decided to stalk them in their lairs. The clouds were at the right altitude for this, and there were gaps in them over which we could hover, examining roads, railroads, villages, cantonments. The danger of attack was negligible. We could easily escape any large hostile patrol by dodging into the clouds. But the wind was unfavourable for such a reconnaissance. It was blowing into Germany. We would have it dead against us on the journey home.

We played about for a half-hour, blown by a strong wind farther into Germany than we knew. We walked down the main street of a village where we saw a large crowd of German soldiers, spraying bullets among them, then climbed into the clouds before a shot could be fired at us. Later we nearly attacked a hospital, mistaking it for an aviation field. It was housed in *bessonneau* hangars, and had none of the marks of a hospital excepting a large red cross in the middle of the field. Fortunately, we saw this before any of us had fired, and passed on over it at a low altitude to attack a train. There is a good deal of excitement in an expedition of this kind, and soldiers themselves say that surprise sorties from the air have a demoralizing effect upon troops.

But as a form of sport, there is little to be said for it. It is too unfair. For this reason, among others, I was glad when Davis turned homeward.

While coming back I climbed to five thousand metres, far above the others, and lagged a long way behind them. This was a direct violation of patrol discipline, and the result was, that while cruising leisurely along, with motor throttled down, watching the swift changes of light over a wide expanse of cloud, I lost sight of the group. Then came the inevitable feeling of loneliness, and the swift realisation that it was growing late and that I was still far within enemy country.

I held a southerly course, estimating, as I flew, the velocity of the wind which had carried us into Germany, and judging from this estimate the length of time I should need to reach our lines. When satisfied that I had gone far enough, I started down. Below the clouds it was almost night, so dark that I could not be sure of my location. In the distance I saw a large building, brilliantly lighted. This was evidence enough that I was a good way from the lines. Unshielded windows were never to be seen near the front.

I spiralled slowly down over this building, examining, as well as I could, the ground behind it, and decided to risk a landing. A blind chance and blind luck attended it. In broad day, Drew hit the only post in a field five hundred metres wide. At night, a very dark night, I missed colliding with an enormous factory chimney (a matter of inches), glided over a line of telegraph wires, passed at a few metres' height over a field littered with huge piles of sugar beets, and settled, *comme une fleur*, in a little cleared space which I could never have judged accurately had I known what I was doing.

Shadowy figures came running toward me. Forgetting, in the joy of so fortunate a landing, my anxiety of a moment before, I shouted out, "*Bonsoir, messieurs!*" Then I heard someone say, "*Ich glaube*—" losing the rest of it in the sound of tramping feet and an undercurrent of low, guttural murmurs. In a moment my Spad was surrounded by a widening circle of round hats, German infantrymen's hats.

Here was the ignoble end to my career as an airman. I was a prisoner, a prisoner because of my own folly, because I had dallied along like a silly girl, to "look at the pretty clouds." I saw in front of me a long captivity embittered by this thought. Not only this: my Spad was intact. The German authorities would examine it, use it. Some German pilot might fly with it over the lines, attack other French machines with my gun, my ammunition!

Not if I could help it! They stood there, those soldiers, gaping, muttering among themselves, waiting, I thought, for an officer to tell them what to do. I took off my leather gloves, then my silk ones under them, and these I washed about in the oil under my feet. Then, as quietly as possible, I reached for my box of matches.

"*Qu'est-ce-que vous faites là? Allez! Vite!*"

A tramping of feet again, and a sea of round hats bobbing up and down and vanishing in the gloom. Then I heard a cheery "Ça *va, monsieur? Pas de mal?*" By way of answer I lighted a match and held it out, torch fashion. The light glistened on a round, red face and a long French bayonet. Finally, I said, "*Vous êtes Francais, monsieur?*" in a weak, watery voice.

"*Mais oui, mon vieux! Mais oui!*" this rather testily. He didn't understand at first that I thought myself in Germany. "Do I look like a Boche?" Then I explained, and I have never heard a Frenchman laugh more heartily. Then he explained and I laughed, not so heartily, a great deal more foolishly.

I may not give my location precisely. But I shall be disclosing no military secrets in saying that I am not in Germany. I am not even in the French war-zone. I am closer to Paris than I am to the enemy first-line trenches. In a little while the sergeant with the round red face and the long French bayonet, whose guest I am for the night, will join me here. If he were an American, to the manner born and bred, and if he knew the cartoons of that man Briggs, he might greet me in this fashion:—

"When you have been on patrol a long way behind the enemy lines, shooting up towns and camps and railway trains like a pack of aerial cowboys; when, on your way home, you have deliberately disobeyed orders and loafed a long way behind the other members of your group in order to watch the pretty sunset, and, as a punishment for this aesthetic indulgence, have been overtaken by darkness and compelled to land in strange country, only to have your machine immediately surrounded by German soldiers; then, having taken the desperate resolve that they shall not have possession of your old battle-scarred *avion* as well as of your person, when you are about to touch a match to it, if the light glistens on a long French bayonet and you learn that the German soldiers have been prisoners since the battle of the Somme, and have just finished their day's work at harvesting beets to be used in making sugar for French *poilus*—Oh, BOY! Ain't it a GRAND AND GLORYUS FEELING?"

To which I would reply in his own memorable words,—

"*Mais oui, mon vieux! Mais Oui!*"

Chapter 11

The Camouflaged Cows

Nancy, a moonlight night, and "*les sales Boches encore.*" I have been out on the balcony of this old hotel, a famous tourist resort before the war, watching the bombardment and listening to the deep throb of the motors of German Gothas. They have dropped their bombs without doing any serious damage. Therefore, I may return in peace to my huge bare room, to write, while it is still fresh in mind, "The Adventure of the Camouflaged Cows."

For the past ten days I have been attached—it is only a temporary transfer—to a French *escadrille* of which Manning, an American, is a member. The *escadrille* had just been sent to a quiet part of the front for two weeks' repos, but the day after my arrival orders came to fly to Belfort, for special duty.

Belfort! On the other side of the Vosges Mountains, with the Rhine Valley, the Alps, within view, within easy flying distance! And for special duty. It is a vague order which may mean anything. We discussed its probable meaning for us, while we were pricking out our course on our maps.

"Protection of bombardment *avions*" was Andre's guess. "Night combat" was Raynaud's. Everyone laughed at this last hazard. "You see?" he said, appealing to me, the newcomer. "They think I am big fool. But wait." Then, breaking into French, in order to express himself more fluently: "It is coming soon, *chasse de nuit*. It is not at all impossible. One can see at night, a moonlight night, very clearly from the air. They are black shadows, the other *avions* which you pass, but often, when the moonlight strikes their wings, they flash like silver. We must have searchlights, of course; then, when one sees those shadows, those great black Gothas, *vite! la lumière! Pop-pop-pop-pop-pop! C'es fini!*"

The discussion of the possibility or impossibility of night combat continued warmly. The majority of opinion was unfavourable to it: a useless waste of gasoline; the results would not pay for the wear and tear upon valuable fighting planes. Raynaud was not to be persuaded. "Wait and see," he said. There was a reminiscent thrill in his voice, for he is an old night bombarding pilot. He remembered with longing, I think, his romantic night voyages, the moonlight falling softly on the roofs of towns, the rivers like ribbons of silver, the forests patches of black shadow. "Really, it is an adventure, a night bombardment."

"But how about your objectives?" I asked. "At night you can never be sure of hitting them, and, well, you know what happens in French towns."

"It is why I asked for my transfer to chasse" he told me afterward. "But the Germans, the blond beasts! Do they care? Nancy, Belfort, Châlons, Epernay, Rheims, Soissons, Paris,—all our beautiful towns! I am a fool! We must pay them back, the Huns! Let the innocent suffer with the guilty!"

He became a combat pilot because he had not the courage of his conviction.

We started in flights of five machines, following the Marne and the Marne Canal to Bar-le-Duc, then across country to Toul, where we landed to fill our fuel tanks. Having bestowed many favours upon me for a remarkably long period, our aerial godfather decided that I had been taking my good fortune too much for granted. Therefore, he broke my tail skid for me as I was making what I thought a beautiful. atterrissage. It was late in the afternoon, so the others went on without me, the captain giving orders that I should join them, weather permitting, the next day.

> Follow the Moselle until you lose it in the mountains. Then pick up the road which leads over the Ballon d'Alsace. You can't miss it.

I did, nevertheless, and as always, when lost, through my own fault. I followed the Moselle easily enough until it disappeared in small branching streams in the heart of the mountains. Then, being certain of my direction, I followed an irregular course, looking down from a great height upon scores of little mountain villages, untouched by war. After weeks of flying over the desolation of more northerly sectors of the front, this little indulgence seemed to me quite a legitimate one.

But my Spad (I was always flying tired old *avions* in those days, the discards of older pilots) began to show signs of fatigue. The pres-

Motors for illuminating the field of a
night bombarding squadron

A hangar at the aerodrome of the Escadrille Lafayette
after a night bombardment

sure went down. Neither motor nor hand pump would function, the engine began to gasp, and, although I instantly switched on to my reserve tank, it expired with shuddering coughs. The propeller, after making a few spins in the reverse direction, stopped dead.

I had been in a most comfortable frame of mind all the way, for a long cross-country aerial journey, well behind the zone of fire, is a welcome relaxation after combat patrols. It is odd how quickly one's attitude toward rugged, beautiful country changes, when one is faced with the necessity of finding landing-ground there. The steep ravines yawn like mouths. The peaks of the mountains are teeth—ragged, sinister-looking teeth. Being at five thousand metres I had ample time in which to make a choice—-ample time, too, for wondering if, by a miscalculation, I had crossed the trench lines, which in that region are hardly visible from the air.

I searched anxiously for a wide valley where it would be possible to land in safety. While still three thousand metres from the ground I found one. Not only a field. There were *bessonneau* hangars on it. An aerodrome! A moment of joy,—"but German, perhaps!"—followed by another of anxiety. It was quickly relieved by the sight of a French reconnaissance plane spiralling down for a landing. I landed, too, and found that I was only a ten-minutes' flight from my destination.

★★★★★★

With other work to do, I did not finish the story of my adventure with the camouflaged cows, and I am wondering now why I thought it such a corking one. The cows had something to do with it. We were returning from Belfort to Verdun when I met them. Our special duty had been to furnish aerial protection to the King of Italy, who was visiting the French lines in the Vosges. This done we started northward again. Over the highest of the mountains my motor pump failed as before. I got well past the mountains before the essence in my reserve tank gave out. Then I planed as flatly as possible, searching for another aviation field.

There were none to be found in this region, rough, hilly country, much of it covered with forests. I chose a miniature sugar-loaf mountain for landing-ground. It appeared to be free from obstacles, and the summit, which was pasture and ploughed land, seemed wide enough to settle on.

I got the direction of the wind from the smoke blowing from the chimneys of a nearby village, and turned into it. As I approached, the hill loomed more and more steeply in front of me. I had to pull up at a climbing angle to keep from nosing into the side of it. About this time, I saw the cows, dozens of them, grazing over the whole place. Their natural camouflage of browns and whites and reds prevented my seeing them earlier. Making spectacular *virages*, I missed collisions by the length of a match-stick. At the summit of the hill, my wheels touched ground for the first time, and I bounded on, going through a three-strand wire fence and taking off a post without any appreciable decrease in speed. Passing between two large apple trees, I took limbs from each of them, losing my wings in doing so. My landing chassis was intact and my Spad went on down the reverse slope—

Like an embodied joy, whose race is just begun.

After crashing through a thicket of brush and small trees, I came to rest, both in body and in mind, against a stone wall. There was nothing left of my machine but the seat. Unscathed, I looked back along the wreckage-strewn path, like a man who has been riding a whirlwind in a wicker chair.

Now, I have never yet made a forced landing in strange country without having the mayor of the nearest village appear on the scene very soon afterward. I am beginning to believe that the mayors of all French towns sit on the roofs of their houses, field-glasses in hand, searching the sky for wayward aviators, and when they see one landing, they rush to the spot on foot, on horseback, in old-fashioned family phaetons, by means of whatever conveyance most likely to increase expedition their municipality affords.

The mayor of V.-sur-I. came on foot, for he had not far to go. Indeed, had there been one more cow browsing between the apple trees, I should have made a last *virage* to the left, in which case I should have piled up against a summer pavilion in the mayor's garden. Like all French mayors of my experience, he was a courteous, big-hearted gentleman.

After getting his breath,—he was a fleshy man, and had run all the way from his house,—he said, "Now, my boy, what can I do for you?"

First he placed a guard around the wreckage of my machine; then we had tea in the summer pavilion, where I explained the reason for my sudden visit. While I was telling him the story, I noticed that every window of the house, which stood at one end of the garden, was crowded with children's heads. War orphans, I guessed. Either that or the children of a large family of sons at the front. He was the kind of man who would take them all into his own home.

Having frightened his cows,—they must have given cottage cheese for a week afterward,—destroyed his fences, broken his apple trees, accepted his hospitality, I had the amazing nerve to borrow money from him. I had no choice in the matter, for I was a long way from Verdun, with only eighty *centimes* in my pocket. Had there been time I would have walked rather than ask him for the loan. He granted it gladly, and insisted upon giving me double the amount which I required.

I promised to go back some day for a visit. First I will do acrobacy over the church steeple, and then, if the cows are not in the pasture, I am going to land, *comme une fleur*, as we airmen say, on that hill.

CHAPTER 12

Cafard

It is mid-January, snowing, blowing, the thermometer below zero. We have done no flying for five days. We have read our most recent magazines from cover to cover, including the advertisements, many of which we find more interesting, better written, than the stories. We have played our latest phonograph record for the five hundred and ninety-eighth time. Now we are hugging our one stove, which is no larger than a length of good American stove-pipe, in the absurd hope of getting a fleeting promise of heat.

Boredom, insufferable boredom. There is no American expression—there will be soon, no doubt—for this disease which claims so many victims from the Channel coast to the borders of Switzerland. The British have it without giving it a name. They say "Fed up and far from home." The more inventive French call it "*Cafard*."

Our outlook upon life is warped, or, to use a more seasonable expression, frozen. We are not ourselves. We make sarcastic remarks about one another. We hold up for ridicule individual peculiarities of individuality. Someone, tiring of this form of indoor sports, starts the phonograph again.

Wind, wind, wind (the crank)

Kr-r-r-r-r-r (the needle on the disk)

La-dee-dum, dee-doodle, di-dee-day (the orchestral introduction)

Sometimes when I feel sad
And things look blue,
I wish the boy I had
Was one like you—

"For the love of Pete! Shut off that damn silly thing!"
"I admire your taste, Irving!"

"Can it!"

"Well, what will you have, then?"

"Play that Russian thing, the *Danse des Buffons*."

"Don't play anything."

"Lord! I wish someone would send us some new records."

"Yes, instead of knitted wristers—what?"

"And mufflers."

"Talking about wristers, how many pair do you think I've received? Eight!"

"You try to head 'em off. Doesn't do any good. They keep coming just the same."

"It's because they are easy to make. Working wristers and mufflers is a method of dodging the knitting draft."

"Well, now, I call that gratitude! You don't deserve to have any friends."

"Isn't it the truth? Have you ever known of a soldier or an aviator who wore wristers?"

"I give mine to my mechanician. He sends them home, and his wife unravels the yarn and makes sweaters for the youngsters."

"Think of the waste energy. Harness up the wrist-power and you could keep three aircraft factories going day and night."

"Oh, well, if it amuses the women, what's the difference?"

"That's not the way to look at it. They ought to be doing something useful."

"Plenty of them are; don't forget that, old son.

"Anybody got anything to read?"

"Now, if they would send us more books—"

"And magazines—"

"Two weeks ago, Blake, you were wishing they wouldn't send so many."

"What of it? We were having fine weather then."

"There ought to be some system about sending parcels to the front."

"The Germans have it, they say. Soldier wants a book, on engineering, for example, or a history, or an anthology of recent poetry. Gets it at once through Government channels."

"Say what you like about the Boches, they don't know the meaning of waste energy."

"But you can't have method and efficiency in a democracy."

"There you go! Same old fallacy!"

"No fallacy about it! Efficiency and personal freedom don't go together. They never have and they never will."

"And what does our personal freedom amount to? When you get down to brass tacks, personal freedom is a mighty poor name for it, speaking for four fifths of the population."

"Germany doesn't want it, our brand, and we can't force it on her."

"And without it, she has a mighty good chance of winning this war—"

When the talk begins with the uselessness of wristers, shifts from that to democratic inefficiency, and from that to the probability of *Deutschland über Alles*, you may be certain of the diagnosis. The disease is *cafard*.

The sound of a motorcar approaching. Dunham rushes to the window and then swears, remembering our greased-cloth window panes.

"Go and see who it is, Tiffin, will you? Hope it's the mail orderly."

Tiffin goes on outpost and reports three civilians approaching.

"Now, who can they be, I wonder?"

"Newspaper men probably."

"Good Lord! I hope not."

"Another American mission."

"That's my guess, too."

Rodman is right. It is another American mission coming to "study conditions" at the front.

"But unofficially, gentlemen, quite unofficially," says Mr. A., its head, a tall, melancholy-looking man, with a deep, bell-like voice. Mr. B., the second member of the mission, is in direct contrast, a birdlike little man, who twitters about the room, from group to group.

"Oh! If you boys only knew how *splendid* you are! How much we in America—You are our *first* representatives at the front, you know. You are the vanguard of the *millions* who—" etc.

Miller looks at me solemnly. His eyes are saying, a How long, O Lord, how long!"

Mr. C., the third member, is a silent man. He has keen, deep-set eyes. "There," we say, "is the brain of the mission."

Tea is served very informally. Mr. A. is restless. He has something on his mind. Presently he turns to Lieutenant Talbott.

"May I say a few words to your squadron?"

"Certainly," says Talbott, glancing at us uneasily.

Mr. A. rises, steps behind his chair, clears his throat, and looks down the table where ten pilots,—the others are taking a constitutional in the country,—caught in *négligée* attire by the unexpected visitors, are sitting in attitudes of polite attention.

"My friends—" the deep, bell-like voice. In fancy, I hear a great shifting of chairs, and following the melancholy eyes with my own, over the heads of my ten fellow pilots, beyond the limits of our poor little mess-room, I see a long *vista* of polished shirt fronts, a diminishing track of snowy linen, shimmering wineglasses, shining silver.

My friends, believe me when I say that this occasion is one of the proudest and happiest of my life. I am standing within sound of the guns which for three—long—years have been battering at the bulwarks of civilization. I hear them, as I utter these words, and I look into the faces of a little group of Americans who, day after day, and week after week (increasing emphasis) have been facing those guns for the honour and glory of democratic institutions (rising inflection).

We in America have heard them, faintly, perhaps, yet unmistakably, and now I come to tell you, in the words of that glorious old war song, 'We are coming, Farther Woodrow, ONE HUNDRED MIL-LION strong!'

We listen through to the end, and Lieutenant Talbott, in his official capacity, begins to applaud. The rest of us join in timidly, self-consciously. I am surprised to find how awkwardly we do it. We have almost forgotten how to clap our hands! My sense of the spirit of place changes suddenly. I am in America. I am my old self there, with different thoughts, different emotions. I see everything from my old point of view. I am like a man who has forgotten his identity. I do not recover my old, or, better, my new one, until our guests have gone.

******

On January 10, Captain Hall, after many inquiries from his publishers in regard to his progress on his story, wrote them as follows:—

> As for the manuscript, I have great hope of being given time to finish it before the end of the month. . . . . . I am almost certain that I shall have enough leisure. I wish that I were as sure of the happy inspiration. For oh! man, but this is a whale of a story! I shall never be able to do it justice, at least not during such stirring times as these. As I said before, however, I'll do my best. What I need is at least six weeks of leisure, that I might shut myself in a hotel room and live with it. This is out of the question, of course.

German airmen's grave at Ham

Sometimes in moments when the mood is on, and I have no opportunity to write, I'm an awfully miserable chap. Then I remember my purpose, the reason why I'm here. I cool off, grit my teeth, and think about tomorrow's high patrol.
Why am I so eager to tell this story? Doubtless because it's such a corker. This is bad, for it makes me too much in love with easeful life. An aviator has no right to make plans beyond tomorrow.

The weeks passed, and with them came, from time to time, batches of manuscript, each accompanied by a vivid letter telling quite casually of adventures above the clouds. On the 16th of April, a brief cable was received:

> Final ten thousand words posted. Hall.

Nothing more was heard until the 8th of May, when the morning papers contained the startling news that Captain Hall was missing after a fight with four German planes ten miles inside the German lines. The Associated Press report described the fight as follows:—

> Captain Hall, with two others, was patrolling this morning between St. Mihiel and Pont-à-Mousson. When they were over Pagny-sur-Moselle, four enemy albatross airplanes, painted with black and white stripes, were seen.
> The Americans attacked, Captain Hall singling out one of the enemy and driving him downward while firing with his machine-gun. The pair made a spiral dive from six thousand metres to four thousand, when the German suddenly reversed his machine and started to rise. In a quick turn, he poured a deadly stream of machine-gun bullets into the bottom of Hall's machine. Captain Hall promptly came out of the spiral and made a dive for the earth. He was last seen attempting to complete this manoeuvre.

Every effort was made, through both official and unofficial channels, to obtain further news, but the next information came in the following dispatch from a staff correspondent of the International News Service:—

> With the American Army in France, May 21.—Captain Norman Hall, the American aviator, who was brought down behind the German lines on May 7, is reported alive, a prisoner

in a German hospital. He was slightly wounded when brought down with his machine.

For military reasons the correspondent is unable to give the source of this information.

On the same day a long letter reached the publishers, written by Captain Hall two days after he had given instructions for the sending of the cablegram already quoted, he wrote:

> I'm an awful liar. This batch of manuscript isn't the final one. I have just a little more to add, to round off the story. . . . However, the last two chapters will be posted to you within a week's time, *without fail*. . . .
>
> The only reason my story is not completed is that some hardhearted military magnate at aviation headquarters, to whom I am only a name or a number, pulled me out of the Escadrille Lafayette—my beloved squadron—and sent me as a flight commander to a newly formed American squadron. It was an awful wrench.
>
> Two other pilots were sent at the same time to the same pursuit group, which makes the exile a little easier to bear. I have been awfully busy ever since, trying to live up to my new responsibilities. This and the German offensive together have made the task of finishing my yarn a difficult one.

Whether he was unable to finish the two chapters to his satisfaction, or whether they have been lost in transmission, is not known. They have not reached the publishers, and this record of Captain Hall's experiences as an aviator must therefore go to the public without the ending which he had planned.

An encouraging message comes from Washington headquarters of the American Red Cross under date of May 28:—

> Today we received further word from the International Red Cross that Captain Hall had been reported officially by the German Red Cross as a prisoner. We do not yet know his prisoner camp address.

One coincidence in connection with his latest letter lays grim emphasis on the swift vicissitudes of war. Major Raoul Lufbery was attached to the pursuit group to which Captain Hall had been sent, and the latter writes at length about some work that they were planning to do together. But when the letter reached Boston, its writer had been nearly two weeks a prisoner in Germany, and Major Lufbery only the day before had given up his life in a daring air fight in France.

War Birds

LT. JOHN MACGAVOCK GRIDER

Contents

Diary of an Unknown Aviator   163

Diary of an Unknown Aviator

September 20th, 1917
Aboard R. M. S. *Carmania* in the harbour of Halifax.
Well, here I am aboard ship and three days out of New York, waiting for a convoy at Halifax. This seems to be a fitting place to start a diary. I am leaving my continent as well as my country and am going forth in search of adventure, which I hope to find in Italy, for that is where we are headed. We are a hundred and fifty aviators in embryo commanded by Major MacDill, who is an officer and a gentleman in fact as well as by Act of Congress. We are traveling first class, thanks to him, though we are really only privates, and every infantry officer on board hates our guts because we have the same privileges they do. Capt. Swan, an old Philippine soldier, is supply officer.

This morning when we steamed into harbour, which is a wonderful place, we found five or six transports already here. The soldiers on them, all that could, got into the boats and came over to see us. They rowed around and around our boat and cheered and sang. They were from New Zealand and a fine husky bunch they were. One song went:

Onward, conscript soldiers, marching as to war,
You would not be conscripts, had you gone before.

This is a beautiful place. I expect my opinion is largely due to my frame of mind, but it really is pretty. Low jagged hills form the horizon and on the south side of the river as we came up, is solid rock with a little dirt over it in spots but the rock sticking through everywhere like bones through a poor horse.

We went through two submarine nets stretched across the mouth of the harbour. I wish I had words to describe the feeling I had when all the soldiers in the harbour came over to tell us howdy. One New Zealander, I think he was a non-com, stood up in the back of the boat and said, "You fellows don't look very happy." And I guess our boys don't at that—the doughboys, I mean. We've got over two thousand of them on board of the 9th Infantry Regiment of the regular army. Anyway, New Zealand beat us cheering with their full throated, "Hip Hurrah Hip Hurrah Hip Hurrah!" But they said they were five weeks out and knew each other pretty well, while our boys aren't acquainted yet.

I have a stateroom with Lawrence Callahan from Chicago, who roomed with me at Ground School, where we suffered together under Major Kraft and had a lot of fun from time to time in spite of him. We almost got separated at New York as he was going to France with another detachment over at Governor's Island. I got Elliott Springs, our top sergeant, to get the major to have him transferred to us. We had a good crowd over at Mineola and I saw him in town and he told me he was in a rotten bunch over there. I was a sergeant as Springs had me promoted because I took a squad out and unloaded a carload of canned tomatoes after two others had fallen down on the job.

We got him transferred all right and then he got mad as fury at Springs because he made him peel potatoes for four days for chewing gum in ranks. On the fourth day Cal told Springs how much trouble he had taken to join his outfit and that he hadn't come prepared to be a perpetual kitchen police. Springs said he was very glad to have him but if he wanted to chew gum in ranks he'd have to peel potatoes the rest of the day every time he did it. Cal said he'd already been assigned to the job for four days. Springs said he knew it but that so far he hadn't peeled a single potato and he was going to get one day's work out of him if he had to chain him to the stove to do it. Cal won though, because Springs was too busy to watch him and he never did finish one pan of spuds.

I've got to go to boat drill now. We practice abandoning ship every day.

That's over. My platoon is assigned to the top deck and Captain La Guardia is in charge of our boat. He is a congressman from New York City and learned to fly last year. He is an Italian so was sent over with us. He managed to bring along two of his Italian ward bosses as cooks. One of them owns a big Italian restaurant and yet here he is as a cook. And he can't cook!

I probably won't write much in this thing. I never have done anything constantly except the wrong thing, but I want a few recollections jotted down in case I don't get killed.

I am going to make two resolutions and stick to them. I am not going to lose my temper any more—I fight too much. And I am going to be very careful and take care of myself. I am not going to take any unnecessary chances. I want to die well and not be killed in some accident or die of sickness—that would be terrible, a tragic anti-climax. I haven't lived very well but I am determined to die well. I don't want to be a hero—too often they are all clay from the feet up, but I want to die as a man should. Thank God, I am going to have the opportunity to die as every brave man should wish to die—fighting—and fighting for my country as well. That would retrieve my wasted years and neglected opportunities.

But if I don't get killed, I want to be able to jog my memory in my declining years so I can say, "Back in 1917 when I was an aviator, I used to—!"

I'll probably not write any more for a week, or perhaps no more at all.

September 21st

We left Halifax in a haze just as the sun, blood red, broke through the clouds for an instant before it set behind those rock-ribbed hills. It was a wonderful sight seen from our ship, one of a convoy of fourteen strung out, as we left the harbour in a stately majestic procession. All hail to Mars, the *Kaiser's* godfather!

As we came through from the inner basin down the river south to the sea, we passed the British battle cruisers, their bands all playing the Star Spangled Banner and their crews cheering with their well-organised "Hip Hurrah," the "Hip" being given by an officer through a megaphone. As we were coming out of the inner basin, one of our convoy steamed past us with one lone bugler playing our national anthem and everyone on board standing rigidly at attention. I never had quite such a thrill from the old tune before and I am really beginning to love it. The bugler played, "God Save the King," too, and not a sound was made on either ship as the clear, sweet, almost plaintive notes stole out over the water. I am sure every man on board was affected no matter how hardboiled he was.

There is a cottage to the right of the river going up where only three women live. I am sure no men are there and they must be Americans for they had a big U. S. flag. When we passed they dipped their flag on the house and one of them wigwagged, "Goodbye, good luck, God bless you!"

September 22nd

We haven't done much today except watch the other ships. They changed their formation every little while during the morning and finally settled down in three lines of four ships each with one ship leading and the *Carmania* bringing up the rear. That makes fourteen in the convoy not counting our escort. It rained all morning but held up this evening. It remained cloudy and the wind blew. Everyone thought we were going to have some rough weather tonight. I was just on deck and the stars were peeping through the clouds and they were as bright as diamonds. I never saw sky more beautiful. I tried to count the other thirteen ships but could not. I was arrested by the guard for smoking on deck. He saw my wrist watch. No lights, no matter how faint, can be shown except the red and green navigating lights on the masts. A British commander told us that one ship was torpedoed because someone carelessly struck a match on the deck.

There is never an intermission of cards in the smoker. We shoot crap in our staterooms and I am gradually collecting all kinds of money,—Italian, French, English and best of all, a little American. We don't know what all this foreign money is worth so we have to shoot it by the colour,—green against green, and yellow against yellow. The coins rank by size. I guess it's all even in the end.

September 24th

I wrote nothing yesterday. Nothing happened except I saw a fight on the lower deck from above and heard a quartet and a speech down below. Quite a sea has been running today, or so it seems to me, and several of the boys have been sick. Especially Leach from Tuscaloosa, who is awfully low. They put a sign on him as he lay in his chair on the deck: "I want peace and quiet."

We spend two hours a day studying Italian. La Guardia and the two cooks and Gaipa are the instructors. I am way behind and will never catch up. I am discouraged about it. I learned all sorts of queer things at Ground School without much trouble so guess I can catch up but I sure hate to think of the hard work I have to do.

There's a full moon tonight and the sea is beautiful. Oh, for words to describe it! It makes me sad and makes me ache inside for something, I don't know what. I guess it's a little loving I need. There are twenty nurses on board but they are all dated up for the rest of the voyage. They certainly ought to get all the attention they need.

The wind is rising and whining through the rigging of the ship.

We can hear it crying down here in our staterooms. I am going on deck to see what goes on. It's a wonderful night, as clear as a bell and this big old ship rising and falling, sloughing its way through the sea. This must be a wonderful life at sea. I shall always carry the picture in my mind of the damp decks and masts rearing along under the stars with the white foam spreading from both sides every time she dips.

I wish I could soak it all up and keep it. God, I am young, life is before me, and if I have wonderful memories, when I get old I will be happy. I have spent all my life so far in harsh surroundings and had so much hard work that I think some good time is coming to me. And I have always longed for better things but didn't I know how to go about getting them. But now Fate has tossed me this opportunity. I must make the best of it! All I have to pay for it is my life! I must make it worth the bargain! I am always feeling sorry for myself, a poor habit and one I am going to cut out. Well, I'll try this thrice accursed Italian for a few minutes now.

September 25th

Something queer went on this evening. The Painted Lady, as we call the camouflaged cruiser that is escorting us, turned around and circled behind us and fired a few shots. We don't know what she was firing at. She sure is a queer-looking boat. She's painted all different colours in lines and squares and you can't tell which way she is going or what she is until you get close to her. Another boat in our convoy is painted the colour of the ocean and then has a smaller ship painted over it going the other way. From any distance it is very deceptive. Another ship has the same arrangement except the deception is in the angle of her course.

We went below, Cal and I, to hear the Steerage Quartet, as they call themselves. Enlisted men they are and natural born entertainers. One boy sang "I ain't got nobody" wonderfully well. Spalding played one of his own compositions for us. One day at Mineola, Springs was looking about as usual for some kitchen police. He put the first six men to work peeling potatoes. While they were manicuring the spuds he checked up their service records. One record caught his eye. The name on it was Albert Spalding and he gave his profession as musician. He was sent to our detachment as an Italian interpreter.

Springs went out to the kitchen and asked him if he was the guy that played the fiddle. Spalding allowed as how he was. Springs asked him where his pet instrument was. He said he'd left it in town. So

Springs pardoned him from the peeling and sent him back to town after it. He isn't a cadet but an enlisted man and isn't eligible for a commission as we are. I hear that he lost a $35,000 a year contract. I guess he will be figured into a commission somehow, though. He should be. They put him down in the steerage and won't allow him up in the first class with us. Springs and MacDill are trying to get him up but the regular army colonel of this regiment won't hear of it. But he plays for the enlisted men every night down below.

I feel safe from seasickness now and would enjoy myself immensely if it were not for this Italian. I never will learn it unless I do some work so here goes! I thought my troubles were over when I got rid of that wireless.

September 26th
Nothing much doing. We have to do submarine watch after tomorrow and I am sergeant of the second relief. At last I will get a chance to go up on that little trick platform on the front of the ship and also on the bridge.

September 29th
I haven't written anything for the past two days. Nothing really of noteworthy importance has happened until this evening. I was sergeant of the guard yesterday or rather of the submarine watch. We had a watch posted at five points on the ship. Each man had a certain arc that he was to keep his eye on. No man was to take anything to drink for twelve hours before he was to go on watch. We were supposed to look out for gulls which they say usually follow in the wake of a sub. Everybody has to take their turn at it except Springs, who is sort of perpetual officer of the day and runs the show. We did have a guard mount at five in the afternoon but MacDill and Springs and Deetjen are the only ones that know how to do it so we had to abandon that after the first day.

 No periscopes have been sighted yet though one boy got all excited over a big piece of timber that was sticking up. The signal for take to the boats is five whistles and yesterday while our company barber was shaving one of the boys, it blew three times. It scared the barber so bad that he couldn't finish the shave. Nervousness has been growing for the last few days about subs. There has been a kind of tension barely noticeable. No one is actually scared but we all feel a little nervous about it. We have had to wear our life preservers all the time since yesterday morning. They are very uncomfortable and are a great nuisance but the order is strictly enforced. We wear them to meals and put them beside our chairs while we eat. No refuse of any kind is thrown overboard except at night when it is all thrown over at one time. That's to prevent leaving any trace.

Everybody felt funny about the thing until four this afternoon, right after Italian. I went up on deck and the sea was swarming with submarine chasers. Lord, how happy everyone was at the sight of them! They are the prettiest little ships I ever saw, about a hundred and twenty feet over all, I would say. They cut through the water instead of riding the waves but there were no waves today. You can't feel the motion of the ship at all. They say we have three American chasers with us but we couldn't tell which they were. Lord, those little boats are fast; they fairly fly through the water and cleave it so clear and clean. I would give a leg to own one. They are all run by steam. I thought there would be gas boats, but I guess we are too far out for them.

I never slept as much in my life as I have on this ship. Must be the salt air.

I hear we will sight the coast of Ireland tomorrow about twelve o'clock and be in Liverpool Monday. It can't be too soon for me, I'm sick to death of this Italian.

Everybody on board makes fun of my laughing. I never knew before I joined the army that there was anything unusual about it, but it seems to waken everyone on this side of the ship. Poor McCook, the ugliest man alive, is worried to death about subs. The boys, Curtis and McCurry, have kidded him until he sleeps in his clothes including his puttees and shoes. Curtis says he'll be mad as hell if the ship isn't sunk.

We have an ex-cowboy with us named Bird, who has been having a terrible time behaving himself. Bob Kelly was a cowboy out in Arizona for a while when he was trying to shake off the con and every time they get together the storm clouds gather. They are good friends of Springs's and whenever they get started he joins them and tries to quiet things down. One night last week Bird got tired of this paternal supervision in the bar and went down below. Then he started giving his cowboy yell and the matter was reported to the major.

The major said he didn't want to be hard on anybody but he couldn't overlook it, so he left the punishment to Springs. Springs put him on the wagon for a week. Since then he has been sitting around the table in the bar drinking ginger ale and looking at Springs in a pleading tone of voice so he let him off tonight in honour of the prospects of seeing land tomorrow. We had a big crap game later in our staterooms. First Jake Stanley took all the money and then Springs took it all from him and finally Stokes ended up with it all. I don't know how much it was but there were a couple of handfuls of assorted paper.

How I hate those Italian lessons. They finally got Spalding up in the first class on the excuse that he has to be there for private instructions. All he does is play bridge with Springs, Cal and the major. They say that he is the fastest bridge player in the world, whatever that means. Crap is my game but the major outlawed that. We can gamble at bridge and drink all we want as long as we don't get drunk. Now isn't that a fine distinction! I don't know how to play bridge and I like to get drunk.

October 1st

Tomorrow we will wake in Merrie England. Oh, boy! This voyage is nearly over. I am sorry in one way and glad in another. I am growing restless and want a change. This ship is too monotonous.

We left the other ships about nine-thirty last night and steamed off at full speed. We are making nineteen knots now and it seems high speed after the snail's pace we have had. We picked up a lighthouse shortly after leaving the convoy and Cal and I fancied we saw land by the light of the moon away off on the starboard. The sea is as green as grass and has been all day. It's beautiful, and the foam from our wake is as white as snow. We have only one chaser with us and it is streaking along in front. I found out that they are not as small as they look. They are nearly three hundred feet long. I am rather excited about arriving in Liverpool tomorrow and going across England by train to London. I know it will be a peach of a trip.

October 3rd

So this is England. We landed yesterday morning and took a train right at the dock for Oxford. We aren't going to Italy after all. We've got to go to Ground School all over again. Our orders got all bawled up in Paris and MacDill, La Guardia, the doctors, the enlisted men and Spalding have gone on to France. MacDill said he would go on to Paris and get the orders straightened out and come back for us. Somebody had made a mistake. All our mail is in Italy, all our money is in *lira* and our letters of credit are drawn on banks in Rome and we've wasted two weeks studying Italian and two months going to Ground School learning nonsense for now we've got to go through this British Ground School here. And we hear that everything that we were taught at home is all wrong. Gosh, I hope someday I get a chance to tell Major Kraft that. We left all our baggage and equipment at Liverpool because we couldn't wait until it was unloaded. Springs left Kelly in charge of it and he picked Bird and Adams and Kerk to stay with him to help. I'll bet they don't show up for a month. They are fools if they do.

We came through the most beautiful country I ever saw. It made me think of *Grimm's Fairy Tales*. The greenest fields imaginable and no fences, just hedges and occasionally a stone wall. We did see some fences too, but very few and they were board, no wire. I think the biggest field I saw was about sixty acres and they ranged down to about one and a half acres. Most of the fields were pasture lands or seemed so. They were covered with this intensely green grass. I saw a good many hay stacks, so I guess they must cut this grass and cure it. There was never a frame house, all the houses were the softest red brick, I mean the colour, and all pretty too, or I should say, picturesque, and never an inch of ground wasted even on the railroad right-of-way, which was all in grass except where it was planted in vegetables.

I am living at Christ Church College in a room with Callahan, Jim Stokes and Springs. Stokes and Springs had a stateroom together on board ship. Our barracks are a million years old, I know, because it took it that long to cool off to this temperature. The stone is crumbling away and the whole place is very ancient and has all that charm and dignity that only antiquity can give. Cardinal Wolsey and Henry VIII built it or had something to do with it. I haven't found out whether they got fired from it or gave money to it. Either one makes a man famous. Our mess hall is like a chapel, with stained glass windows and the most wonderful paintings all around the walls. The ceiling is very high and is beamed. It's an inverted V and has the old black wood inside with the cross fancy work showing on it.

We have champagne with our meals at $2.10 a bottle! We get the vintage of 1904. This is indeed the life! I am full of it now and that's why I can't write very well. Everyone over here is so damn polite. I know now why they always think of us as savages. This is the most charming country I ever dreamed of. Cal and I went canoeing on the Thames this evening and saw some sights. I tell you this is the home of the brave and the land of free love.

Most of the boys are pretty mad. We all came over as volunteers and we volunteered for service in Italy and not in England. There seems to be a good deal of prejudice against the British.

This is Sunday. I don't know the date but I am sober so it must be Sunday. The description of this country is so far beyond me that I will have to leave it to a better pen than I wield. It suits me!

Yesterday the old fellow, the dean of Christ Church College, took us all through the church and showed us the interesting things there. The newest part of the church is only about four hundred years old but it is built on the ruins of an old Norman church and one of its present walls was built in 700 *A. D.* being then a part of the priory of St. Frideswide. This quadrangle where we live is called Peckwater Quad and where the mess hall is, Tom Quad. The architecture over there is Moorish and is the work of Sir Christopher Wren. I would love to know all the old English gentlemen who spent, or misspent their youth here at Oxford and slept in this very room. I'll bet they love the wasted part of their youth best.

I hear today that we will only be here five weeks. I think that will be long enough but I won't mind as long as the champagne holds out. Fry, Curtis, Cal, Brown, and I took a bicycle ride over to the Duke of Marlborough's palace at Woodstock. It is a beautiful place and was given to the old Duke by Queen Anne, I think, for winning a battle. It fulfils my idea of what a palace ought to be. It's on a hill overlooking a beautiful lake with little islands in it and a most imposing picturesque bridge across it. He has erected the statue of Victory or some such idea on the far side of the bridge to commemorate his victory. The Duchess is an American girl.

It's a ten-mile ride from Oxford and about every two miles there is the most delightful wayside inn where you get this English ale and Scotch whiskey and cheese and bread. We made all the stops going and coming and I never saw such quaint places or quaint people. We stopped in Woodstock and had a bottle of port and lunch. The woman who ran the place could hardly understand our American way of talking.

I went to the barber shop yesterday and asked for a haircut. I got a haircut, shampoo, singe and a big revolving brush run over my head for the equivalent of fifty cents. They don't have any regular barber chairs over here. They sit you down in a regular office chair, and they never heard of a hot towel.

Everything over here is dirt cheap. The English don't run up the price on anything just because it's scarce. I think there're some laws on the subject. There's no candy for sale except in small lots at a few places, yet the price is the same as if it were plentiful. I tried to buy all the chocolate they had at one little shop. They told me they couldn't sell but one piece to a customer and when that was gone they couldn't get any more. I told them I would buy it all and they could close up and go on a vacation. But they couldn't see it that way and all I got was one piece.

We met a private last night in the Carlton Bar who seemed to resent the presence of American troops in Oxford. He was Irish and seemed to be looking for trouble. I was all for helping him find it. He wanted to know where we had been for the last three years. I wonder how much of that feeling there is. Everyone else has seemed more than glad to see us and is more than cordial. I wonder if some of the boys have been going around bragging. No one gives a damn, but I had rather these people would think well of us and feel kindly towards us for after all, we are their cousins. The British cadets are as nice as can be and go out of their way to help us when they have the opportunity.

I am going over to the library and read some old books. The last time troops were quartered here was in Oliver Cromwell's time.

We have no commissioned officer here so do about as we please. Springs is a good hard worker and does the best he can to keep order but he hasn't the proper authority to back it up. Everybody realises that if we don't obey him we'll catch hell from somebody else later. But there are a few roughnecks in every outfit that will cause trouble and get the whole bunch in wrong. I've got my eye on one of that sort and the first break he makes is going to be his last. I can't put him in the guard house, but I can put him in the hospital. Springs is only a sergeant so can't legally discipline any one and according to the Constitution no officer of a foreign army can discipline an American soldier, so if anything goes wrong they'd have to send to London for an American officer. Stokes was a lawyer before he took wing and keeps finding all sorts of trouble. He may have had a law office but I'll bet he made his living shooting crap. He cleaned out the whole crowd last night.

Some of the boys are getting reconciled to England but there's still a lot of cussing about it and a lot of them are looking for trouble.

October 8th

Cal, Stokes, Springs and I went to supper and a show tonight. Dismal failure. This has been our first day of real work. I believe the course will be easy as we've had it all once except the Vickers machine gun and rotary motors. Both of these are used extensively by the Royal Flying Corps.

I hear that the Germans have the goods in airplanes and A.A. guns. I guess it's the North and South over again. Of course, no one doubts our winning out in the end but it will be a long hard fight and few of us will be left to enjoy the fruits of our victory. I surely am lucky not to be in the trenches. Some, in fact, most of the cadets have been out and they say it's hell. "Only we young chaps can stand it," they say. Most of these English cadets are kids and the instructors themselves wouldn't average over twenty-two. Our machine gun instructor has a bullet hole through the flap of his ear. He says he's going to get one in the other ear so he can wear earrings.

Kelly and his squad arrived today with our baggage. They look like they had a good time. Bird was telling some story about their driving a coach until Kelly fell through the top of it.

The only thing that confuses us is this English alphabet. Instead of saying: A, Bee, Cee, Dee, they have a different way of designating the letters. They say: Ak, Beer, Cee, Don, E, F, G, Haiches, I, J, K, Ella, Emma, N, O, Pip, Q, R, Esses, Toc, U, Vic, W, X, Y, Zed. And as they call everything by initials it's very confusing.

They also drive on the left-hand side of the street. If there was any traffic we'd all be run over.

October 16th

I am neglecting this important volume lately, I am afraid.

The last few days have been crowded with events. A regular army West Point major came over from Paris to look us over Sunday and straffed hell out of us in front of the British Colonel and his staff. Besides the hundred and fifty of us, there are sixty more American cadets over at Queen's College that came here two weeks before we did. They have a sergeant named Oliver in charge of them. He is a son of Senator Oliver and is only five feet high. When he marches along beside the first squad it's an awfully funny sight because none of them are less than six feet five. All the Englishmen like him and cheer every time they see him marching the detachment around.

This major had a parade of both outfits and inspected us and then got us in the mess hall and pitched into us as if we were convicts. He said he had heard that we were grousing because we had to go to Ground School again and hadn't gotten our commissions as we had been promised. He said if any of us didn't like it, he would send us over to France and send us up to the trenches as privates. He said he could do what he pleased to us in time of war and would. He said he had heard that there was some objection to having the colonel discipline us but that we were going to take it and going to like it. He said he'd asked the colonel as a special favour to him, to give us all the discipline that his own cadets got. He certainly did despise us in public with a loud voice.

He didn't like our uniforms. He said they were all right at home but they wouldn't do over here where everybody has to be smart. So we've got to buy tailor-made uniforms and pay for them ourselves. If we haven't got money enough, we've got to borrow it and any man who refuses to buy one of these special uniforms, is to be sent to France for discipline. Springs has a big letter of credit and has offered to lend it to us as far as it will go. And we've got to wear these funny little monkey hats and R. F. C. belts. Our detachment will be the funniest thing when they blossom forth in their bastard British-American get-up. Springs was the first to adopt the monkey hat and we all nearly died laughing when he showed up.

Our belts were issued today and they look awfully funny with these short blouses. We don't like the idea of adopting the British uniform and looking as much like an Englishman as possible. But that's what the major was after. We will sure look funny as the devil as every man has designed his own uniform and picked different material and colours. These tailors ought to give that major a commission. I hope someday I meet him again. He's one man that ought to have his face shoved down his throat. If we ever meet as equals I'm going to break my resolve about keeping my temper. He'll always retain possession of my goat and as an American, I'm as ashamed of him as he was of us. I'll bet he never does any fighting! He got hightoned by the colonel and lost his head and indulged himself in an orgy of bootlicking. That was the reason for the whole thing.

If he wants us to look like officers, why doesn't he get us our commissions? They were promised to us. If we have to obey army rules and regulations, why doesn't he? If he has authority to violate the Constitution, why hasn't he authority enough to give us our commissions and pay? How can he make enlisted men buy their own uniforms? By calling us cadets. The cadets are the mulattoes of the army. They get the privileges of neither enlisted men nor officers and get all the trouble coming to both. MacDill dressed us as we are; what business is it of his if the colonel wants to doll us up like Englishmen?

October 19th

A British major with the D.S.O. and the M.C talked to us the other day. He said as I remember it:

You men are starting on a long trip. It's a hard trip and will require a lot of courage. You'll all be frightened many times but most of you will be able to conquer your fear and carry on. But if you find that fear has gotten the best of you and you can't stick it and you are beyond bucking up, don't go on and cause the death of brave men through your failure. Quit where you are and try something else. Courage is needed above all else. If five of you meet five Huns and one of you is yellow and doesn't do his part and lets the others down, the four others will be killed through the failure of the one and maybe that one himself.

This individual hero stuff is all tommy rot. It's devotion to duty and concerted effort and disciplined team work that will win the war.

War is cruel, war is senseless and war is a plague, but we've got to win it and there's no better use of your life than to give it to help stop this eternal slaughter.

It's a war of men—strong determined men and weaklings have no part in it.

He looked just like he talked.

None of the men I've talked to curse the Hun particularly. So far, I've met no eye witnesses of atrocities and not much is said of them.

I hope I can stick it through. I know I'm not afraid to die. I'm pretty young to be ready for it and I'm not. Why, I'm just beginning to live! And after going to all this trouble to help make history, I want to live a little while to be able to tell about it. If we make the world safe for democracy, as some salesman remarked, brandishing a Liberty Bond in one hand and a flag in the other, what price salvation if we are not here to be democratic? Glory is hardly a passport to paradise. I can't imagine a man with a lot of rank and a lot of medals and a lot of dog, getting through the eye of a needle any easier than a camel. I'll have to consult Springs on the matter. He was an honour man in philosophy at college and is the authority on heaven, hell and hard licker.

I was talking to a little English cadet who had on an old battered Sam Browne and I asked him was he trying to look like a veteran. He smiled and said, "My brother wore it two years. He was killed by

Richthofen." There seem to be a lot of them after that bird. Wonder how long before somebody sneaks up behind him and drops him. It will take a good man from all I've heard. There's no price on his head but I'll bet the fellow who gets him gets a lot of decorations.

Kelly and Bird got started again. We were all over in the R. F. C. Club doing a little quiet drinking,—Cal, Stokes, Jake and myself. Kelly and Bird came in with a good start. Bird said he couldn't enjoy his drinking unless he had Springs to watch him and tell him when he had enough. Kelly said that in that case the best thing to do was to send for Springs. They wanted to know where he was so we told them he was over in the room writing some letters. They found someone who was going back to the college and sent word to him to come right over or Bird would start giving his cowboy yell and keep it up until he got there.

By the time Springs got there they were well oiled. They are both six feet three and would rather fight than eat. I had visions of them both being sent to Leavenworth in chains. They nearly killed Springs with an affectionate greeting and he had to do some fast thinking. Bird said he supposed he was going to be put on the wagon for another week and he wanted his portrait painted doing it. Springs ordered a round of double brandies. Then Kelly, who always has to pay for more than anybody else, ordered triple whiskies. Then Bird called for some port and they started a round again. It was a good battle while it lasted. We had to put Springs in a cold tub before he could call the roll for dinner and Kelly and Bird never raised their voices again until the next morning. They are on the wagon all right and it didn't require any orders either.

We met a French officer from Chicago tonight who came over from France to see his brother Paul Winslow, who's over at Queen's College with the first outfit. He's in the French Air Service and says the Hun has the supremacy of the air on the French front without a doubt. It seems that we will be the goats as France has about shot her wad. He says we are lucky to be here as all the cadets in France are having a terrible time. They haven't done any flying but live in tents and do manual labour. They help build the flying fields and have to do the same work as the German prisoners and get the same food. Their letters are censored and they aren't allowed to write home how they are being treated. They had a German spy in command of them for a while. He says he expects to hear of a mutiny any time.

October 22nd

We have moved to Exeter College. And why? Thereby hangs a tale. Bim Oliver and his crew had finished their course and made the highest marks in the examinations on record. So the officer in charge of Queen's gave them all passes Saturday night to go out to dinner and celebrate. That was also Jake Stanley's birthday and he gave a party at Bud's that night to celebrate it. It was a right good party. He had a private room on the third floor and there were present: Cal, Springs, Stokes, Paul Winslow and his brother Alan, Hash Gile, Dud Mudge, an English staff officer and myself. Dwyer and a bunch of others came in later. Everybody was all teed up before they got there and then we had cocktails by the quart and champagne and then each man got a half gallon pitcher of ale. We sang that old song and made everybody do bottoms-up by turn. Jake had a cake and he kept announcing that he was going to "tut the twake." When he did cut it, Hash Gile insisted on helping Springs to eat it and got most of it down his neck and in his ears. I never laughed so much in my life.

When the party broke up and we were all getting out, the English officer and the French officer were assisting each other home. The colonel came up with a flashlight and tried to stop a bunch of them. The English officer gave the colonel a push and ran and the colonel made a flying tackle at him but missed and grabbed Winslow. The colonel insisted on knowing who it was that ran and when Winslow refused to tell him, he went down to Queen's and ordered a formation of all of Bim's detachment.

They say it was the greatest sight that Oxford ever witnessed,—sixty American soldiers in all sorts of costumes, in all stages of drunkenness, trying to get into line and stay there, in a dark and ancient courtyard, hallowed by the scholars of the ages, with a British colonel dashing about with a flashlight and bellowing like a bull at each man as he came in, "Are you the man that pushed me and ran?" The first sergeant that tried to call the roll passed out cold in the middle of it and had to be carried off. The second one got the British and American commands mixed up and was led away babbling something that sounded like a cavalry drill.

The colonel tried to question them but all one man would say was: "I wasn't on the third floor; I was on the second floor." No matter what the colonel would ask him, that was all he would say.

Another one asked the colonel, "What do you mean run, sir? How fast is a run?"

Finally, the colonel had to give it up but he made the French officer leave the college and he wants to make a complaint to the French Ambassador. It certainly was an international mess. Bim and his crew left the next day to go to Stamford to learn to fly and the colonel moved us over here to Exeter where we can't corrupt any of his cadets and turned the place over to us. We have the whole college to ourselves. There are a million rumours flying around about what is going to happen to us. The colonel sent over one of his staff officers to help Springs. And who did he send but the very same officer that pushed him and ran! You can't laugh that off. He and big Shoemaker, who used to drive a dog-team in Alaska, are great friends and I foresee trouble.

Ten of us went to a dance Saturday night at Miss Cannon's. She's a real English girl and wears a monocle. I'm going riding with her Wednesday afternoon. Oxford isn't such a bad place after all. Stokes came to the dance illuminated and did an Indian war dance in the middle of the floor. He nearly passed away next day over the kidding he got. We have a way of getting in late at night by climbing over a high wall with the assistance of a limb of a tree that hangs over from the inside. Fulford and I were coming in by that route and we heard a plaintive call for help. It was Brownie and he had tried to get over at the wrong place and had got hung by the seat of his trousers on a nail. We had a time getting him down and putting him to bed.

We brought four boiled lobsters back with us and a couple of bottles of port. We woke Springs up and he was as mad as hell. He said if the rest of the crowd got on to the fact that he was letting us come in when we pleased, he wouldn't be able to control anybody. We told him that everybody was out anyway and to go back to sleep and forget it. So we ate the lobsters and drank the port ourselves. About that time Kelly and Bird came in with Capt. Swan. He had come up from London to pay us off and they had run into him and brought him on over the wall with them. He told us some funny stories of the Philippines. Kelly and Bird were all lit up and had a bottle of whisky which they had brought to Springs. He wouldn't take it so they drank it themselves with Capt. Swan.

We finished the lobster and put the shells in a big bucket outside the door. Bird saw it and decided it was a football and took a terrific kick at it and scattered it all over the courtyard outside. Springs got up steaming like a scalded hog and told Bird that he had to get a flashlight and go out and pick up every piece or he'd have to put him under arrest in the morning for it. Bird thought it was a joke at first but Springs made him do it. It sure was a funny sight, that big cowboy out in the court with a flashlight, down on his knees looking for lobster claws. We all went out and helped him.

Sunday morning, we were all just as sick as we could be from that lobster. Cal, Stokes and I couldn't get out of bed and couldn't get to drill. Springs was raging. Along about noon we got up and managed to stagger in to lunch. Then Springs informed us that we were under arrest and couldn't leave the college. And the damn fool made us stay in all the afternoon and evening too. He said if we were too sick to drill we were too sick to go out and get drunk again. I'll get even with him. He says he is going to demote all three of us. He's just mad because he's missing all the fun. Kelly and Bird go out every night and take off their white hat bands and say that they are mechanics from this squadron outside of town. They throw a big party and then come in and wake Springs up to tell him about it because they say they don't want to do anything behind his back that they wouldn't tell him about to his face. Some morning this detachment is going to wake up and find they haven't got any sergeants.

We had a boxing tournament last week. Springs and I went in and won our first bouts, but got knocked out in the second round. Pudrith and Jake Stanley each won in their classes and got a trip to London over the weekend as prizes.

October 24th
We had mail from home today which seemed to sadden the boys more than cheer them up. It sort of made us realise how far away we are. Springs certainly had a funny collection. He ought to save them for publication some day when people get their senses of humour back.

November 6th
Harroby Camp, Grantham, Lincolnshire.
I wish I could have stayed at Oxford for the horseback ride with Miss Cannon but we were all suddenly sent up here to Grantham to the machine gun school. All except Springs and twenty who have gone to Stamford to learn to fly. Springs had to pick the twenty and naturally everyone wanted to go. He picked those who'd done the most flying already. He took only those who were ready to go solo and Deetjen, Garver and Dietz because they have done a lot of hard clerical work for the detachment. I couldn't see why he wouldn't take

Cal and me and I told him so. What's the use of having friends if you don't stick by them and do things for them? And what's the use of having authority if you can't use it to help your friends? I'm a Jackson democrat and I believe the victim is entitled to what is spoiled. And when I fight, I fight to win. I don't want to know anything about the Marquis of Queensberry's ideas. When I fight I only hit a man once and the first thing he knows about it is when he reads about it in the papers. And when I swing, somebody gets 199 of my 200 pounds where they least expect it.

Mit wanted to go to Stamford and he kicked up an awful row. He claims that he is a friend of General Wood's and he wanted to call up the American Ambassador when Springs wouldn't let him go. He stood out in the court and cussed for half an hour because he said there was a conspiracy against him. Finally, I went over and told him that he was about to be crowned and that if there was any partiality in it I would be going to Stamford myself. He says he's going to spend the rest of his life getting even with Springs.

We all chipped in to buy Springs a parting gift. We couldn't see wasting $75 on a cup that he couldn't use so we bought him a big silver flask.

We had to leave poor Jim Stokes behind. He was operated on for appendicitis the day we left. He got through it all right.

We were met at the station here by a band and escorted to our barracks. The English rank us as officers now and we don't have to salute anything under majors. Some of us are rather embarrassed because we are treated as officers when we really aren't, though it isn't our fault. We just aren't nephews of the right people in Washington. Mit is in his glory. He has blossomed out in boots and swaggers about in the bottom half of a Sam Browne belt and cusses his batman. We have a regular servant who cleans our hut and shines our shoes. We have our own mess—a regular officers' mess. The classes are terribly boring and take all the daylight hours but we do as we please in the evening and don't have to be in until twelve o'clock.

Cal, Schlotzhauer, Leach and I went over to Nottingham Sunday and had supper. Believe me, it is some town. There have never been any troops quartered in Nottingham and there are no camps near it and all the men have been gone for three years. I never knew there was such a place. The women clustered around us all the time and talked to us as if we were a new species.

Stillman is in charge now and I am a platoon commander still.

When Springs was trying to decide whom to appoint in his place, everyone wanted Bird as top sergeant. Springs likes Bird but isn't so particularly keen about Stillman but he said he was afraid of Bird so he put Stillman in as top and made Bird second in command. I guess it's just as well. Somebody has got to hold this crowd down and Bird has been in too much devilment already to be effective on his own responsibility. Stillman is a fine fellow and certainly looks the part. He's six feet seven and a half and weighs over 200. He used to play end on Yale.

McCurry came in tonight and begged me with tears in his eyes to go with him and cut off Ken's moustache. He sure was tanked. He ran into the barbed wire between this hut and the next one and nearly tore his brand new uniform off.

I miss Kelly and Springs and Jim. This is the first split and I guess there will be many more.

November 7th

We have Raftery in our hut. He is going to bed now, putting his money belt on over his pyjamas and wearing a knitted helmet. He's the funniest thing I ever saw.

I heard that Jim is getting on all right.

November 8th

I got four letters from home today and they seem to have travelled a little bit further than the others. Poor old Fat Payden hasn't gotten even a postal since he left the States. His eyes are inflamed and he doesn't go to classes but sits in here all day and gossips with Fry and our batman. He laughs at everything any one says, no matter how stale it is. I just found out today that he is just twenty.

Cal, Herbert, Fulford and Fry are sitting around the table now drinking port out of their canteens and writing home. Everyone is fed up. I don't see how we are going to stand three more weeks of this. Aren't we ever going to fly? There was some talk of making ground officers of some of us. Some of the married men decided they wanted to be ground officers but nobody else would consent. An English general made us a talk and said this war was no great adventure: you were either scared to death or bored to death all the time.

This camp is sort of a pretty place. When I look down at Grantham nestling between these pretty checkered hills with the sky all coloured up by the setting sun and the clouds so low you can hang your hat on them, it kind of gets up in my neck and I think this old world is a damn fine place to live in. The hill on the other side of town we see from here is checkered up with little fields—every one a different colour and it's very pretty. If the sky wasn't filled with aeroplanes all day, you'd never think of war. I hope I never see another machine gun. I came over here to fight—not to sit around and talk about it forever.

November 9th
Lord, I have the blues, the worried blues. Anderson was in here playing his steel guitar. How that boy can play! A couple of the English instructors have been going to see a couple of girls and not making much progress. So they took Andy along with them and put him in the next room and made him play soft Hawaiian music to keep them in the proper frame of mind.

Morrison came in tonight with a beautiful bun and a new pair of boots. They were tight too and it took four of us to pull them off.

I've got the blues so bad I think I'll get drunk tomorrow and see if that will help things.

November 10th
One of the boys came in the other night after midnight without his Sam Browne belt. He was last seen walking down the street with a girl and he had it on then. So everybody got to kidding him about bushwhacking. He couldn't remember where they had gone but he had to have a belt and was broke so he decided he'd go back and ask the girl where he left it. But when he went back he woke up the girl's father and he came out and chased him down the street. But he had his belt back the next day so I guess love found a way.

November 13th
Well, the old man is himself again. Jack Fulford, Cal, Morrison, Leach and I went to Nottingham over the week-end. We didn't get very drunk.

Springs flew up from Stamford to see us while we were away.

Last night was guest night in our mess and we had all the English staff over. These Englishmen sure have a funny idea of a party. They want to smash everything. Fulford got the idea that he was a baseball pitcher and he knocked the end out of our hut throwing whisky bottles at it. We caught Ken and cut his moustache off at last.

November 18th
Cal and I went down to Stamford to spend the day and nearly died laughing. Our stomachs are still sore. Springs and Kelly are rooming

together over a millinery shop. They spend all their time at a club there.

There was a sort of straff going on that day. They had a new C. O. and he was an ex-Guards officer and had a grudge against the Huns and wanted to get on with the war. There were a lot of young English kids that had been there some time swinging the lead and he sent for them all and lined them up. He told them that there was a war on and that pilots were needed badly at the front and that they were all going solo that afternoon. They nearly fainted. Some of them had had less than two hours of air work and none of them had had more than five.

We all went out to the airdrome to see the fun. I guess there were about thirty of them in all. The squadron was equipped with D. H. Sixes which are something like our Curtiss planes except they are slower and won't spin no matter what you do to them.

The first one to take off was a bit uneasy and an instructor had to taxi out for him. He ran all the way across the field, and it was a big one, and then pulled the stick right back into his stomach. The Six went straight up nose first and stalled and hung on its propeller. Then it did a tail slide right back into the ground.

The next one did better. He got off and zigzagged a bit but instead of making a circuit he kept straight on. His instructor remarked that he would probably land in Scotland, because he didn't know how to turn.

Another one got off fairly well and came around for his landing. He levelled off and made a beautiful landing—a hundred feet above the ground. He pancaked beautifully and shoved his wheels up through the lower wings. But the plane had a four-bladed prop on it and it broke off even all around. So the pupil was able to taxi on into the hangar as both wheels had come up the same distance. He was very much pleased with himself and cut off the engine and took off his goggles and stood up and started to jump down to the ground which he thought was about five feet below him. Then he looked down and saw the ground right under his seat. He certainly was shocked.

Another took off fine but he had never been taught to land and he was a bit uncertain about that operation. He had the general idea all right but he forgot to cut off his motor. He did a continuous series of dives and zooms. A couple of instructors sang a dirge for him:

The young aviator lay dying, and as 'neath the wreckage he lay
To the Ak Emmas around him assembled, these last parting words did

he say:
'Take the cylinder out of my kidney, the connecting rod out of my brain,
From the small of my back take the crankshaft, and assemble the engine again!'

There were a lot more verses but I can't remember them.

We thought sure he was gone but he got out of it all right and made a fairly decent landing but not where he had expected.

The next one didn't know much about landing either. He came in too fast and didn't make the slightest attempt to level off. The result was a tremendous bounce that sent him up a hundred feet. He used his head and put his motor on and went around again. He did that eight times and finally smashed the undercarriage so that next time he couldn't bounce. Then he turned over on his back. The C. O. congratulated him and told him he would probably make a good observer.

They finally all got off and not a one of them got killed. I don't see why not though. Only one of them got hurt and that was when one landed on top of the other one. The one in the bottom plane got a broken arm. I got quite a thrill out of that.

A flying field is not at all what I expected it would be like. They all seem to do pretty much as they please, go where they please and fly when they please. The chief occupation seems to be passing the flowing cup.

There is a cemetery right in the middle of the town and since the Americans came the ghosts walk about it all night. Kelly has a joke on Springs about it. I saw Horn, Knox, Taber, Roth, Neely, Watts and a couple of others.

November 17th

Cal, Curtis, Brown, Fry and I are ordered to Thetford to learn to fly at last. This is the final bust-up of the Italian Detachment. I am lucky to get a good gang. I had Ken but I swapped him for Curtis. Fry said it was just like swapping horses.

November 18th

I went to Stokes Castle this afternoon for lunch and stayed for tea. I think this has been the best day I have spent in England. I met a Mrs. Chapin out there from Louisiana. She is a sure-enough Southern aristocrat and I am proud of her. She reminded me of Gramma. She dominated the whole table at dinner and was so interesting and made everyone feel at home. She took me to her room and showed me the picture of her old home in Louisiana. It was an old Italian villa on the banks of the Mississippi. I certainly enjoyed talking to her. It was like a visit home. I wonder if I will ever see the Mississippi again. It flows through another world like the River Styx that Springs talks about.

The castle was a wonder, too. It was full of old paintings and relics—some of them a thousand years old. There was a picture of a woman kissing Christ's feet by Rubens. The library was about forty by eight and lined with books and relics. The best part of the place was the grounds, about three acres, I guess.

We leave for Thetford tomorrow at eight-thirty and at last I am really going to learn to fly. It's over six months since I enlisted to fly and I am not sorry they are past.

November 20th

Arrived at Thetford *via* Peterborough and Ely. We had about four hours at Peterborough and went to see the cathedral. It's the most magnificent thing I have seen so far. I saw where Mary, Queen of Scots was buried before she was moved to Westminster.

Thetford is not much. We are going to start on Rumptys as these Henry Farman planes are called. They say that you test the rigging by putting a bird between the two wings. If the bird gets out, there's a wire gone somewhere. They are so unstable that they never go up except when the air is very smooth. No one flew today except Roberts.

These old short-horn Farmans are awful looking buses. I am surprised they fly at all. We have the same sort of wild kids here for instructors that we had at Oxford, only more so,—wilder and younger. I was told that they kill off more instructors in the R. F. C. than pupils and from what I've seen, I can well believe it. I have a Captain Harrison for an instructor. He seems to be a mere kid. He's about nineteen and is trying hard to grow a moustache. Classes are a joke.

This is real country here. The fields are bigger and rougher. I like it better too. This is Norfolk—I wonder if the jacket originated here.

Cal and I are posted for early flying tomorrow. He just came in and said in a shaky voice, "Well, let's get ready for our last sleep." The fool plays bridge all the time for the good of his soul. While he's playing I usually do my writing on this thing. Fry is in the same room with us and is terribly funny.

November 25th

Just returned from my first leave. I went down to London to get my teeth fixed. It cost me forty pounds. These teeth of mine certainly are expensive, my sweet tooth being the worst. London is a town after my own heart. I stopped at the Savoy. I tell you it is a wonderful sight to sit in the dining room and see all the women in evening gowns—all the soldiers on leave, airmen, observers, artillerymen, infantrymen, sailors and marines. It's a wonderful sight. Think of the sacrifice laid at the feet of the God of War!

Today I saw my first scout machine, a Sopwith Pup. It's the prettiest little thing I ever laid my eyes on. I am going to fly one if I live long enough. They aren't as big as a minute and are as pretty and slick as a thoroughbred horse. Tiny little things, just big enough for one man and a machine gun.

It snowed today and it's as cold as a nun's lips. The wind is rattling the stove pipe. I guess I'd better turn in.

December 6th

I have been flying for three days and Capt. Harrison says I can solo tomorrow if it's calm. I tell you it's a great life. I am absolutely ruined for anything else. I wish I could describe it. The thing most surprising to me is the feeling of absolute safety. I have put in two hours and twenty minutes in the air and I would have soloed this evening if it had been calm enough.

I have been to London again. I went to Murray's nightclub with the Chinless Wonder. Cal and Fry joined us at the court later where we had a suite. Then I took the Wonder to a dance we heard about at the Grafton Galleries.

I saw Jake Stanley, who was down from Stamford. He told me a funny story. Springs and Kelly went to a dance after a party the staff officers gave to the Americans. Kelly didn't want to go home and threw a bicycle at Springs which missed him. Then Kelly sat down on the side of a ditch and said, "If you want me to go home, let's see you take me." Every time Springs would try to pick him up Kelly would push him in the ditch. Kelly would make two of Springs and can push him all over the place. About that time Jake came by and Springs called for help. They decided that the best thing to do was to knock Kelly out and then carry him home peacefully. So Jake got behind him and put his hands under his arms and lifted him up on his feet. Then Springs got in front of him and tilted Kelly's head back and adjusted his jaw to just the proper angle and hawled off and took a terrific swing. Just as he swung, Kelly's feet slipped and instead of landing on the jaw, Springs hit Jake on the nose and they all went over in the ditch. May Dorsey was going home with a big package of his own and saw Springs hit Jake and thought there was a fight on and jumped on Springs. Before he knew what was happening Springs had a black eye and Dorsey was working on the other one. Then Springs got on top of Dorsey and nearly killed him. He was bumping his head on a piece of cement when they pried him loose.

A couple of Bobbies came up and helped Springs get Kelly over his shoulder and then he carried him home quietly.

I met Dora at Murray's and had lunch with her the next day. She is very pretty and witty and smart. She came up to Thetford and brought another girl with her. Fry called her the Long Lean Lanky Devil. We had dinner and they caught the eleven-thirty train back to London. The landlady at the Bell Hotel refused to take them in at the indecent hour of ten-thirty.

January 1st, 1918
London Colney, Hertfordshire

This is New Year's Day. I haven't written up this diary for quite a long time—nearly a month, and many things have happened.

I have done my four hours solo on Rumptys and am done with them forever, thank God. I have done two hours on Avros. They are entirely different and I have to learn to fly all over again. We had four days' leave in London before we left Thetford. Cal and I finished the same day and came to London together. Cal rolled into a Roman dugout on his last landing and I thought sure he was killed. Fry wrote off a bus by pancaking from two hundred feet.

We met Jim in London and had a wild party. Jim is living there now and is attached to headquarters. After the show we had Beatrice Lillie and the entire cast of *Cheap* up in our suite at the court and they brought along Lord Somebody or other. Cal salaamed before him and shook hands and said, "Hello, God." He was much shocked. That was the first lord I ever met. They all got to fraternizing among themselves so we split up. Cal has fallen in love with a sweet little thing called Peggy. She is very pretty but that's the best I can say for her.

We have been posted to London Colney, which is the greatest place yet. It is only twenty miles from London and they have Pups and Spads and Avros. There's no discipline or wind-up at all. One class a day in machine guns and one in wireless but we know more than the instructors and nobody cares whether we go or not. We go to London when we please. There are only two Avros for about thirty of us so we will be here for some time. Americans are not popular with the C. O.

and adjutant. I guess they've got a good reason to dislike us.

It seems that the U. S. Army has bought a lot of Curtisses at home for primary training planes and they are building a lot of planes like Sopwith Pups but they don't want to build any Avros if they can help it. So they sent orders over to take the best men that finish on Curtisses and put them on Pups without letting them go up in Avros. Springs and DeGamo were the first two to finish on Curtisses so they sent them down here to London Colney to be used as experiments.

The C. O. and adjutant said it would be plain murder and refused to let them have Pups. There was a U. S. lieut. here named Gaines and he forbade them to try it. The London Headquarters called up and told them to go ahead anyway. The C. O. ordered them off the tarmac and said he was fed up on funerals and the U. S. Army would have to conduct its own executions. A British general came over and backed up the C. O. so they compromised by sending Springs and DeGamo back to Stamford for further instructions. The C. O. at Stamford got sore as a boil and said there was nothing more he could teach them on Curtisses and that they were ready for anything.

The adjutant at London Colney tried to put it off on the two of them so Springs and DeGamo wrote a letter and said they were always willing to do it and were ready at any time and had been ordered off the tarmac at London Colney but they were still ready to try it. There was a big row over it and the adjutant caught hell for not carrying out orders. Then the Paris Headquarters sent over orders that they were to loop and spin Curtisses and then be put on Pups anyway—the worst that could happen would be two funerals. Don't these non-flyers love us! What are a couple of aviators, more or less?

Up at Stamford, Springs and DeGamo were duly ordered to go up and loop and spin those ancient crates. They couldn't get any of the instructors to go up and show them how to do it. They knew better! Besides the orders came from American Headquarters and the British didn't approve of them. But up they went and looped and spun anyway. Springs did ten loops in succession and landed. Ainsworth went up later in the same machine and was coming over the top of his loop when the wings fell off. He was killed instantly. He's the first of the American cadets to go. I'm afraid there'll be many more before the *Kaiser* is pushed over backwards.

The C. O. at Stamford refused to permit any further foolishness and Paris backed down and sent orders over for DeGamo and Springs to stop all flying until it could be decided what form the experiment would take. So they had to sit around for a month doing nothing while everybody else was going on. DeGamo is instructing on Sixties and Springs is ferrying. A great system we have. Everything we have had to do so far has been messed up. I'll guarantee our noble commanders will kill more Americans than Germans before it is over. But what can you expect when they promote the jackasses on seniority and put men in charge of important technical affairs just because they have spent their lives doing infantry drill in the Philippines and transferred to the aviation section a week ago to get a soft berth and more pay? Why should they worry about mistakes? They aren't the ones that get killed. An order from the adjutant general can't make a pilot out of a quartermaster.

Last night Cal and I and four English officers went to a dance at an Insane Asylum. Cal became fascinated with a charming young Welch nurse.

January 3rd

There's a U. S. lieut. here that certainly is looking for trouble. He enlisted the same time we did, but he did his flying first and got out of going to Ground School and got his commission right away. He's quite impressed with his exalted rank and makes us all salute him continuously just because the government hasn't kept its promise to us and we are still cadets.

The English can't see any difference between us and it makes him foam at the mouth. He was an instructor at home and has done two hundred hours on Curtisses. But he's no good on Avros. Two instructors turned him down and he's got to have a lot of dual. I wish they'd send him up in a Pup as an experiment!

Machine gun class is awfully boring. Kent Curtis draws pictures of everything in his notebook. One of the lecture headlines is, "The tripping of the lock." Instead of taking down the lecture, Curtis drew a picture of it. The next paragraph is headed, "The depression of the seer." He drew a picture of an old soothsayer looking into a crystal ball and biting his nails. Then he drew a picture entitled "The care of the piece," and another, "The return of the *fusee*." The sergeant caught him at it and got mad and reported him to the C. O. The C. O. had him up on the carpet and made him bring the notebook. He nearly died laughing. So for punishment he made him draw the same pictures on the walls of the office. Now every time a general comes over to inspect they get in the office and get to laughing and there's no inspection.

January 12th

Springs and DeGamo showed up today. They were as welcome as the measles. The adjutant will probably file their flying wires. The experiment is all off and they are to fly Avros if they ever get a turn. Springs looks bad and says Kelly has been getting his revenge for that party in Stamford. Joe Sharpe was killed over at Waddington on a D. H. 6. There was a fine fellow for you.

January 14th

Yesterday was washout day so we all went into town and threw a party at the court. The traveling is so congested over the weekend that the flying corps takes its holiday during the week and works on Sundays.

Dud Mudge had a funny crash over at Northholt. He was up on his first solo in a Rumpty and lost his head coming in and flew right into the side of a hangar. The nacelle came on through and pitched Dud on the floor. A mechanic was at work in there and was smoking and he was so frightened at being caught smoking in a hangar that all he could do was to stammer and make excuses while poor Dud lay on the floor with a broken arm. The engine was full on outside and the throttle was on the inside and before anybody could get to it, the Rumpty slowly pushed the side of the hangar in and the roof fell on top of it. No one could get to the throttle then and it ran until the cylinders overheated and froze up. It must have been a funny sight to see that box-kite pushing madly at that hangar and then jump on top of it.

Hash Gile cracked up a Curtiss but didn't get hurt. His instructor had bawled him out for not getting his tail up when he was taking off, so the next time he started off he pushed the stick forward up against the dash and held it there. His tail came up and kept on coming. It got higher and higher and still Hash kept the stick forward. The poor old Curtiss did the best it could and turned a forward somersault. When they fished Hash out of the wreckage he was still holding the stick forward. I also hear that Al Rothwell distinguished himself by spiralling into the ground.

January 20th

We all went into town and tore off a real raspasass party at the Court. Everybody was there for dinner. Springs's beauty nearly broke up the party. She got mad when he started drinking and then got insulted when some other girls came in to join us. She said she couldn't be seen with such girls—they were not respectable. I told her that there was only one place in London she could go to a party and that was Buckingham Palace and I wasn't sure about that. She referred to us as "your uncouth friends," and made Springs take her home.

January 24th

I'm feeling pretty much at home in the air now. But after doing very many vertical banks I feel rather sick and dizzy. If tomorrow is a good day, I am going up to ten thousand and shut offend spin down and see what happens. I am quite good at spinning but it makes me a little sick. I guess I'll get over that, though, and I think a lot of it is due to the castor oil from the motor.

Springs, DeGamo, Nathan and Barry have all finished Avros and gone on Pups. Barry and Springs crashed the first time but got away with the second try.

Dora and another girl, who was so big that Fry called her a Handley-Page, came up and had dinner with us at the Peahen Inn at St. Albans. They went back on the eleven-thirty train. There was a snowstorm and we had to walk back the five miles. Fulford and Fry insisted they were going to sleep in the snow so we left them in a big drift.

I am afraid that this diary will not be of any value as an historical document. I don't write it the way I date it always. Sometimes I don't get a chance to write in it for a week or so, and then I take a couple of hours off when Cal is playing bridge or it's raining, and then I go back and write it up properly. I'm getting so I really enjoy writing in here. It makes me realise how lucky I am. And some day it will be my greatest pleasure to read it over. Maybe someday I'll read parts of it to my grandchildren and tell them all about the war.

We went into London again last night, Capt. Pentland, the wild Australian, Fry, Cal, Springs and myself. We went down to Jim's hotel for dinner. Then we all went to the Flying Corps dance at the Grafton Galleries. The whole flying corps was there, with a good sprinkling of our crowd. All the American cadets manage to cluster themselves around London. We spent the night at Jim's hotel and caught the seven-thirty train back. Jerry Pentland and Springs stepped into the St. Pancras Hotel opposite the station for something to eat. They couldn't get any service so Jerry put Springs in the dumbwaiter where he promptly went to sleep. Some maid on the top floor pressed the button and up went the waiter.

Jerry got scared and started up the stairs and climbed six flights.

The maid started to put some dishes in and saw Springs and let out a yell and pressed the down button just as Jerry burst in. Down went Springs with Jerry in hot pursuit. The dumbwaiter got stuck in the basement and they had a time getting Springs out of it. The manager wanted to turn him over to the military police, but Jerry swore that he was Russian and Springs quoted a little Latin and the manager saw all the eagles on his buttons and believed it and let them catch the train without any further argument.

I saw little Halley and Newt Bevin and Matthiesen at the Savoy.

January 28th
I took my altitude test today. I went up through thick clouds to nine thousand five hundred feet and damn near froze. The bus was covered with ice where it had been touched by the clouds coming up.

The sky up there was the bluest I ever saw, absolutely glassy blue with just a few cirrus clouds about five miles up, snow white, and this beautiful snow white plain of clouds beneath me. I felt awfully lonely. I could see, I know, at least a hundred miles. I saw another plane about ten miles away and I thought it was a bird at first but it started spinning and I knew it was a plane. I spun down and came out of the spin in the clouds. It was the nastiest sensation I ever had. I didn't know whether I was upside down or not. At last I got into a straight dive and came out of the clouds at a hundred and fifty miles an hour right over the airdrome.

There's a little captain here with the M. C. and a bar named Keller, just back from the front, who loves to stunt close to the ground. He seems to be daring the ground to come up and hit him. He took me up with him in an Avro and for thirty minutes we never got above fifty feet and only then to clear the trees. His specialty is flying under bridges. The other day one of his friends was getting married in the centre of London and he flew down in a Pup and broke up the wedding procession by diving on them. He was looping and rolling between the church spires.

Some general was a guest and got excited and put in a complaint about it so the wing sent around orders for us to stay away from London below five hundred feet. That boy has been knocking on the golden gate for some time and if he isn't careful as well as lucky, he's going to push too hard and get in. He and MacIntaggart chased each other all over the country for an hour at an altitude of fourteen inches. Scared me to death to watch them.

Roy Garver was killed on an Avro day before yesterday.

January 29th

A girl who is a friend of Springs's in New York wrote over to some people that live near St. Albans and they called him up and invited him to dinner and told him to bring along a couple of others. So Cal and I went along with him to dinner last night.

They have a beautiful place about three miles north of St. Albans. Their name is Drake and they are direct descendants of Sir Francis Drake, who did something famous, either discovered the North Pole or licked the Spaniards. I've forgotten which. There were three Drake brothers there, back from the front on leave, and their wives. A fine looking trio they were, two captains and a major, two M.C.s. and one D.S.O., three years in the trenches. Another brother was killed.

Dinner was a very formal highbrow affair. A lot of dog but very little food. They asked us the usual questions: How do you like England? Do you get enough to eat? Don't you miss the sugar? Do you ever get frightened when you are up in the air? We answered yes to all of them.

Food is getting very scarce in this country and even the rich can't get what they need. That poor hostess didn't have enough to go around.

After dinner was over the atmosphere underwent a decided change. The ladies withdrew and our host brought out a bottle of real pre-war whisky that had the kick of Brown's mule. Then we all got to acting natural.

Later Cal got at a piano and the poor thing was nearly shocked off its legs. How that boy can play!! He can make "Nearer My God to Thee" sound like "Georgia Camp Meeting." The ladies wanted to learn the latest dance steps, so Springs and I tried to teach them how to do them. It's a long jump from the Boston and the hesitation to the giant swing, but we had them all fox-trotting in no time.

The party was concluded by the three Drake brothers putting on a pukka drill with some of Sir Francis's own muskets. Gosh, it was great and those men certainly could drill. They were in blue dress uniforms and looked snappy as the devil. I wish we could strut a little.

We had to walk all the way back—eight miles. We stopped at the Peahen in St. Albans long enough to get a warm drink and give Cal time enough to kiss his Peggy goodnight.

Springs went back this morning to pay his party call in a Pup. He chased the children around the yard and nearly scared them to death running his wheels on the front driveway. I don't guess we'll be invited back again.

An Australian lieutenant was killed this morning flying a Pup.

January 31st

We put on a real circus at the Court night before last. Kelly and his instructor, Capt. Bell-Irving, came down from Harling Road for the occasion. Cal, Springs, Tommy Herbert, Capt. Morton and myself went in from here and Budge Weir and Atkinson, two Scots, came down from Thetford. Anderson and Jim and three Englishmen and a U. S. lieut. named Fuller, a friend of Cal's from Chicago joined us later.

We got under a full head of steam at tea. We had the whole chorus from the Shaftsbury theatre up in the suite. Kelly and Springs got caught out one night last week in a bomb raid,—the same night they dropped a bomb on the front entrance to Jim's hotel about fifteen minutes after they had all been standing there watching the searchlights. They were walking down the street and a bomb fell about a block away from them and they jumped for shelter. They got in the stage entrance and went behind the scenes in the Shaftsbury theatre.

The show was over but the actors hadn't gotten out and the chorus was all huddled over in one corner of the wings scared to death. Kelly and Springs got someone to play the piano and started a dance and before long they were having a regular party. They got them after the matinee today and brought them up to the Court for tea and early dinner. The Chinless Wonder and Dora and Peggy were all there,— passing nasty remarks backwards and forward, and a couple of Sheilas. All the girls in London are named Peggy or Sheila.

Cal played the piano and we had a big dance later. We had four suites on the same floor and everybody kept running from one to the other. Next morning, we were too near dead to get out of bed before eleven. We had a big champagne breakfast in our suite and didn't get back to the squadron until after two.

The C. O. sent for us at once. He and Capt. Horn, our new flight commander, were all set for a big straff because we were supposed to be back at nine.

The three of us lined up in the orderly room.

"Why are you so late in getting back today?" the C. O. asked us.

"To tell you the honest truth, sir," I said as he was looking at me, "we had such a hangover this morning we couldn't have gotten out of bed before nine if our lives had depended on it."

"That's at least original," Capt. Horn remarked, "usually it's a bomb raid or a sick aunt. Where were you last night?"

"In the Court," I told him.

"What suite?" he asked.

"Oh, 103, in, 115 and some other odd ones," I told him.

"Well, you certainly made a lot of noise," said Capt. Horn, "I was in 104 myself."

"You weren't exactly quiet on your side of the fence," Springs chirps up, "I thought someone was making boilers in there for a while."

The C. O. got to laughing and said he guessed he'd have to pardon us this time for telling the truth. Capt. Horn says he wants to go in with us the next time we throw a party.

February 5th

Yesterday was washout day so we all went into town again.

Springs had a big suite in the Court and was giving a private party for his girl.

They had a big dinner and were just beginning to start to argue when the Huns came over and dropped a bomb on the Court bar. Springs said he heard the bomb go whistling by his window and when it exploded two stories below the poor girl was scared stiff. She was so badly scared that she made Springs take her home as soon as the raid was over and he joined us in disgust later.

February 9th

I got off in a Pup yesterday. Gosh, what a thrill! They are not so different, but they are so quick and sensitive that they will crash taking off or landing before you know what they are going to do. I didn't bust anything but I pancaked like the devil landing. I hate to think what would have happened to DeGamo and Springs if they had been allowed to go up that day. I doubt if they would have gotten off the ground. If they try to take them from Curtisses to Pups back home, the undertakers will sure do some tittering.

A horrible thing happened today. We were all out on the tarmac having our pictures taken for posterity when somebody yelled and pointed up. Two Avros collided right over the airdrome at about three thousand feet. God, it was a horrible sight. We didn't know who was in either one of them. I was glad I was sitting next to Cal. They came down in a slow spin with their wings locked together and both of them in flames. Fred Stillman was in one machine and got out alive but badly burned and Doug Ellis was in the other one and was burned to a cinder.

As I sat there watching, I kept trying to imagine what those poor devils were thinking about as they went spinning down into hell. It made me right sick at my stomach to watch. We all went up later and felt better after a little flying.

We went into town for a party with Capt. Horn. He had a girl with him from Georgia named Halley Whatley and it sure did my heart good to hear her talk. He couldn't understand her and Springs and myself when we dropped into the vernacular. Springs made a julep for her and she positively cried when she tasted it.

We all had dinner together and went down to Murray's. When it closed we went to a dance at the Grafton Galleries. Dora and Sousa and Peggy and the L. L. L. D. were all there. I met a sweet little thing with bobbed hair named Lily and we went to another dance at a private place for a while. She is a wonderful dancer and seems to know everybody that ever left the ground.

Hash was there and he and Springs had their weekly Princeton reunion. They drank toasts to old Nassau in enough champagne to float a battleship. It was a right good party. Wonderful music and I'd rather dance than eat. The British officers were either in evening dress or wearing their blue dress uniforms, and looking very smart in their snappy jackets with bright coloured wings and decorations. We looked like hell in our little khaki jackets. Our army isn't worth a damn for anything but fighting but I guess we can hold our end up when it comes to the cool of the evening. But these American women over here get away with murder. There was a girl there last night from St. Louis that sure was the *belle* of the ball.

I have always heard that the English were a tactless blunt people. That's all wrong. Here is an example of what I call tact. The other evening up in the room one of the girls took off her ring to wash her hands and forgot about it and left it on the shelf. She called me up the next morning and told me about it and said it was a very valuable diamond solitaire and asked me please to try and find it. I called up the manager of the hotel and asked him about it. When I was in yesterday I stopped in to see him and he told me it had been found and if I could identify it, I could have it. I identified it and he gave it to me in an envelope and on the envelope was marked, "Found in Main Dining Room." That's what I call tact. Try and laugh that off!

An Englishman spun an Avro into the ground this morning and got out of it alive but broke both legs.

February 10th
Big straff around here. One of our bright young cadets who is little Lord Fauntleroy in his home town, got to cussing in the bar the other night after he got a snoutful and the barmaid objected to his language and made a complaint. This brought on real trouble. The C. O. had to report it to the U. S. Headquarters. The cadet got thirty days' confinement and this American lieut. is put in charge of us. He takes his duties very seriously and is going to have roll call morning and night.

You can cuss before any lady in England and she will probably cuss back at you, but if you let your tongue slip before a barmaid, woe be unto you! They tell the world they are ladies and allow no liberties—during business hours. I always heard they were good at repartee but all I've seen so far have acted Lady Godiva holding on to her hair in a breeze.

Twelve of us were up in our suite at the Court having dinner last night and we decided we ought to have some girls. So after dinner we all went out in different directions to round up the girls after the theatre. As we needed so many we thought that everybody should get as many as possible in case the others had no success.

By twelve o'clock we had twenty-two girls in the suite! Everybody was successful! Then they all got to fighting among themselves and each one said that the others were not ladies and it ended up by all of them leaving. By that time, we were glad to see them go.

February 12th
I've done five hours on Pups and am ready for Spads as soon as they get one in commission.

This lieut. is a prime ass net. It was raining this morning and no one got up to answer his roll call. So he had us all in his room after lunch to bawl us out. He announced last week that no one could leave the squadron without permission from him. I don't know where he got the idea that it was any business of his because there are no restrictions anywhere else. He wanted to sit at the head table with the instructors but the major wouldn't let him and he hates to eat with us. Capt. Morton bawled the life out of him the other day and stood him easy. In spite of all his time on Curtisses, he's still on Avros, while Nathan, Barry, DeGamo and Springs are all through with Pups and Spads and they started after he did. He also thinks he should have the preference of machines but he doesn't get it.

He told us that we were not taking the discipline seriously. He told Springs that he had been to London twice without permission from him and that he was going to punish him. Springs said he had finished his course in flying and was ready to go to the front. He said that made no difference. Springs said he thought that an aviator was supposed to fly and that what he did when the weather was unsuitable was his own business.

As a matter of fact, Springs got in all his time by flying in bad weather when no one else wanted the planes and has put in more hours in the air than any other cadet. And he would go without lunch to get a plane while the rest were eating. He asked what the charges against him were. The lieut. said A. W. O. L. Springs said he wanted a court martial because he knew the lieut. didn't know how to hold one. They argued half an hour over the technicalities and Springs bluffed him out of it by quoting imaginary regulations. He tried to confine the rest of us to quarters and we all demanded court martials. He's postponed judgment until he can go into London and find out just what he can do.

February 15th

Flew a Spad today. Easy to fly but dangerous as hell. Just like flying the famous barn door that Beachy used to talk about. And it has the gliding angle of a brick. I've always laughed at the regulars wearing spurs to fly in but I needed a pair in this Spad. It bucked just like a bronco.

The lieut. went into London and Dwyer told him to shut up and mind his own business and do a little flying himself. So Milnor told Cal.

Springs and Nathan and Barry are through and went to Scotland at midnight last night to the machine gun school. Springs went hog wild yesterday afternoon. He and a little English kid named Rogers were raising hell all over the place in Spads. They were running their wheels on the ground and then pulling up just in time to try and run them on the hangar roofs. It was a great exhibition of damn foolishness. Then Springs got a Pup and began chasing a machine gun class in and out of the firing pit. He'd dive in the pit and chase them out and then run along the ground and chase them back in. In the midst of the party he lost his pressure and before he could pump it up his engine conked and he pancaked in a flower garden between a windmill and a summer house. The C. O. called him in the office and told him they needed fools like that in France and to pack and get going. Then

Spad SVII

MacIntaggart made him go over and fly the Pup out.

February 16th

DeGamo was killed today. Nobody knows how it happened. He was up in a Spad and it was found about five miles from here in a small field over near Ratlett. It wasn't crashed badly but his neck was broken.

I've done five hours on Spads now and I feel I can fly them.

Tommy Herbert took us up to Bedford to a really nice dance with some friends of his. We had a fine time and he met a sort of vamp. Tommy asked us to go up there to dinner with him last night and we thought we were going to his nice friend's house. Imagine our surprise when we walked into the vamp's house. We all got lit and had a hell of a time. Cal took up with one Helen who could dance. Tommy amused the vamp and I was alone except for one Alice, who was the mistress of a general in private life. She had to go home early.

February 19th

We were getting dressed for DeGamo's funeral when the lieut. came in and bawled us out for being late. Cal looked up at him sheepishly and held out a box of candy. "Have a piece of candy," he said.

The lieut. looked like he was going to bust. "Have you no sense of propriety?" he asked.

"Maybe not, lieutenant," I said, fixing a *puttee*, "but I can at least thank God for a sense of humour!"

He glared at us and slammed the door as he went out. I hear he was once an All-American football player.

February 20th

Bulkley and Carlton have been killed. Two good men gone West. Bulkley was flying a Pup over at Hounslow and ran into an Avro. The landing skid on the Avro tore his centre section out and the plane came to pieces in the air. Carlton spun an R. E. 8 into the ground at Spiddlegate.

Cal had a forced landing with a Spad today. His elevator controls jammed and he had to do some quick thinking. He was flying around the insane asylum trying to see his nurse. He used his head and managed to flop down on a golf course. Some old duck was mad as hell when his game was interrupted. He got behind a bunker when he saw the Spad coming and Cal hit it and the Spad went over on its back. He said that when the Spad settled down he was looking right into this fellow's face and it was awful red.

Cal and I went into town again with Capt. Horn. Cal got mad

at Peggy after dinner and she went off to a dance with a Canadian colonel and he started back for the squadron. But there was a bomb raid on and the Huns dropped three bombs on the station so Cal had to come back.

February 22nd
Fred Stillman died after a gallant struggle. They thought he was going to pull through but poisoning set in. A fine fellow! Also Montgomery was killed. Montgomery was killed when the pilot fell out of the front seat in an Ak.W. in a loop. Montgomery was in the back seat and crawled up into the front cockpit and just had his hands on the controls when it crashed. Think of watching the ground coming up at you for two or three minutes while you wiggle up the fuselage. Makes my blood run cold!

March 3rd
Here we are at Turnberry in Scotland. It's on the coast and is cold as hell. We go to machine gun classes for ten hours a day for ten days. They run us to death and we freeze and starve. There's a bunch of Americans up here and a few of them have gotten their commissions. I wonder what's happened to ours. Tipton got his and they had to close the bar for three days afterwards.

Nichol was killed at Stamford on his first solo.

March 5th
No time to write. They work us too hard. I'm starved. Nothing to eat here but Brussels sprouts and vegetable marrow.

We went down to Girvan for a party. The Woman's Army Auxiliary Corps has a training school there. We watched them drill. Gosh, it was funny. A Barbados sergeant major was giving them close order drill and he was absolutely speechless with rage. He was used to flaying a company with his tongue mercilessly and there was nothing he could say to this crowd. There were no words in his vocabulary he could use. He just stood there and sputtered like a wet wick. He had a hundred and fifty Waacs of all sizes and contours and he was trying to line them up and couldn't because he didn't know what part of their anatomy to line on. He had my sympathy. It had taken him twenty years to acquire his drill vocabulary and now he could not use it. But why try to drill women anyway? I don't see the idea at all. They pay them the same as Tommies and give them the same discipline. A Waac officer can't walk out with a Tommy any more than an army officer can be seen with a Waac private. There weren't enough officers to go around with us so we took privates anyway.

March 10th
Heard today that Ludwig was killed flying an S. E. He got into a spin close to the ground.

March 12th
Thank God that's over. We are now at Ayr at the school of Aerial Fighting. The pilots' pool is also here. When pilots are ready to go to the front they are sent here and then sent out when needed. We are quartered at Wellington House. Springs, Nathan, Barry, Landis, Zistell, Oliver, Capt. Morton, Hash Gile, Hammer, Winslow, Whiting, Tipton, Kissel, Mathews, Ortmeyer, Frost, Evans, Mortimer, Armstrong, and Clay are all here. Most of them have finished and are waiting for commissions before being posted overseas. We hear a lot of rumours about how we are going out.

The British won't take us unless we are commissioned and we hear that Pershing has recommended that pilots be sergeants and not officers and that flying pay be abolished. He has stopped it in the A. E. F. Springs, Oliver and Winslow got second lieutenancies and refused to accept them and asked for their discharges instead. Everybody here wants to get out of the U. S. Army and join the R. F. C. where they'll get a square deal. We certainly have gotten a rotten deal from the U. S. A. and the British couldn't have treated their own field marshals any better. We owe the British a lot and have a lot to get even with our own army for.

MacDill and Jeff Dwyer are the only two officers that have made any effort to treat us decently. Jeff is sure our friend.

There's a big party going on here in spite of the wholesale funerals. Six American naval pilots were sent over from France to take the course here. They thought that Camels were as easy to fly as the Hanriots they had been flying in France and they wouldn't listen to any advice from the instructors here. Three of them were washed out one week.

Then Ortmeyer, who had three hundred hours on Curtisses at home as an instructor, spun a Camel into the ground and killed himself. Dealy spun into the ground the next day and before they got him buried, two Englishmen killed themselves. All in Camels and all doing right hand spins.

Col. Rees is in charge here and he tried to put pep in the boys by giving a stunting exhibition below five hundred feet. He certainly did fight the tree tops and he wouldn't come out of a spin above fifty feet. Then he made all the instructors go up in Camels and do the same thing. It was a wonderful exhibition and then he made us a little speech and told us there was nothing to worry about, to go to it. Several of the boys were so encouraged that they took off in Camels and tried to do the same thing. Only one was killed.

March 16th
Everybody had gone crazy over eggnog. Springs and Oliver found a dairy where they got some cream and they made some eggnog. Everybody demanded more. The next day they made five gallons and it lasted ten minutes. Then we got a big dairy vat and put all the Waacs to work beating eggs. All the cooks and maids up here are Waacs. Springs's father sent him ten pounds of sugar and we had three cases of brandy. It must have made fifteen or twenty gallons. Everybody from the colonel down came over to drink it. By lunch time every officer in Ayr was full of eggnog.

We all went out to the airdrome after lunch and tried to fly. They are short of magnetos and the only way they can get more is to steal them off crashes. There were three Spads so Capt. Foggin asked for Spad pilots. He sent Springs up in one hoping he would crash it. He had a quart bottle of eggnog and he took it up with him to drink. The motor conked all right, but he made a nice landing in the field with a dead stick without crashing so Foggin sent him up in another one.

Springs decided he'd steeplechase. The field is in an old race course so he came down wide open and ran his wheels on the track. He tried to bank with the track for a turn but they had put up some heavy wires and his top wing caught them. He went straight up three hundred feet and stalled and fell out of the stall right into the middle of the field. God certainly took over the controls. He wasn't hurt but the Spad was a write-off and Foggin got one mag.

Springs was mad as a hornet because he had the bottle of eggnog in his pocket and when he saw he was going to crash he threw it out to keep from cutting himself up.

The colonel sent for Springs to bawl him out, "Ah, listen here," said the colonel, "I really have enough trouble running this school without you youngsters interrupting my telephone connections. Don't do it! By the way is there any of your priceless concoction left?"

March 20th
Cush Nathan killed. He was flying an S. E. and the wings came

off at five thousand feet. He went into the roof of a three-story house and they dug him out of the basement. A real fine fellow. I liked him. So did everybody. He and Springs have been rooming together and that's the second roommate he's lost in two weeks. He doesn't want to ask anybody else to room with him but Reed Landis said he's not superstitious and moved in.

March 22nd

Last night one of the boys had a date with a staff officer's wife and couldn't get rid of him so brought him around to Wellington and asked us to get him tight and pass him out.

Springs and I took him on. We would each mix a drink by turn. When it came to my drink he did bottoms up and got nasty about it. He said American drinks were all too weak and he picked up a glass of it and threw it into the fire! It exploded! About a half hour later he went out on a shutter. That Scotsman was so tight he couldn't hoot no more than a dead owl.

Armstrong, the wild Australian, came in and said he had two lassies outside and needed help. Springs went out with him. The girl he drew was only sixteen and was sweet and innocent so he bawled her out and gave her a lecture on the perils of folly and the danger of trusting any man after dark. Then he took her home.

Armstrong came back tight and got into the Waacs' quarters by mistake. There was a straff over it this morning. The Waacs saved the day by not complaining officially. They have several rooms in the basement.

Cush's funeral was this morning. The staff officer who went out last night feet first was supposed to have been in charge of it but he couldn't make the grade. There was a long delay and then Springs took charge and somehow we got through with it. One of the escort planes had a forced landing and one of the firing party got nervous and fired too soon and scared everyone to death.

March 24th

For three weeks before Cush was killed, he and Springs had been going to a Scot dentist here to have their teeth reworked. We went to see him today to pay Cush's bill. We told him about the crash and do you know, that Scot wouldn't accept a penny! We explained that we had been directed by the court of inquiry to pay his bills but still he wouldn't take anything. He said he couldn't take money from a man who'd died for his country. Yet they crack jokes about the Scots loving money above all else. I'm glad that my blood is Scotch. If they don't hurry up and send us on out to the front a lot of German-Americans are going to have their veins full of Scotch too.

Springs said he'd pay his own bill right then as he might get killed too and didn't want to cheat him.

"But, mon," says the dentist, "I'm na through wi' yer."

"Oh, yes, you are," says Springs, "whether you know it or not. I'm not going to all the trouble and expense of having my teeth fixed when I'm this close to Lethe's waters. Every morning when I wake up I reach out to shake hands with Charon."

"And dinna ye take na thought for yer soul when the day draws nigh to return it to its maker?"

"I've been to the kirk with you every Sunday since I've been here," said Springs, "and I'm helping to support a couple of distilleries. What more can I do for my immortal soul in Scotland?"

"Hoot, mon," says he, "Americans must be heathens. Ye dinna ken where to find the text in the Bible."

Springs told me later that the dentist wouldn't work on his teeth unless he'd go to church with him. Then he shocked the dentist by pretending to look for Matthew in the Old Testament.

These Scots may be canny but they are a trusting lot. Any of the banks here will cash checks without asking for any identification. Yet down in England they won't even accept money for deposit until they've got a picture of you and know why your grandfather had to marry the girl.

Pansy hasn't taken a step since he's been here. He rides out to the field and back in the only taxi in town. He hasn't paid a penny to the driver yet and that poor fellow is going to get an awful jolt some day when he tries to collect.

This town is full of statues of Bobby Burns and bars. That's the principal industry. The barmaids are the *belles* of the town. I looked around at the show the other night and there were our three leading social lights, all escorting barmaids. The one down at the station hotel is the favourite. She takes a personal interest in each drink and every drinker.

The other night Springs went down to the station to see Gile and Hammer off and she thought he was going too. She came out from behind the bar and threw her arms around his neck and cried over him. We've been kidding her about it and she's as mad as a hornet. Ayr is really a beautiful spot and I'd like to stay here a while but they kill off pilots too fast for anyone to linger very long. Springs says he's been to twelve funerals. One more coming tomorrow. All the flying here is stunting and we have service machines. Every time we go up, we are supposed to find another machine and have a dogfight with it. The colonel stays up in the air a lot and is about the best at scrapping,—he and Foggin and Atkinson. Foggin is a wonderful pilot and only has one eye.

March 26th

Springs and Oliver got their commissions as 1st Lieutenants yesterday. It was Bim's birthday so they decided to give a party and invited everyone to a dinner. It was a nice dinner party but our hosts never appeared until it was all over. They were back in the bar with the Waac barmaid experimenting with a new drink they had just invented. Every now and then they would send us in a sample by Minnie. It was a potent beverage, judging by the results, though it tasted harmless enough. It had Benedictine, cognac, champagne, vermouth and pineapple juice. They called it "The Queen's Favour."

Later on the adjutant's wife and sister came over with Alec to call. Bim came up to speak to them. He came in the door and bowed. Then he reached out to close the door. He reached short by about four feet. You could have knocked his eyes off with a spoon. Cal plays bridge all the time. Curtis says he is suffering from the Woofits, that dread disease that comes from overeating and underdrinking.

George Vaughn cracked up an S. E. in splendid style. The engine conked with him over the town and he pancaked in a vacant lot and climbed up on top of a building. Later on, somebody wanted a picture of the crash and wanted him in it. He got back in the seat and the fuselage collapsed and the whole thing toppled over. He got his arm skinned up then, though he hadn't gotten hurt in the original crash.

Pansy run into a chimney with a Camel and scored one complete write-off. Practically everyone that has been killed in a Camel has done it from a right hand spin.

Hagood Bostick came down here from Turnberry looking like the Queen of Sheba's favourite husband. He had on everything but the monocle to make him Hinglish. He had pale pink breeches, light tan tunic with skirts down to his knees and boots and gloves and cane to match. He comes from Charleston, S. C, so doesn't have to cultivate the accent. Plucky little kid, he's only nineteen. He and Pansy are our sartorial stars. Pansy really looks more dashing, due to his sabre moustache. He talks too much about his yacht and his flunkeys.

Thank God we are through with wireless forever. And just think of the valuable time we've wasted learning that damn code! Eight words a minute! Bah! An hour a day for eight months! *Da-da-da diddy da!* Bah some more! I knew I was going to be a scout pilot all the time!

March 27th

I am ordered to France on Spads even though I haven't got my commission. I leave tomorrow. Hoorah! Hoorah!

The lieut. from London Colney blew into Wellington last night. He was all lit up like a new saloon. He asked for Springs and me. We weren't too cordial. He told us that he had come to see us and he realised we thought he was an ass and that he wanted to show us that he was a regular fellow. He said he wanted to give us a party and prove what a good sport he really was. We slapped him on the back a few times and carried him home after he passed out. He's learning some of the values of this life, but a sense of humour is a divine heritage and can't be cultivated.

Springs's little girl came back for further instructions so this time I undertook her education. I took her down on the beach and gave her a short lecture. She's young and innocent all right,—but ambitious.

March 30th

I came down to London and was told that Spads are being washed out at the front and replaced with Dolphins so I am ordered to Hounslow to learn to fly them. Springs came down from Ayr with me. Captain Horn is a flight commander out there in the squadron that the great Major Bishop V. C, D. S. O., M. C. is organising to take overseas. He wants the three of us to go out with him. They are letting Bishop pick his own pilots and he went with us to the U. S. Headquarters to try and arrange it. Col. Morrow said it couldn't be done. The whole staff nearly lost their eyes staring at us when we strolled out, arm and arm with the great Bishop.

He has a very pretty chauffeur and I made a date to take her to a dance Saturday night. All the cars in England are driven by girls.

The lieut. came down from Ayr and gave his party at Murray's. Gawd, it was terrible! He wouldn't have anything but individual bottles of everything. He was certainly determined to be a good fellow and everybody obliged him by getting soused to the eyeballs. He ended up the night sitting on Lillian's doorstep singing love songs through the keyhole.

I went to a big dance and managed to collect a redhead. She gave every indication of being ready to burn my fingers so I left while the door was still open. I had lunch with her the next day and she sure is a good-looking woman. But my grandfather told me never to get mixed up with a redheaded woman who wears black underwear.

Springs went back to Ayr after a very unsatisfactory conference with a major at headquarters, who is an officer all right but even an act of Congress couldn't make him a gentleman.

I hear that Nial and Lavelle and Jake Stahl are in the hospital pretty badly smashed up.

April 2nd

Springs came back down last night and has orders to go overseas to an S. E. squadron. I got Bishop and we went into London and he arranged to have him sent out to Hounslow when he reports to the Yard.

I have taken an apartment at the Piccadilly Mansions and am quite hot these days.

April 6th

The dirty deed is done. Springs came out here mad as a hornet because they told him at the Yard that he was no good and would have to have some more instructions before he could go overseas. He didn't tumble at all and insisted that he was a damn good pilot and offered to prove it. But they had a report on him that was unsatisfactory so sent him out here. He didn't find out until he got to Hounslow that Bishop had had that report sent in. Now to grab off Cal as he passes through.

April 7th

Sanford, Kissel, Zistell, Whiting, Frost, Tipton, Campbell and Hamilton are going out on Camels to regular British squadrons just as if they were R. F. C. pilots. The Hun has played hell with the troops in France and they need help. So we are to be commissioned at once and sent out to the R. F. C. as they need us. I got my commission today and Cal's is here too.

Everybody is discouraged over the continued bad news that comes through. It's clear now that the war will be won or lost in the next two months. You certainly have to hand it to the British for keeping a stiff upper lip.

Cal arrived this morning from Ayr and we had everything fixed at the Yard like a greased chute.

We arrived at Hounslow in triumph and a one lung taxi. Bishop says he doesn't care where we stay,—so we are going to get some place in town and spend our last days on this earth in peace and comfort. Halley says she can get a house for us for less than one suite at the Court. That would be warm.

April 8th
We have a house! You can't laugh that off! Halley had a friend, a Lordship, who had a four-storey house in Berkeley Square that he was willing to rent to us for ten pounds a week. We also have a cook and butler. Gangway!

We moved in and gave a big party Saturday. Major Bishop, Nigger Horn, MacGregor, MacDonald, Capt. Benbow and Capt. Baker came in from Hounslow for dinner and Col. Hastings and Col. Hepburn of the Canadian General Staff.

We found out too late that we couldn't get any meat without meat coupons. And there was little else we could buy. We got around the food problem easily. All we had cooked was soup and fish. Then we made a big tub full of eggnog and a couple of big pitchers of mint julep. To make sure that no one got beyond the fish course, we shook up cocktails too.

Our guests arrived about six and we started doing bottoms-up in rotation. It was a riot.

Springs was at the head of the table and served. Everybody had a bottle of port and a bottle of champagne. The butler brought in a big platter of fish and Springs served them by picking them up by the tail and tossing one to each guest as if they were seals. At the end of the fish course, I was alone at the table. The rest were chasing each other all over the place.

His Lordship has a wonderful collection of ancient war weapons. Before going to the theatre, where we had a box, all these ruffians armed themselves with swords, machetes, shillelaghs, maces, clubs, bayonets, sabres, pikes, flintlock pistols and various daggers and dirks. They looked like an arsenal. It's a wonder they weren't all arrested. Cal dropped a club on the bass drum in the middle of the show and Benbow nearly fell out of the box. Springs and Vic Hastings and I improved the idle hours by taking a Turkish bath and joining the rest of them later back at the house, as fresh as a spring morning.

April 11th
Springs has given birth to another idea. It may be all right. Some

of his are good and some are awful bad. Information has been received that the Germans have developed a parachute that can be used from an aeroplane. Springs got all excited about it and went to see Calthorpe the inventor of the Guardian Angel parachute that all the balloonitics use. Calthorpe is working on the idea. Springs offered him two thousand dollars if he would make one for him according to his idea. Calthorpe said he couldn't do it as the War Office wouldn't let him work for individuals, but that he would be glad to have any assistance or ideas. Springs offered to test out Calthorpe's and take it to the front for further tests and they are working on the same idea.

Calthorpe's idea is to have the parachute arranged in the trailing edge of the wing like an aileron.

The trouble with that is that it is liable to foul on the tail and it would take some time for the pilot to get out of his seat and get the straps on. And he would have to get out in a spin or a steep dive. Calthorpe is developing it primarily for the big planes where there is a crew and all of them could possibly get out except the pilot.

Springs wants one made to fit on an S. E. where the steam-line for the pilot's head is on the top of the fuselage. Then the pilot could wear the harness all the time and all he would have to do would be to unfasten his safety belt and jump. The objection to that again is the possibility of fouling. He figures on having a long cord between the parachute and the plane so that it would be free of the plane before it started to open. As the pilot fell away from the plane the cord would open the parachute and then the pilot could cut loose. It might be very difficult for the pilot to cut loose and Calthorpe figures on doing it with a series of rubber bands or an unravelling device.

I like the idea. It would certainly help at the front. Most pilots are killed by structural defects or by having the plane catch fire in the air. It would also be a great device for testing.

Springs tried to get permission from the U. S. Headquarters to go ahead with it but they said nothing doing.

We also hear rumours of a new machine gun invented by a Russian which uses larger bullets than the present ones and they are little shrapnel shells. This war is getting more dangerous every day. There is only one other American at Hounslow, Loghran from North Carolina.

April 12th
We've all been up in Dolphins and they aren't so hard to fly but are very tricky. They have the two hundred and twenty horse power His-

pano motors and the prop is geared which reverses the torque. They don't turn as well as an S. E. but better than a Spad. There's one great danger with them. They have twenty-four inches of back stagger and the top wing is very low. They have no centre section and your head comes up through the top wing where the centre section ought to be. If anything goes wrong and it turns over, the whole weight of the plane will rest on your head. If you crash, the gas tank is right at your back like in a Camel and your legs are up under the motor. There's not much hope for the pilot. Capt. White was landing last week and a tire busted and the wheel gave way and he turned over. The plane caught fire and he was nearly burned to death before we could get him out. They spin very easily from a left-hand turn. Cal gives me the willies by always taking off in a left-hand climbing turn.

I heard a funny story about Tracy Bird. Two old maids got frightened at the air raids in London and moved out to the country. The third day they were there Tracy crashes into their roof in an Ak. W. and lands in their room. They were so frightened they moved back to London. Tracy wasn't hurt.

April 13th

Roberts and Al came around to the house last night after Murray's closed. Sheila and Peggy and the Queen Bee and the Brainless Wonder were all here. We were doing a little serious drinking and Al and Sheila got to cussing at each other. Al was coming back pretty hard and Sheila was determined she was going to have the last word. I didn't like it. I can't bear to hear a man use bad language to a woman. I told him to shut up. He kept on and I told him again to shut up. He said something to me and we both jumped up and I saw blue for a moment. I took a swing at him and I'd have killed him if Springs hadn't jumped between us and my fist hit his shoulder and he hit Springs in the back. All three of us went down on the floor and got tangled up in the bearskin rug and Cal jumped on me. We got up and shook hands. Damn my temper anyway! It gets away from me in spite of all I can do.

Middleditch and Pudrith have been killed on D. H. Fours. The Lord sure is a good picker!

Stratton got smashed up. He was in a Camel and his machine gun ran away so he crashed to keep from shooting another machine.

April 14th

There's a new order out from headquarters that no U. S. pilot can come to London without orders. Now isn't that nice? Here we are stationed within the city limits, the tube station is right at the entrance of the field and yet we are forbidden to go down to the centre of the town. In other words, we are confined to our quarters as if we were under arrest.

The U. S. Army is a great institution. I have been treated like an enlisted man for ten months though I was never supposed to be one. But I didn't expect the treatment to continue after I became a 1st lieutenant. I suppose if we ever get to be captains, the regulars will all be colonels and captains will be enlisted men still. We all realized that there was a war on and that Washington was too busy to give us our commissions as they promised and we did the best we could in the meanwhile in the best of spirits. We lost our seniority and our pay.

A man that was in the same class with me at Ground School and who wasn't good enough to come over with us, went to a flying field and got his commission in six weeks and came over here and was put in charge of some of us. We have all the responsibilities that the British pilots have, we have to do the same work they do, we die the same way they do, we accept orders from the same officers they do when it comes to duty, yet we have none of their privileges. It isn't fair. If Bishop can order me to go up and get killed, which he can, he should be able to give us permission to go into town, which he can't.

I'm glad I had the pleasure of knowing Major MacDill and Colonel Morrow but I can't understand what they are doing in the army. They are gentlemen! There was a major out here yesterday that certainly couldn't qualify. If we had to choose between fighting the Prussian Guard and the West Point Alumni Association, I know where at least two hundred and ten aviators would assemble.

I guess majors are like children around eight and ten. They are just passing through an ugly age. And these present ones have been hatched so recently that their gold leaves itch.

We are going to the front and get killed off like flies. Two or three get killed in England every week. Yet these great Moguls are so afraid that we will have a little fun before we do go West that they have forbidden us to come to London to see a show or join our friends and try to forget for a little while what is going to happen to us. It's an outrage. They think we are so much dirt. We went to the American Officers' club for lunch for a while. They ought to call it the majors' and admirals' free lunch. They think we have leprosy. The club is just around the corner from the house and is very convenient and the food is good but I don't like the company. When Lord Leaconsfield donated his house for the purpose I didn't hear anything said about what officers were to be allowed in it. Well, we should worry.

I'd rather eat one meal with Bishop than have Admiral Sims and General Biddle pay my board eternally. Thank God the British can recognise a gentleman despite his rank.

These little tin majors give me a pain. They can't find enough aviators in France to cuss at, so they have to run over here every little while and show off their authority by cussing us out before the British. And I must say for the British that they resent it as much as we do.

I'm an American and I'm proud of it but I'm damned if I can take any pride in the boobs that are running the flying corps. For instance, how can we fly when our necks are being choked off by these 1865 model collars? The staff must think they are still in Mexico wearing O. D. shirts.

Springs called up and got permission to go down to Headquarters. He came back with three sets of orders for us to go to the dentist until we get our teeth fixed. I guess that will see us through. Dwyer certainly is a friend in need. He said he's heard about our house unofficially and that we'd better keep it quiet. We will.

Loghran has gone to Turnberry.

We are all broke at the moment and have all cabled home for funds. Cal has a rich grandmother and he and Springs got together and composed a letter to her that was a masterpiece. They told her about the young aviator that had been over here for six months and had been broke and had a rotten time. Then he went out to the front and his father sent him five thousand dollars for a birthday present but he was killed before he had a chance to get leave and enjoy it. If Springs isn't hung first, he'll be a great writer someday. That letter was the work of a master hand.

Wheelock and Berry crashed a Bristol Fighter at Ayr and it caught fire. Wheelock was in the back seat and had a broken arm but managed to get out of the wreckage. Berry was in the front seat and couldn't get out so Wheelock went in after him and pulled him out. Both were badly burned.

April 18th
Gawd, what a life! We get up at noon, breakfast and go to Hounslow on the tube if it's a good day, if not we go down to the Savoy bar and join the gang there. At six we are back at the house unless there's

a party at Murray's. Vic Hastings usually comes around before dinner with Col. Hepburn or Cecil Cowan or Nat Ayres and we all go out to dinner after getting well oiled. Vic sent around a couple of cases of Canadian Club from Canadian H. O. yesterday. That ought to last at least three nights. We went down to see His Lordship's own private wine-merchant when we first moved in and he keeps us supplied with some marvellous 1880 port. At least he says it's port. I call it the "answer to a drunkard's prayer."

Then we usually get in our evening dancing at Murray's or the Elysee and then all come back to the house when they close. Anywhere from five to twenty-five of the old detachment usually drop in and we simply can't keep up with our engagements.

We had a full-blooded Sioux Indian in the squadron but he killed himself yesterday by spinning into the ground from a left-hand turn.

Nigger Horn had a crash. He was flying an S. E. and had just gotten off the ground when the engine conked. He was headed straight for the town and couldn't turn back. It looked as if he was going to crash into a crowded street but he stuck his nose down and deliberately dove between two little brick buildings on the edge of the field. The buildings tore his wings off clean and he and the fuselage slid along.

Springs has a new girl and my Gawd, what a beautiful thing she is. But she's so stupid it's ludicrous. Nothing but a doll. He says he's suffering from a reaction. The last one had too much brains.

April 20th

It looks like we were going to be delayed. 84 squadron on the same field at Hounslow is ready to go over but the factory is short on Dolphins as they have been using all the new ones to replace Spads at the front. They have taken our Dolphins and we have to refit with S. E.s. I'm not sorry to get S. E.s but I hate the delay. If we don't get to the front pretty soon there won't be much use in taking us,—we'll be too busy fighting off the purple crocodiles.

Mathews, Oliver, Eckert, Newhall, Gile and Hammer are ready to go out to the front today. There was a big party last night and we went to a dance at the Elysee Gardens. The whole flying corps was there and all tight as a nun's corset. Hash and Springs held their usual reunion. Springs has something wrong with his left eye and when he drinks too much it closes. I went downstairs in the bar and found Hash holding Springs's eye open with his hand so he could have another drink to Old Nassau. When they meet in hell those two will organize a Princeton reunion.

Cecil gave a dinner party in honour of Peggy and the Doll the same evening. This is a new Peggy,—the third. This one came as a present in Murray's the other night. Vic and Barney and Dora were there too. Then we all went to the dance. We decided to go back to the house about one o'clock and the Doll was dancing with some Englishman and Springs and I went out to get her. She didn't want to leave and her partner got the idea that she was objecting to me breaking in. He got very nasty about it and told us to run along and gave me a gentle push. I saw red and took a long swing.

Springs saw me swing and jumped in the way. I knocked him flat and then Cal grabbed me. Gosh, it's funny how we three stick together in a crowd. But I wish they'd jump on the other fellow for a change. That's three times they've jumped on me in a fight. We need better team work! Hash has the right idea. He's about six feet four and an old Princeton tackle. He saw the argument and came up and towered over this fellow while Cal was holding me and looked him over and said, "Listen here, young fellow, when he's through with you, I'll take on what's left."

We abandoned the Doll and all left including Hash and Eckert. We couldn't find but one taxi so all nine piled into it. When we got back to the house we all got out and payed off the driver. Just as he was about to drive off, the door opened again and out stepped Bim. Nobody knew he was with us.

I heard that Stanberry was killed last week on a Camel. He and I were always good friends after our fight at Ground School. There was only one blow struck in that fight and he went out like a candle in the wind. We both apologised and have been good friends ever since.

April 25th

We gave a farewell dinner for 84 at the Criterion. I'll bet the bill for breakage will be more than the one for food. Mac brought back a sign, "Ladies Room" and hung it over our spare bedroom.

A little girl came around to the house the other night that I've known for some time, named Lily. She's a cute little kid and a good dancer. She's been living with one of the boys for a couple of months. She went up to his squadron and took a house for a while. He's nutty about her and would have married her if she'd tried to make him. She has a sort of past that wouldn't sound well at home but doesn't seem to make much difference over here. At home every woman that isn't a virgin has a past, while over here they've got to shoot somebody, be divorced by somebody who is somebody or get run over by a train.

Well, this particular cadet had just gotten his commission and he celebrated the happy event by diving into the ground from five thousand feet. The poor little girl is all broken up and is scared to death because she thinks she is going to have a baby. She wanted me to tell her what to do. She wanted to know whether to write his people or not. I told her not to. He had done the best he could and it would be a shame to spoil his family's solace in sorrow. They've probably got a dozen artists busy painting wings on all his pictures by this time. I told her if she loved him to say nothing about it and carry on. I gave her what money I had—not much, I'm sorry to say.

Tommy Herbert and Paul Winslow were in the other night full of rumours. They have a scheme for getting switched from Camels, or rather Winslow has. They are ferrying and always take a Bristol Fighter. They are going to pass themselves off as Bristol pilots. Tommy is not so enthusiastic as he crashed a Bristol last week and broke a couple of ribs and sprained his back. I wish he'd sprain his throat so he couldn't sing.

The other evening before going out to dinner we heard a terrific explosion up on the third floor and we dashed up the stairs thinking we were being bombed. 'Twas only Springs trying to take a bath and the geyser had exploded. The gas in the water heater had blown out and he lit it again after the room was full of gas. Funny things, these geysers. The English stick a tank over the tub and when you turn on the water it turns up the gas to heat it. Springs is short his eyelashes and eyebrows. He didn't have much to start with. Dora says he looks perpetually startled and she's afraid every minute that he's going to run away.

Tom Mooney has been killed. So has Brader.

April 28th
Cal got a cable from his grandmother today which called for a hundred pounds. A lot of famous writers would like to get paid at that rate for their work.

Springs and I went out to a hospital in the suburbs to see Bostick who's back from the front all shot to hell. He flew a Camel into the ground and his face looks like a scrambled egg. His jaw is broken in two places, his arm is broken, and he may lose one eye. On top of that, he's had pneumonia. He couldn't talk much but all that worried him was getting back to the front. He'll never see the front again, poor kid. We took him some strawberries. They are worth their weight in gold over here.

The Royal Flying Corps and the Royal Naval Air Service have been merged into one service known as the Royal Air Force which is to rank equal with the army and navy and be under neither one. From now on it will be the Army, Navy and Air Force. I understand the Navy doesn't like the idea at all. It ought to save a lot of confusion and duplication of work. Some of the non-flyers will lose their jobs which will be a good thing.

May 3rd
Lily, the widow came around again. It was a false alarm about the baby and she acts as if she might be consoled very easily. However, none of us wanted the job. We wanted to get rid of her but we didn't know how to do it. Then one of these bold, bad, handsome woman stealers came in to call. With a little careful arranging we permitted him to steal our girl right out from under our eyes. Weren't we mad? I hope he gets into trouble as the last time he pulled that little trick he got one that didn't have any label on her addressed to him.

If these boys can fly two-bladers like they can fly four-posters, there'll sure be a shortage of Huns before long.

Springs had a narrow escape. He was about to go up in an S. E. and he just happened to notice in time that his elevator turnbuckle was broken and the controls were held only by a safety wire. He would have gotten off and then it would have broken in the air.

We had a game of follow the leader. Mac was the leader. We had an old two-twenty S. E. and he took it up first. He dove it at the ground wide open and levelled off and ran his wheels along the ground and pulled up in a long zoom and looped. The trick of the stunt is to get over the top of your loop. An S. E. will zoom fifteen hundred feet from the level and that's why they are so good at the front.

Cal was next. The idea was that each man should do the stunt of the preceding man and then set another one for the next man. Cal did Mac's and then half rolled at the top of the loop.

Springs was next and his stunt was a full roll at the top of the loop. Of course he was up above a thousand feet.

I was next and I put my nose down to about two hundred after I did my full roll, and as soon as I started up for my zoom I kicked on full right rudder and pulled the stick back into the right-hand corner.

I didn't know what I was doing but I sure did it. I whirled around a couple of times with my nose up and then I whirled around with my nose down and ended up stalled upside down. The motor stopped and I just did get in the field with a dead prop.

It was Thompson's turn next. Mac said what I did was an upward spin followed by an outside spin, whatever that is. I told Thompson how I did it and he went up and started into it with terrific speed. The propeller shaft broke and his prop flew off, just nicking the leading edge of the wing. He got into the field all right. That ended the afternoon performance. Mac and Cal certainly can fly.

About eleven o'clock last night the phone rang and Springs answered. It was a lady and she wanted to speak to His Lordship. Springs got to chewing the rag with her and ascertained the fact that there were two of them and they were alone and would be agreeable to gargling a little champagne. So he and Cal got some pop and went over to call. In about an hour Cal came back without his hat. Springs came in about half an hour later with it and kidded the life out of him. Cal says the lady made an improper proposal to him so when she wasn't looking he departed. Springs says Cal had been making improper proposals himself for half an hour and as soon as the lady began to take them seriously, he lost his nerve. He sure is funny with women. Give him a piano or a dance floor and a girl and he's like a snake with a toad,—just fascinates them! But as soon as they surrender, he gets stag fever or stage fright or something and takes his foot in his hand.

May 4th

London was too much for us; the house was getting too crowded every night so we decided we'd better leave for a few days and send out the rumour that we had left for good. Everybody in the flying corps knew about the house and came around for a drink after hours and brought their brothers and sisters. The story goes that we three have been picked by Bishop for his circus, which is going out to fight Richthofen's circus, because of our great skill as pilots. Isn't that a joke? Particularly after the stunt I pulled the other day.

Bishop had a little Bristol Scout that the general gave him to play around in—pretty little thing, all painted silver and it had a Le Rhone motor.

He let me fly it the other day. I took off and the motor cut out cold at about two hundred feet. I tried to land short but I didn't have room enough to even sideslip and I couldn't turn and there was a high fence right in front of me that I couldn't glide over. Then I had a brilliant idea. I pointed the nose at the ground in front of the fence and deliberately bounced. And I bounced over that fence. All would have been well if there hadn't been a football goal-post on the other side of the fence. I hit the cross-bar and the Bristol was reduced to matchwood and I got a bruised knee and a split lip.

Yes, London was getting to be too much for us and so we came down here to Eastbourne to rest up for four days.

This is a beautiful place down by the sea, quiet and restful.

We had a funny party the night before we left. Sir Somebody or other and Lord Somebody and their wives came around to the house to call on His Lordship. I explained that His Lordship was in the country and that we were holding down the fort. Then I asked them to come in and crack a bottle with us. They came in and I opened some pop. They were very nice and were much interested in the American Army and asked a lot of questions.

About that time, Cal and Halley and Nigger came in. A nice time was had by all though no one could figure it out. I believe they thought that Halley lives here too. But they didn't say so, and we couldn't just volunteer the information that she didn't. The titled contingent left and we went down in the kitchen and cooked sausage and mushrooms and made some eggnog.

Vic Hastings came in with two Canadians and two girls. One of them was a raving beauty and the other one wasn't so bad. The beauty and Springs cooked up a mess that was easy on the palate. After a while the Canadians got tired of our kitchen and their dignity got restless and they left. We kept the girls and took them home ourselves. You can't laugh that off!

I wonder what the boys in Texas are doing for amusement. You chase me and I'll chase you! We called the girls Cherubim and Seraphim.

May 6th
We did rest for two days and felt a lot better. Cal, the nice boy, took up with an old gentleman and his charming young daughter. While he was telling them all about the war this morning, Springs and I went out for a stroll. We saw a bottle of ancient pre-war Haig and Haig in a pinch-bottle sitting in a bar window and we went in and tried to buy it. They wouldn't sell it except by the drink. So we bought it by the drink and sent a messenger after Cal and started on another one. Cal arrived and in order to catch up, he poured out half of the other

bottle and took it neat. It took effect like a dentist's drill and by the time we finished the second bottle, we were ready to fight a buzz saw. We hired a limousine and told the driver to show us the sights. He took us out to Beachy Head which is a cliff three hundred feet high and showed us Lovers' Leap where all the suicides do their stunt. Cal and Springs began chasing each other around and got over the side of the cliff on a gentle slope. They slipped in the soft dirt and slid right on down the first stage of the cliff to the perpendicular drop above the rocks a hundred feet below. I was scared stiff. They managed to check themselves right on the edge. Cal was all right because he was on his stomach and dug his toes in the soft dirt, but Springs was on his back and the dirt kept crumbling away under his heels, and he slowly slid on down to the very edge.

Cal and I were yelling at the top of our lungs but we couldn't go to his assistance. He held on to a bunch of weeds until he could get his knife out and dig a slot for his heels. I yelled for help and the chauffeur got some officers to come and help us. We made a chain out of our Sam Brownes and some rope and they lowered me and I pulled Cal up easily. But we had an awful time with Springs because he couldn't turn over and didn't dare let go either hand because he was still slipping a little. I don't see why he wasn't killed. We had to lasso him and pull him up backwards.

We decided that since our lives were in jeopardy we ought to have our pictures taken to preserve our likenesses for posterity. The photographer nearly had a fit at our poses. Then we went down to an indoor swimming pool. There was a flying trapeze over it and Springs insisted on getting up on it as he used to be a trapeze expert at college. He isn't so good now and he missed his jump over shallow water and took all the skin off one side his face, where he cracked the bottom.

Then we went roller skating. That's where I shine. Everybody got off the rink for me and I put on an exhibition for them that was an exhibition. I had on my new pink breeches and when I tried a double reverse, I tripped. My beautiful pink breeches are ruined! When the place was ready to close the band played "God Save the King." Cal was sitting on the side-lines talking to a girl and he forgot he had skates on and jumped to attention. His feet went out from under him and he lit on the floor on his back. Springs embraced a post for support.

May 10th
The good effects of the Eastbourne trip didn't last long. Kelly

came down to town from some ungodly hole and we had a terrible battle. Kelly didn't have a girl so Springs called up and said he was sick and sent Kelly around after his girl. That pair certainly are funny. They aren't satisfied by trying to give each other the shirts off their backs but they want the other to have everything. This time the girl didn't like the idea so well so Kelly came back and they started out together.

We had a fine bomb raid last night. Springs, Cal and I were over at Cherubim's flat. Sherry was there too, and they were playing bridge while I was writing some letters. The Maron, which is the raid warning, went off about ten-thirty. The girls jumped like they had been hit already. They grabbed some camp stools and said they were going down in the tube station. We said we weren't going but they begged us to go with them, so we did. We took along a bottle of whiskey and a plate of cake. The girls were hysterical with fright. Cherry had a sister killed in a raid last year and Sherry had some friend bumped off.

When we got to the station it was already packed. We couldn't get down to the platform so camped on a landing half way down. The air was as foul as the Black Hole of Calcutta and those people certainly were scared. We cheered the girls up and drank the whiskey and felt better. Everyone had brought camp stools and it sure was a funny sight. I hadn't realized before how successful the raids are. It doesn't matter whether they hit anything or not as long as they put the wind up the civilian population so thoroughly. These people wanted peace and they wanted it quick. Possibly Lord Lansdowne got caught out in a bomb raid.

The air got so bad that we said goodnight and left. Outside, the town was absolutely deserted. We waited fifteen minutes for a taxi but there wasn't any so we had to walk home. The city was like a sepulchre except for the terrible racket of the anti-aircraft guns. Not a light anywhere. We didn't hear any bombs explode but Archie kept up a lot of fuss. There wasn't the tiniest crack of light to be seen anywhere. They certainly do enforce the law about lights. They don't have many laws in this country but they certainly enforce what they do have.

There is a battery over in Hyde Park a couple of blocks from the house and it shakes the panes in the windows when it fires. When there's a big raid on, you can sit at our window upstairs and hear the pieces of shrapnel falling in the street like hail. It's just as well to stay indoors. Archie has quit trying to hit anything. They just put up a barrage and hope the Huns fly into it. They have certain areas which they range and certain areas which they leave clear so they won't hit our planes that are up after them. Our night-flying Camels are doing a lot of damage to the raiders and that's the only way they will ever stop them. Armstrong, the Australian stunt pilot, was over at Hounslow the other day in his specially rigged Camel and gave an exhibition for us. He's certainly a wonderful pilot. He runs his wheels on the ground and then pulls up in a loop and if he sees he hasn't got room enough, he just half rolls at the top. I saw him land from a full roll and he glides and does S turns upside down. I don't think he has long to live, though, just the same. He says night flying is not so difficult after you once get used to it. And he says it's just as easy to fire at night as in daytime. I don't see how he figures that though.

After the raid was over an assorted crowd came around to the house. Two of mamma's own little darlings came around with two wild women. I eased them towards the door gently but firmly. One of the boys was highly insulted when I told him that we were glad to have him any time but he'd have to leave his girlfriend at home. He got real nasty and said he didn't know that we were running a nunnery and from what he heard he didn't think we were in a position to object to anything. Then he took a couple of nasty cracks at a few of our friends and regular callers. I told him that after all it was our house and I was sorry that he couldn't see the thing right. We were trying to keep our house respectable.

I told him that since we had moved in here, not a woman had spent the night in the house and while I wasn't any inspector of the public morals and hadn't snooped around any, still I'd be willing to guarantee that no one had indulged in any horizontal refreshments here. I wasn't concerned with what they did elsewhere, but this was an amateur gathering and we didn't allow any professional talent or union workers. If he wanted to leave five pounds with his card when he called, it was all right by me, but as for us, alcohol was our weakness. So they left. I should have crowned them. Gosh, it's wonderful the way I control my temper now. I used to like that kid. I remember his mother came out to Mineola to pack up for him and she asked MacDill to please write to her if he didn't behave.

But what I told him was the truth. Some of our guests may be a bit unconventional in their mode of living but they have certainly all been ladies around here. And considering the number that have drifted in and out, I think it's right remarkable. These London women are in a class by themselves. They are good sports, good looking, good dancers, well educated, act like ladies, and they don't sit around and worry about their honour all the time. They aren't a bit conceited about the matter as they all are at home. Virtue over here isn't even its own reward.

Springs and I flew over to London Colney for lunch and heard that Waite killed himself by driving a Spad into the Elstree reservoir. He was firing at the ground target which is in the centre of it and his controls must have jammed for he never came out of his dive. London Colney is sure an unlucky place.

Clarence Fry is funnier than ever. He was telling a story on Barksdale about how he went over in a Pup to stunt for his girl. He came out of a spin below the tree tops and couldn't get his motor again and crashed right in her yard. Barksdale is so long he can hardly get in a Pup and flies without his *puttees* so as not to interfere with his legs. When he crashed he got out of the wreck and confronted his girl with his long underwear sticking out below the breeches. He was so embarrassed his girl thought he was knocked out and wanted to take him to a hospital.

May 11th

The lady that owns the house next door has come back from the country and she wrote a letter to His Lordship complaining about the racket over here. He sent the letter to us and said we had to do something about it. So Springs went over to call on her this afternoon. He was gone a long time and we thought she must have proved to be young and attractive but when he came back he said she had invited him to stay for tea. He said she was awfully nice and her son was killed last year in the Battle of the Somme. He explained to her how we were just waiting around to go out to the front and expected to go any day now and were just trying to have a little fun before we left. She got to crying and said that was just how her son felt about it before he went out the last time. She ended up by wanting to give us a dinner party and invite some nice girls for us to meet. Springs told her that we knew too many already and that we craved quiet just as much as she did. So we are not going to play the piano after midnight and she is going to withdraw her complaint. You can't beat these English women!

They are having hard luck over at London Colney again. I saw Barksdale in town and he had a long tale of woe. A big two-engined Handley-Page landed on top of an Avro over there the other day. The pilot in the Avro was hurt but not killed and the pilot of the Handley was killed when it nosed on him. The next day the Handley was still standing on its nose and a pilot was taking off in a Spad. The Spad swung 90° taking off and flew right into the tail of the Handley. The Spad turned the Handley over on its back and wrecked the fuselage. The Spad was a write-off, of course. The pilot may live.

Clarence Fry killed himself by stalling a Spad over there. That's too bad. I thought a lot of Clarence. He certainly was a peach.

May 12th
Last night we had another choice assortment of callers. Halley, as usual, was responsible for it. 'Twas a motley crew. But one of them, *oh, la, la*, what a knockout! Her name is Billy Carlton. She and I got on like Antony and Cleopatra. How that woman can dance! Well, she ought to be able to, seeing as how she is leading lady in a musical show. She is about twenty-three and has been on the stage since she was eighteen. She sure is witty. She kept us laughing all evening. She had a general in tow that wasn't at all friendly to me. There was a little monologue she gave.

"What, you coward," she would say, "how dare you strike a poor defenceless woman! You contemptible cur, why don't you have courage enough to hit a man? Why don't you hit me? Whow!" And with that she would throw herself on the floor as if she had been knocked down. She had a lot of little stunts like that.

Then she has a cockney song she sings:

She was poor but she was 'onest,
Victim of a rich man's crime,
First 'e wooed 'er and then 'e left 'er,
Ain't it all a bleedin' shime?

Chorus
It's the sime the whole world over,
It's the poor wot tikes the blime,
It's the rich wot tikes the pleasure,
Ain't it all a bleedin' shime?

Then the girl went up to London,
For to 'ide 'er bleedin' shime,
There she met another squire,
And 'e dragged 'er down agine.

See 'er in 'er 'orse and kerridge,
Ridin' daily through the park,

> *Though she 'as a dozen rubies,*
> *They don't 'ide 'er bleedin' 'eart.*
>
> *There she stands upon the corner,*
> *Sellin' flowers to the gent,*
> *She's grown fat about 'er middle,*
> *And 'er golden locks 'as went.*

There are a lot more verses and variations to it but these are the only ones I know.

I took her home and the general wasn't very mad! It's getting to be a disgrace the way we welcome our friends and then put them out and keep their girls. Well, they ought to know better!

She has a gorgeous flat and there was a supper waiting for us when we got there and a maid to serve it. She slipped on a negligee and looked like a million dollars.

> *I was sitting in jail with my back to the wall,*
> *And a redheaded woman was the cause of it all.*

About ten of the boys have given it up and just quit flying. No nerve. They never should have enlisted if they didn't intend to see it through after they found out it was dangerous. Jeff Dwyer gets them jobs at Headquarters or puts them in charge of mechanics. But yellow is yellow whether you call it nerves or not. I'm just as scared sometimes as any of them.

May 13th

The great McCudden, now Major McCudden V. C, D. S. O., M. C, E. T. C, just back from the front to get decorated again, came into Murray's last night for dinner and, oh, boy, what a riot he caused. All the officers went over to his table to congratulate him and the women,—well, they fought to get at him just like they do at a bargain counter back home. He's the hottest thing we have now,—54 Huns, five more than Bishop and he's just gotten the V. C. and a bar to his D. S. O. He held a regular levee. I think there are only five airmen living that have the V. C. The first thing you have to do to get it is to get killed.

The girl with him thought she was the Queen of Sheba. She started to pretend she didn't know us. I should have reminded her where we met but I didn't. I saved her life once.

Well, I'm not jealous. I'm going to be hot myself someday.

I'm either coming out of the war a big man or in a wooden kimono. I know I can fight, I know I can fly, and I ought to be able to shoot straight. If I can just learn to do all three things at once, they can't stop me. And Bishop is going to teach me to do that. I've got to make a name for myself, even if they have to prefix "late" to it.

The groundhog captain at London Colney finally got his wish and killed himself in a Pup. He was rolling over the tree tops and his motor cut out and he didn't have enough speed to get around and went into the ground.

I hear that Kissell has been shot down and killed at the front. He was the best Camel pilot we had. He could fly upside down as well as right side up.

Cherubim and Seraphim invited us down to Maidenhead for the weekend at Cherry's house. Vic, Jack May, Barney, Cecil, Dora and the three of us went down Saturday afternoon.

Cherry has a cottage right on the river with a pretty little garden in the back. Jack brought the food down from Murray's and a good time was had by all. Vic found attraction next door and left us for a while. We called on His Lordship and he showed us his country place but I'm not sure he was glad to see us. We were supposed to go to a dance but none of us ever got there, or even came near it. Everybody went back to town Sunday except Cherry and Sherry and the three of us. We chartered an electric punt and spent the day on the Thames. It's a beautiful spot, a regular fairyland. Little estates come right down to the water's edge and at night it's beyond description. These punts are big flat-bottomed canoes and are run by storage batteries. They have no seats but the bottom is filled with cushions. Anybody can paint the rest of the picture.

Somebody gave Springs a bottle of Canadian Club and he got up in the bow and remained there all day like a bowsprit. Cal gave a good imitation of a young man in love. We had lunch on the terrace at Skindle's, which is a big restaurant with a terrace down to the water's edge. We had tea in the punt up at some place above the locks. We went back to Skindle's for dinner and Springs got chummy with a girl over at another table and made a date with her to meet him there later.

We all got back to the cottage after dinner and then Springs got a rowboat and went back to Skindle's after the girl. He couldn't find her and went in the bar. There were a couple of Guards officers in there and they all got to chewing the rag. The Guards officers began taking cracks at the American Army. One of them, a long tall bird, said, "I've been reading in the papers until I'm bloody well sick of it, about the number of American troops that have come over. But what I can't understand is why none of them will fight. Paris is full of them, London is full of them, but they all jolly well stay away from the front. None of them will fight."

"Well," says Springs, "here is one of them that will." And with that, he hauls off and stretches the long tall bird on the floor. The other one makes a pass at him but he ducks and beats it out and jumps in his boat and shoves off. But in his haste, he forgot his oars. He floated down the river and missed the falls by a miracle. There were no lights showing anywhere and I don't see how he found his way back, but he did. He's got more lives than a cat and needs all of them.

I heard today that Hash Gile is missing at the front.

Bob Griffith is dead. The wings of his D. H. Nine came off at ten thousand feet.

May 14th

All aboard for France. Our orders have come through and we leave next Wednesday.

A ferry pilot brought over my new machine day before yesterday and smashed it all to pieces landing. He got tangled up in the wires coming in. So I decided I'd fetch my own service machine and got Springs to fly me over to Brooklands in an Avro yesterday and I flew it back. It certainly is a beauty. I like these 180 Viper Hispanos made by Wolsey much better than the 220 Peugeots. Brooklands used to be an automobile race track but is now the depot and test park for the R. F. C. I saw some of the new experimental planes down there. One was the Snipe, which has the 200 Bentley motor and is going to take the place of the Camel at the front. Another was the Snark which has the big A. B. C. air-cooled radial. It has a wonderful performance but I understand there's some hitch about it. The Salamander and the Hippo and the Bulldog were all there too. The Hippo is a sort of two-seater Dolphin.

I gave my new plane a work-out in the air today. It flies hands off; I put it level just off the ground and. it did 130. Then I went up high and did a spinning tail slide. Nothing broke so I have perfect confidence in it. I've been cleaning and oiling the machine guns, tuning up the motor and testing the rigging. The best part of it is that it's mine— no one else has ever flown it and no one else ever will. It's painted green and I have named it the Julep and am having one painted on the side of the fuselage. Nigger has the Gin Palace II and Springs has the Eggnog First.

Larry has had trouble with his motor and is losing sleep over it.

Tomorrow, I've got to synchronize my gun gear, set my sights, swing my compass and then I'm ready. Death bring on your sting, oh, grave hoist your gold star!

The bus certainly is plentifully supplied with gadgets. The cockpit looks like the inside of a locomotive cab. In it is a compass, airspeed indicator, radiator thermometer, oil gauge, compensator, two-gun trigger controls, synchronized gear reservoir handle, hand pump, gas tank gauge, two switches, pressure control, altimeter, gas pipe shut-off cocks, shutter control, thermometer, two cocking handles for the guns, booster magneto, spare ammunition drums, map case, throttle, joystick and rudder bar. That's enough for any one man to say grace over. It has two guns: one Vickers and one Lewis. The Vickers is mounted on the fuselage in front of your face and fires through the propeller with a C. C. gear to keep from hitting it. The Lewis is mounted on the top wing and fires over the top of the propeller. It has two sights: a ring sight and an Aldis telescopic sight.

I set both sights and both guns so that they will all converge at a spot two hundred yards in front of the line of flight. When you aim, what you really do is to aim the plane and the guns take care of themselves. The Vickers has a belt of four hundred rounds and the Lewis has a drum of one hundred and we carry three spare drums. To change drums, you have to pull the gun down on the track with your hand and then take off the empty drum and put on the full one. It's not hard to do unless you let the wind get against the flat side of the drum, then it will nearly break your wrist. We've practiced changing until we can do it in our sleep. The Vickers is the best gun by far.

Of course, I can't resist the temptation to add a few devises of my own and have also put a cupboard and shelf in for spare goggles, machine gun tools, cigarettes, etc. I am also decorating my cockpit. When you're in the air for two or three hours at a time, you get awfully bored.

We saw *Fair and Warmer* last night. It was opening night and Billy sent us tickets. She's in it. It was quite amusing, especially the audience which always laughed at the wrong time. Their idea of American slang is about as good as our idea of theirs.

Down at Eastbourne we went to a Revue and they sang "Over There" with the chorus dressed in Kilts. You can't beat that!

Yet it is surprising how well Americans are getting along over here,—much better than I expected. Everyone that has come in contact with the British swear by them. And the British will do more for us than they will do for their own troops. Every club in England that is open to English soldiers is open to Americans. We have every privilege that is offered to their own troops. If the English soldiers are entitled to special prices on anything so are we. We ride on the train at half fare and are entitled to anything we want from their canteens. We even draw what we want from their quartermasters.

Yet when the American Commissary was opened up in London, the first rule they made was that no one could buy anything who wasn't in American uniform. To me it hardly seems fair, not to say discourteous. I went down to get some canned stuff the other day but I couldn't get near the counter because the place was so full of the Y. M. C. A. and Red Cross and K. of C. Those boys are going to have the best of everything or know why.

As for me, I'm for the British and I don't care who knows it. Irish papers please copy.

The three of us and Nigger flew up to Maidenhead to call this afternoon. We ground-straffed the place and chased everybody off the terrace at Skindle's. Vic was down there and fell off a haystack watching us. Then we steeplechased all the way back down the river and kept our wheels just out of the water. Nigger dipped his once. Cal missed hitting a bridge by inches and Springs landed with about two hundred feet of telephone wire dragging on his undercarriage. There was one funny thing. At one long open stretch there was a punt in front of us right in the middle of the river. A man in a bright blazer was standing up in the stern punting and a girl was sitting in the bow with a big pink parasol. As we dove on them, the man fell overboard and the girl lost her parasol. I looked back to see it floating down the river and the man in the blazer floundering about in a regular whirlpool.

We heard that Sanford has been killed out at the front.

When I think of all the good men that have been killed and then see all the bums that are still alive hanging around town, it makes me mad. Justice is blind, all right. And God is not fair about it. Why should he take men like Fry and Stillman and Nathan and all the rest of the good ones and leave bums like me hanging around? It's not right. I feel sort of ashamed to be here still. I'll bet what the government owes me that I can name those that will be the survivors, if any, of our outfit.

One of our crowd got ambitious and not only got married to two different girls, but tried to give both of them an allotment. That takes nerve!

For a while one of the boys was playing around with a very charming young lady who more or less owed allegiance to a big diplomat who was in Holland on a mission of state. She had a beautiful apartment and he was more or less enjoying himself in the absence of the baron. But the gentleman returned suddenly and he was henceforth out of luck. We were all kidding him about it one night and Springs after listening a while retired and penned a poem on the subject. We all told him how rotten the meter was but he said that was charged up to poetic license. Here's a copy of the revised version:

> A portly Roman Senator was sipping his Rock and Rye.
> When a classic Vestal Virgin caught his educated eye;
> "Ah, ha," he cried, enraptured, "that's just about my style,
> Behold the old come-hither look, that makes the wild men wild!"
>
> The old boy was no novice, for he'd served his time in Gaul,
> And he saw she was a chicken and the flapper pose a stall,
> So he flashed a roll of talents and she flashed him back a smile,
> And she shrugged her architecture in a manner to beguile.
>
> While the young bucks wagered drachmae that his game would never win,
> He was letting her drive the chariot and chucking her under the chin.
> They dined at the smart Lucullus, saw the Coliseum show,
> Supped at the Appian Roadhouse where the party's never slow
> They drank a lot of Roman punch and shook a wicked hip,
> For she taught him the Tiber Grapevine and the Herculeum Dip.
>
> Said he, "If you're a Vestal, it's because you've had no chance,—
> I can see that you're ambitious by the charming way you dance.
> I'm getting rather lonely and I've got a tidy bit,
> Oh, really, you must come over." She answered, "Tempus fugit."
> As he gave his chariot number to the chasseur at the door,
> He heard the garcon whisper. "Sine qua non, caveat emptor."
>
> He gave her a three-horse chariot, a flat with a cellar of booze,
> And introduced her as his niece, who had moved from Syracuse.
> He bought her Carthaginian Togas, her sandals came from Thrace,
> And her B.V.D.'s were Grecian and were trimmed with Persian lace.
> Her hair was bound with fillets of platinum and gold,
> And she sprayed her dainty tonsils with a vintage rare and old.
>
> The young bucks were green with envy which but aroused his mirth,

And he boasted, "To hell with all expense, I'm getting my money's worth."
But he had to go to Naples, where some rents were overdue,
While she lingered by the Tiber, complaining of the flu.
And no great time elapsed ere the wise ones slyly winked,
And they whispered, "Habeas corpus," as their golden goblets clinked,
For it was gossiped at the banquets and told o'er games of cards,
That a certain dashing Shavetail of Julius Caesar's Guards,
Was bringing home the bacon, had a latchkey to the flat,
Had soused himself in pre-war stock and was staging a terrible bat.

Now the Senator in Naples was leasing out his piers,
When the gossip from the Tiber was wafted to his ears,
He cursed his Naples real estate and paged his charioteer,
As he scorched along the highway, he pumaced off his spear.
He broke the record back to Rome and arrived with a terrible shout,
But the Shavetail heard him on the stairs and escaped by the gutter spout.
The Senator surveyed his flat, with bottles everywhere,
And picked up some scattered plumage and bits of odd tinware.

The lady wept in anguish, but he only mocked her cries,
"I gave you rings for your fingers, now they're beneath your eyes."
The sweet young thing was cagy, she'd expected his return.
And she explained, "Semper fidelis, won't you ever learn!

"Dear Caesar came to see me, said Pompey's getting hot,
And the Legion's drilling badly and the Navy's gone to pot:
So to stimulate recruiting, I've been flirting with this Wop."
And she slipped her toga's shoulder strap, and displayed a fancy clock.

And the fat and portly Senator bethought himself of Gaul,
And when garrisoned in Egypt how he used to pay a call,
On a dusky amorous maiden with a houseboat on the Nile,
Whose lingering caresses made Army life worthwhile;
His thoughts went back to Britain, and he stroked a scarred chin,
Where an angry Celtic husband had expressed his deep chagrin.
And he recalled how his upright figure and the polish his armour bore
Had intrigued the Spanish maidens on that temperamental shore.

And his anger soon abating, he replaced the truant strap,
And she said, "Carpemus diem," as he gave her—cheek a slap;
He patted the tousled curly locks, that on his shoulder lay,
And thought, "She's not hors de combat, 'tis part of an Officer's Pay."

I hear the American lieut. that was at London Colney distinguished himself the other day. His squadron ran into two layers of Huns and leapt on the top layer. He was trying to turn his Camel to the right and he got into a spin and down he went. He got it under control and came out of the spin right in the middle of the lower flight of Huns. They didn't do a thing but shoot him full of holes. He got back a sadder and wiser man. They say he is stout enough and has made a good man. More power to him!

May 17th

We had a bunch of Brass Hats from the War Office down at Hounslow today and we put on an exhibition of formation flying and stunting for them that was pretty good. Nineteen machines in close battle formation are a stirring sight. Everything went off well except Springs's landing. His wheel hit a soft spot and turned him and the other wheel gave way and he turned over on his back and his head was shoved into the mud. He was a great sight when he came walking back to the tarmac where all the generals were standing. He had on slacks and a white shirt and wasn't wearing helmet or goggles and his face and head were all covered with mud. He's got to go over to Brooklands again tomorrow after another plane. I'm going to fly him over in an Avro.

Mrs. Bishop had a lady with her and she invited us to tea with them. We explained that we were all pretty dirty, which we were, but she said to never mind that and come along as we were; so we did. We all went into the squadron office and had tea brought over from the mess. The lady with her proved to be very nice and was very much interested in Americans and America. She was the most patriotic person I've met over here because she was always talking about the king. When I told her how much all the Americans liked serving with the British, she said she was so glad and she knew the king would be delighted to hear it. That sounded a bit farfetched to me.

We got on fine with her and we told her some funny stories and she nearly died laughing. We had a taxi waiting for us and offered to take her back to town with us as soon as we got dressed. She said she'd rather take a bus and get the air and it would take her right by the palace. I didn't get that either. As we went out we saw Cunningham-Reed's mother and she nearly broke a leg curtsying and I noticed Mrs. Bishop do the same thing when we left her and took the lady out to the bus. I asked Cunningham-Reed why the gymnastics and he told me it was for royalty. I asked him wherefore and he told me the lady was Princess Mary Louise. All three of us have been trying to remember whether we cracked any jokes about the king or not. Mrs. Bishop must have been laughing merrily. She's a peach. We're all crazy about her. Well, I have pressed the flesh of royalty now. My hand has gotten accustomed to the grasp of nobility and now I know the feel of the real thing. Who said we were Democrats? We're all snobs underneath the cuticle.

When we went into tea an American lieut. colonel asked to see Bishop. I think he wanted a plane. Bishop said to tell him to wait and asked us if he should invite him in to tea. We said certainly not; no colonel would ever invite us to anything but a court martial. That colonel got the surprise of his life when he saw these three disreputable looking Americans, with non-reg. uniforms and slacks, coming out with Bishop and realised what had kept him waiting. He wasn't very mad. I hope we never see him again.

May 20th
I've been spending most of my time with Billy. She certainly is a wonder and we get on fine together. I wish I had met her sooner.

Earl Hammer has been killed out at the front.

May 25th France!
Here's where we sober up and get down to real serious work.

Here I am at the front, the victim of many emotions. We had a fine send off and come what may, nothing can ever take away from me the joy that has been mine.

We had a series of farewell dinners and parties. Nigger's father gave us a banquet at the Criterion. He's a fine old fellow, eighty-two years old. He made a pile of money in the wool business in Australia and has five sons in the British Army. Everybody had to make a speech. Bishop kidded Springs about telling the lady next door that he knew too many nice girls. He wanted to know if he had met any more that turned out to be nice. Then he kidded me about playing football with the Bristol.

The next night Billy came around to the house with some friends. She started to kid me and said I was her cave man. She had a little actress named Babs in too that was sweet and girlish. Springs said that if the cave man stuff would work with one, it ought to work with another. Whereupon he starts to grab Babs. Babs thought that was fine and she entered into the spirit of the game with great glee. She responded to the cave man treatment by hitting him playfully over the head with an empty port bottle. She was no sylph and it didn't do a thing but knock him cold. It was a terrific crack and he was out for some time and had a big knot on the top of his head. Babs spent the rest of the evening making a fuss over him and I think she meant it. Springs sent her a nice brick all wrapped up in tissue paper the next morning and a couple of hours later a bunch of orchids.

We left Hounslow about eleven and our take-off was a scream. Billy and Babs were there over at one end, Dora and Lillian and Cecil were also present in another group. Nigger's *fiancée* was there with her family, and the princess was there with Mrs. Bishop. We nearly broke our necks running from one group to another and pretending we didn't know anybody else. Then the staff arrived from the American Headquarters. We hadn't expected them, —Col. Morrow, Col. Mitchell, Jeff Dwyer and a couple of others. We tried to get in the ground but couldn't find a hole.

The princess was very cordial. She said she told the king about us and that he was very pleased to hear that American pilots were so enthusiastic about serving with the R. F. C. and that he hoped someday he would have the opportunity to decorate one of us. Mrs. Bishop made us promise to stick to the major and not let a Hun get on his tail.

That was one morning when I would rather not have been so conspicuous. Our style was badly cramped. Col. Morrow was very nice and spoke of the time I had come to him to enlist and only had one letter of recommendation. But that was from the ex-secretary of war so he wrote the other one for me himself.

Dora was much interested in our silk skull caps that we wear under our fur helmets. She wanted to know whose stocking mine was made from.

All nineteen machines were arranged in position for taking off in formation and the engines warmed up. The major's machine was out front in the centre and the three flights arranged in a V on each side and in back of him. We'd practiced getting off that way and it was all right as long as no machine got directly behind another and hit the backwash.

Bishop lined us up before the crowd and some general made us a little speech. Then Bishop gave us our final instructions. He told us that Lympe would be our first stop and to be sure and take a good look at the wind sock and to land squarely into the wind. But he didn't call it a sock. He called it by the name we always call it on the field when there are no ladies or gentlemen present. He turned red and the ladies lowered their parasols and he ran and jumped in his machine and we all took off together. I got in Springs's backwash and nearly cracked up getting off.

Cal didn't get far. He disappeared from the formation about fifteen minutes after we took off, and didn't get here until today. He had an air bubble in his water line and he had to land in a field south of London to let his motor cool off and get some more water. He got down all right and got out of the field again and decided he'd stop at Croydon and get his radiator drained. He made a bad landing at Croydon and crashed. So he went back to London for another night and got a new machine from Brooklands the next day.

We stopped at Lympe near Folkestone for lunch and Brown cracked up there. We took off after lunch and Canning cracked up on the beach when his motor conked. We landed at Marquis near Boulogne, for tea. We had a beautiful trip across the channel. It was as clear as a bell and we crossed at eight thousand feet. My motor was missing a little and I kept picking out destroyers and trawlers below to land beside in case it gave out. MacDonald crashed at Marquis when he landed short in the rough and turned over and Cunningham-Reed washed out his plane by pancaking.

On the way across, Springs motioned for me to come up close to him. I flew up to his wing tip and he took out his flask and drank my health. I didn't have a thing with me but a bottle of champagne and that was in my tool box and I couldn't get to it.

We arrived at our airdrome about six. It's two miles south of Dunkirk and is an old R. N. A. S. station called Petit Synthe. We are about three miles from the coast and there are two other squadrons on this same airdrome. They are bombers and have D. H. Nines. We had dinner at the 211th squadron which used to be No. 11 R. N. A. S., and they are very nicely fixed in semi-permanent quarters. There is one American over there—Bonnalie, who was in Bim's gang. They bomb Zeebrugge and Bruges every day trying to damage the submarine bases there. Just across the canal is another airdrome. There are two squadrons of night-bombers on it with Handley-Pages and Fees and one squadron of Bristol Fighters.

We are in the 65th wing, which is a part of the 5th brigade. There is a brigade of the Air Force assigned to every Field Army and consists of four or five wings. A wing consists of five to fifteen squadrons.

211 is a good outfit and we had quite a party. Springs and I got a couple of motorcycles and went out in search of eggs and cream. We

found plenty and made a big tub of eggnog. 88 squadron came over to see us with a band and we had a regular binge. Capt. Harrison who was our instructor at Thetford is a flight commander over there and he invited us over to spend the night with him. I finally went to sleep laughing over Springs and Dora. After I told Billy goodbye rather formally as everybody was watching us, Springs went over to Dora and they put on a burlesque tragic parting that was a scream. Everybody nearly died laughing.

They tell me that our sector of the lines, from Nieuport on the coast to Ypres, is very quiet as there is no possibility of a battle up here. All new squadrons are sent here for a month's final training before going south. 84 has just left this airdrome and gone down to Amiens.

After paying all my bills I had just sixpence left when I took off. Now isn't that perfect! I couldn't have used anymore and I couldn't have gotten along on less. That's figuring pretty close. Now I am beyond the reach of money. Eternity has no currency.

May 27th

I'm feeling exceptionally good tonight. I had a nice swim in the moat of Ft. Mardick followed by a glass of eggnog made with real cream, and I can smell a good dinner cooking and I just got some mail,—none from home, just from England. I am at peace with the world. What a strange place to find peace. I can hear the roar of the guns and may be bombed any minute. There was a letter from Dora to us all. She writes:

My dears:
I hope you have all settled down comfortably to your new careers of rape and robbery. It was really a wonderful sight to see you all go off and then turn and dive on us. If my eyes, ears and nose hadn't been so full of dirt and castor oil, I should have cheered loudly but I defy anyone to be festive under those circumstances.
Cal, my dear, I congratulate you most heartily on your somewhat short but extremely concise demonstration of how to crash in safety. You have filled a long needed want and I think it most unselfish of you to take the trouble to come back and take me out to dinner when you had once started over. However, once a gentleman, always a gentleman!
You, you bum: I don't think that in the whole course of my somewhat varied career, I have ever seen such a peculiar figure

as you made on Wednesday. In the old days, knights took their lady's glove into the heart of battle with them; but you, moving with times, wear your young woman's stocking as a helmet. It would have been a touching tribute, methinks, if you had worn a pair of her knickers as cuffs.

I hope that you will live up to your reputation as a cave man and bite any prisoners you secure. I expect it will soon be quite a familiar sight to see you returning to the landing stage, if you have one, with the scalps of six luckless Germans, who have annoyed you, hanging from your Sam Browne.

Springs, last but not least, my blue-eyed baby—you're a stout fellow. I shall never forget the expression of overwhelming sorrow in your velvety eyes as you kissed me goodbye so tenderly under the eyes of the assembled multitude. Thank heaven, whatever happens, I have the thought of your great love to cheer my barren life.

Well, my pin-whiskered and illegitimate trio, all the love of my passionate southern nature. And take care that you all three sit down and write me an epistle at once or it will turn to bitter hatred. We women of Spain are terrible in our rage!

Thine, Dora.

We bought a piano today and have a phonograph so the mess is very cheery and excellently equipped with furniture. We are allowed so much cash by the government for furnishing and then have a big private fund. We received several large donations that will come in well. Springs is vice-president of the mess and O. C. drinks. We took a truck and went into Dunkirk to stock up our cellar. We got some Scotch, Benedictine, cognac, champagne, port, white wine, red wine and beer. Dunkirk is not in the "*zone des armées*" so is under civilian control and we can get what we please. We decided that it was too much trouble to sign chits for drinks, so all drinks are to be free and each man will have to see that he gets his money's worth.

I am certainly glad to be out here at last. I am now going to earn my salt. And there are other reasons I like to be out here. Everybody is in such a good humour and we have a wonderful bunch of fellows. We're about the keenest bunch of fighters that have been gotten together in some time. We're all very congenial and that means a lot. There are three Americans, two New Zealanders, two Australians, one South African, six Canadians, two Scots, one Irishman, and six Englishmen.

Over in England you never could have a cheery mess because everybody was chasing away every evening to see some skirt or other and some of them had wives in the offing that cramped their style. Over here, there are no skirts on our clothesline and there's small chance that we'll see anything eligible for at least three months. That sounds like I am a woman hater, which I am not, but this is the first time in my life that I have ever been entirely removed from feminine influence and for the moment, I like it. I don't expect anybody else would understand this. I want to enjoy my independence a little. I suppose I'll feel different about it before I get my first leave, but just at present, I feel as if I had won the game by default and somebody had arranged a big party in my honour.

Nobody at home seems to be interested in anything but promotions and church attendance.

Our mechanics and baggage have arrived and we are all ready to start work. We did a practice patrol today and had a look at the lines.

The major got a Hun two-seater today the other side of Ypres. First blood!

May 29th

Nigger and Bish each got a Hun today. Brown and Capt. Baker each crashed an S. E. on the airdrome. That makes an even break for the day.

Springs and I went into Dunkirk today to get some things and I listened to him trying to *parlezvous*. He's not so good even if he is educated.

We went into one large store and strolled up to a very pretty little clerk with a big head of blonde hair and opened fire, endeavouring to purchase some toothpaste. She didn't follow him and couldn't interpret his gestures. She thought he was looking for a dentist. She was quite captivating and I commented on how nice she was. She looked as if she knew I was talking about her, so I kept on. I said to him, "She has a pretty face, all right, but fat ankles. Call for a new deal." She gave me a dirty look and Springs tried to brush his teeth with his finger again after his college French failed. I said. "She's sure got the come-hither look in her eyes, but her figure would go better if bustles were back in style. She'd be a knock-out then." She looked mad.

Finally, Springs found some new French words that he'd overlooked and she led the way to a counter and he got his Pebeco and paid for it. Then says she, in perfect English, with a glance in my direction. "Do you wish me to wrap it for you or will you take it as it is?" We grabbed the tube and fled. She sure was keen. I'm going back to see her if I ever break my monastic vows. I overlooked the fact that the British have used Dunkirk as a port for nearly four years and wherever there's a Tommy, there is English spoken. It won't be long before all the French women will be speaking with an American accent.

The squadron amusement is Diavolo. Somebody found a couple of old sets in Calais and now everybody is concentrated on it. Cal is the champion. He also plays tennis over on 211's court.

The major just blew in raising hell because he picked up the wrong tube and used shaving cream for toothpaste.

June 2nd

One of the supernumerary pilots is looking at the war in my machine, so for the present I am occupied and will write a little. I hate for anybody else to fly my machine and this is the first time anyone else has touched it. But Nigger wants Inglis to have a look at the lines and get his bearings so when one of us goes West, he will be ready to take his place. I wonder whose place it will be. He's a nice fellow, a New Zealander, and got the D. C. M. at Gallipoli with the infantry.

There are six machines in a flight. Nigger leads and MacGregor and Cal are on his right, behind and a little above. Springs and I are on the left and Thompson is in the centre in the space between Cal and me. We fly in the form of a triangle with the back corners high. MacGregor is deputy flight commander and takes command in case anything happens to Nigger. We fly pretty close together and have a set of signals. If Nigger is going to turn sharp, he drops his wing on that side. If he is going to dive steep, he holds up his arm. If he wants us to come up close or wants to call our attention to something he shakes both wings.

If it's a Hun, he shakes his wings and points and fires his guns. If he means "yes" he bobs his nose up and down and if he means "no" he shakes his wings. If we see a Hun and he doesn't, we fire our guns and fly up in front and point. We fly at three-quarters throttle so we can always pull up. If he has trouble and wants us to go on, he fires a red light from his Very pistol. If he wants us to follow him out of a fight, he fires a white light. If he wants to signal the other flights, he fires a green light.

MacGregor has been out before. He was out on Pups for six months when they were service machines. He came over with the

RECONNOITRING IN THE AEROPLANE

Australian infantry. Thompson has been out before too. He was out last fall on Camels but crashed too many of them.

We've been doing rather well. We have a score board in the mess and there's a big red 6 staring me in the face now. We don't count any unless they go down in flames or break up in the air or someone sees them crash. The wing commander, Col. Cunningham, is over here all the time and is tickled to death because all this is voluntary for we aren't supposed to get into action the first two weeks. I'm going to get a Hun this week if I pull a wing off in the attempt.

June 3rd

I was censoring some of the men's mail today and I ran across this:

Dear Bill:—

You remember the big dog back at Hounslow? Well, he ain't got no master no more.

That was Capt. Benbow's dog and we all miss his master. He was buried where he fell, "so what the hell, boys, what the hell!" He died with his boots on and his grave is marked with a cross made from a propeller.

He went out the other day alone and managed to get up in the sun above a flight of Hun scouts. He got on the tail of the rear one and would have gotten him but both guns jammed. Then the others turned back on him and chased him home. He was as mad as a hornet and spent the next day oiling and adjusting his guns. He went back to the same place at the same time and found the same Huns again. No one knows exactly what happened but Archie called up and said they saw him coming out of Hunland with five Huns on his tail. Just as he got to the lines two of them fired a burst and his plane dived into the ground on our side of the lines and he was killed. He was certainly a fine fellow.

The English have the reputation of being a phlegmatic unemotional race and they certainly try to live up to the part, though I believe they are very sentimental underneath. It is simply considered bad taste to show it. We all felt pretty bad about Benbow but no emotion was exhibited. I have heard that the *London Times* printed the story of the Battle of Waterloo on the inside sheet at the bottom of the page. That's typical. Unless the people at home get an emotional bath every morning they don't think the war is being conducted properly.

It seems funny for me to be censoring these Tommies' mail. The officer of the day always has to censor the men's mail. Here I am, officer of the day and in one of His Majesty's squadrons and this time last year I hadn't even seen a real live Englishman and sort of regarded them as enemies.

I'm still doing things to my machine. I've taken off the steamlining behind my head so I can see backwards better. I've taken off the windshield steamlining so I don't have to use goggles because the steamline sets up ripples in the air which hurt your eyes and I've put heavier wire on my stabilizer and fin. I've got a new way to fire my guns now that I like much better. I've got a Camel joystick and the triggers are fixed so I can fire both guns with one thumb if I want to. I got tired of my drab looking cockpit, all full of uninteresting labels and gadgets. And I am now decorating it so I won't be bored upstairs. It's quite like old times playing with my bus.

But instead of the spasmodic assistance of a negro chauffeur, I have three expert Ak Emmas, who do nothing else but look after my bus and do my bidding. They never touch another one and so far, I've managed to keep them pretty busy. Unless I bring down a Hun in a few days I'm afraid they'll get fed up with their jobs. You can tell by their letters that they like to have the machine they work on bring down Huns. You can also tell by their letters what they think of their officers.

They are changing the score now as the major has just come down and has shot down two more Huns,—a scout and a two-seater. He's broken the English record and now has more than McCudden. Archie saw one of them go down and another one broke up in the air.

I pulled a good one. Whenever we come back from a trip over the lines, we're supposed to shoot up all our spare ammunition at a ground target to keep in practice. I asked where the ground target was, and they told me it was a silhouette on the beach north of Ft. Mardick. The first time I came back I went over looking for it. I couldn't find it at first and then I saw a rotten attempt at a silhouette of a plane over in a corner of a field and I dove on it and emptied my guns into it. I knew my shooting was poor but I didn't think it was that bad and it took me a hundred rounds to get on the target.

When I got back to Petit Snythe, there was a big straff on. A Belgian major had telephoned over that a plane with my letter on it was over shooting at their landing Tee and they were all in the dugout and to please send over and stop it before their mess was all shot to pieces. That's what I call good camouflage when they can hide a whole squadron. Either that or I am blind as a bat.

There's only one objection to this locality. Dunkirk is only twenty miles from the lines and it has a big harbour with three canals running into it and it is just as easy to find it in the moonlight as in the daylight. And this field is right between two canals and there's a railroad siding back of the mess so they always know where we are. The Huns bomb Dunkirk every clear night and it's gotten tiresome already. And every day about noon, they shell Dunkirk with a long range gun from Ostend. The civilian population live in cellars and spend most of the day down there too. I don't see why they don't all move.

The first couple of raids didn't bother us at all. We stood out in front and watched and thought it was good fun. But one night it suddenly began raining nose fuses around us and some friendly Hun dropped a bomb in the middle of the field. Since then we have swallowed our pride and taken shelter in the dugout. It's carefully sandbagged and has a telephone in it and a special compartment for the officers which is fairly comfortable. But I don't like it. You read too much about bombs falling on dugouts and if they get a direct hit, it will kill everyone in it.

We are doing regular patrols now, one in the morning and one in the afternoon. We stay over the lines two hours each trip and our beat is from the coast to Courtrai, which is about fifteen miles east of Ypres, commonly known as Wipers. It's a comparatively quiet sector in daytime but a lot of dirty work goes on at night. The French and Belgian Armies hold the trenches so look after their own artillery and reconnaissance. Whenever we are looking for Huns we go down south of Wipers in the Salient where they are as plentiful as niggers in a watermelon patch on a moonlight night.

June 4th
Everybody in the squadron has some sort of a dog. Cunningham-Reed had a forced landing and came back with a Belgian fox terrier that can do everything but talk. I have a chow that was born in the hangars at Hounslow,—a real dog of war.

Springs got all full of enthusiasm and went out by himself the other day to do battle with the Hun in spite of what Nigger told him. His ambition was rewarded and he managed to find six Hun scouts south of Courtrai. They chased him all over the sky and he had a time getting away from them. He finally just put his tail plane forward and dove wide open. Not orthodox but if your plane stays together, it's all right. Nothing can hit you while you're doing two hundred and fifty unless they are right on your tail and I guess it would be impossible to get there at that speed. And even more difficult to get out alive after you get there. He tore all the fabric loose on his top wing coming out.

He was still so excited when he landed that he ran into the major's plane and locked wings with it on the ground. The major was all set to bawl him out but Springs walked up to him and ran his finger across his row of ribbons and said, "You see these medals?" Bish nodded. "Well," says Springs, "I just want to tell you that you are welcome to them!" With that he walked on into the bar. Bish laughed though he wasn't pleased about having his machine smashed.

They say Archie is the most useless thing in the war, but that machine gun fire from the ground is greatly to be feared. That's what got Richthofen. I think so too, for I came back today and found a couple of bullet holes in my rudder. I think I know where the fellow lives that did it and I am going back tomorrow and fill his dugout with lead. Machine guns only carry up to about twenty-five hundred feet but Archie can go higher than we can.

It's surprising how personal the war in the air gets. Whenever there's anything going on, you know that each little lead bullet or Archie shell is meant for you personally. And when you fire, you don't just fire towards Berlin and then wait until someone telephones you whether or not a Hun stopped it. No, you wait until you are in the correct position on a Hun's tail and then you open fire and see your tracer bullets going past him or into him and if you get him you see him go spinning down, maybe in flames. Meanwhile Mr. Hun has been practicing target shooting and is ready to do a half roll as soon as you start your dive. Or he may have it all fixed up with Archie to range a certain area and then lure you into it. And Mr. Hun is on the job too. Just do a bad turn or a sloppy half roll and you'll hear him play your swan song on his *Spandaus*.

Archie has a funny sound. A burst near you sounds like a loud cough and as soon as you hear it you start zigzagging. When you hear it you know that burst won't hurt you—it's the one you never hear that does the dirty work and tears the bag,—but it does mean that the battery has your range and the next one is sure to come closer unless you fool him and sideslip, zoom, turn or throttle down. Then he fires where you should have been but weren't. He's easy to fool but you must do something. The best thing to do is to change your course twenty degrees every twelve seconds. That gives you time to get out of the way of the one that's coming up at you that moment and doesn't give the gunners time to get your deflection for the next shot.

I've been out baiting Archie several times and it's great sport. You can make him waste five thousand dollars' worth of ammunition on you in no time. And then think how mad the old Hun gunner must get! I'll never be happy until I get a chance to open up on one of them with my machine guns.

The Huns use shrapnel which bursts black and the Allies use high explosive which bursts white. There is an Austrian naval battery at Middlekerke that bursts pink. Scared me to death the first time I saw it.

There's one Hun gunner over at Dickybush that is so good he never fires but one salvo of four shots at you. If he doesn't hit you the first time, he doesn't waste any more ammunition on you unless there's a big formation where he's got a chance to get a trailer. But he knows it's useless to fire at a plane that is trying to dodge him. He nearly got one of us—a shell burst between Cal and myself. Cal got a piece of it in his arm and we tried to make him put up a wound stripe but he wouldn't do it. It was the first salvo and I was asleep and didn't even know we had crossed the lines. The best thing that Archie does is to signal. You can see an Archie burst twice as far as you can see a plane and our Archie is very good about warning us of the approach of Huns up in the sun when we can't see them. I was out the other day alone and our Archie put a burst up close to me to call my attention to a scout formation in Hunland.

I went up to test out my new engine and landed up north of Dunkirk where I heard there was an American squadron. They didn't seem particularly glad to see me though the C. O. invited me to lunch. These boys certainly are down in the mouth. They think the Hun has won the war and are worrying about their baggage and girls in Paris. Why didn't I just write baggage? Hobey Baker is a flight commander up there. He used to be a great athlete at Princeton. A fine fellow he is. I've heard Hash and Springs talking about him. Poor Hash is a prisoner now.

I asked some of them to come over and have dinner with us. They said they couldn't as they had no way to get over there. They haven't much transport and they have to account for every drop of petrol. I offered to send over our car for them and they said they'd like to but didn't show much enthusiasm. They aren't enjoying the war much. They didn't have a bar and their mess wasn't much to boast of. I gather that Uncle Sam is pretty stingy with his nephews on this side, particularly those in the air. Me for the R. F. C. There's one thing about the British that I like—they realise the importance of morale. The British try to build it up, the Americans try to tear it down. You can't expect men to have any pep after they've been cheated out of their seniority and pay, lost faith in their government after broken promises and been treated like enemy prisoners by the higher officers. Only the enormous patriotism and determination of our young men have prevented serious trouble. Our army seems to think that all they have to do for morale is to send along a couple of Y. M. C. A. secretaries and a few professional song leaders. Wait and see what happens to them.

June 5th

Springs went back after the six Huns that chased him home. Nigger and MacGregor wanted to go hunting so they all went together. My engine was giving trouble so I couldn't go. Just after they crossed the lines Bish joined them and led them down on the same six Huns at the same place where Springs found them before and at the same hour. They must have been the same ones that got Benbow. Methodical, these Huns are. They were in two layers of three each. Bish and Mac took the lower ones and Springs and Nigger took the top ones. Bish and Mac each got one and Springs got one down out of control but no one saw it crash so he doesn't score. It must have been a good fight while it lasted. They were Pfaltz scouts and are easy meat for S. E.s.

The wind shifted and they had to land the short way when they came back. There was a train on the siding when Springs came in and he just glided over the box cars and tried to make a slow landing. His undercarriage crumpled up and stuck in the ground and he slid along in the fuselage like it was a canoe but didn't go over on his nose. Bish told him to fight on our side for a change and to quit bringing down S. E.s. Brown washed out his third today trying to land cross wind. It can't be done in an S. E. Not with the undercarriage where it is. I don't see why they don't move it forward.

Springs says he feels like a little boy that got licked in a fight and went home and got his big brother and came back.

June 6th

The new flight commander for A flight arrived. His name is Randall and he is known as Randy. He was badly wounded at Gallipoli and got trench fever when he was with the infantry. Then he was transferred to the flying corps and was out on D. H. Twos. He was shot down by Richthofen. He says that Richthofen may have the reputation of being a good sport but that he showed him no mercy,—shot his engine up and then followed him down while he was trying to land and shot him three times. He got one bullet in his rear and they had to cut off a slice. He sits down and leans like the tower of Pisa. Cal said he'd be fine for sitting on stairs. He went up to have a look at the lines and crashed landing and turned over on his back. That's the trouble with these S.E.s; they don't like the ground.

I went up and had a private battle of my own. I saw a Hun two-seater away the hell and gone over Roulers. I chased him a bit but I couldn't catch him. Then about three Archie batteries opened up on me! The whole sky turned black. A barrage grew up in front of me like a bed of mushrooms and I swung around just in time to avoid it. Scared? Of course, I was scared. There were heavy clouds below me and I didn't know where the lines were. My compass was spinning around so fast that I couldn't tell anything from it.

Then I forgot whether the sun set in the east or the west and had to stop and figure it out. Every time Archie would get close to me, my heart would skip a beat. It has an awful sound when it's close, like a giant clapping his hands and it has a sort of metallic click. So I put my nose down and ran for it. First Archie would be 'way behind me and then he'd get 'way in front and I'd zoom and he'd be a mile away. I crossed the lines down below Wipers where I didn't know the country and for a few minutes I was lost. I got out my maps and found a town on the map that I located on the ground and then I came on back by Bergues.

Springs is all right until he gets mail from home, then he gets into a terrible rage and wants to fight the wide, wide world. He and his father seem to carry on a feud at long range. He's got so now he doesn't open any letters until after he's had a few drinks and some of them he doesn't open at all. His father writes him full details and instructions in triplicate about how to do everything and finds fault with everything he does. He showed me a couple of them and they certainly were nasty. Springs is no saint but he isn't nearly that bad. I don't see why he cares what's going on at home. He worries about everything his father says and takes all his criticism to heart, though why he should worry over it when he's three thousand miles away is beyond me. He's three thousand miles closer to hell.

He must be awfully fond of his father to care what he thinks about things he doesn't know anything about. And the idea of losing sleep because someone three thousand miles away hasn't got sense enough to understand English when you write it to them, is absurd!

There was a bomb raid on last night and the dugout was stuffy so he and I went out and crawled under a boxcar on the siding. It's about as good shelter as you can get. A direct hit will kill you anyway in the dugout and the boxcars will protect you from the nose-fuses and fragments. We got to talking about home. He said that he had to get killed because he couldn't go home. He said if he got killed, his father would have a hero for a son and he could spend all his time and money building monuments to him and make himself very happy and proud.

But if he lives through it and goes home, he says his father will fight with him for the rest of his life. No matter what he does, his father will say it's wrong and worry over it. I told him he was crazy but he was quite serious about it. He says it's a family trait. He says he wants to last long enough to make a name for himself so his father will have something to build a monument to, and then get bumped off with a lot of fireworks the last week of the war.

He says if he lives through it, his father is determined to make him go down in a cotton mill and work five years as a day labourer and live in the mill village. Some sort of foolishness about starting in at the bottom and working up. And the slightest mistake he makes will break his father's heart. He says he owns one mill himself but that won't make any difference to his father who won't want him to have it. I asked him what he wanted to do. He said he wanted to write but his father is determined to make a horny-handed hardboiled superintendent out of him. He's all the time scribbling now. He's always stopping something important to jot down a plot, as he calls it, for future reference. He's got a brief case full of them already,—plays, short stories, poems, sketches or what have you. He's tried to read me some of them several times.

His grandfather left him a big plantation in South Carolina, about three thousand acres, and he wants to go there to live. There's a big brick house on it that was built by his great-grandfather and he wants to fix it up like it was originally. We talked it all over. He wants me to come and live with him and run the farm in case we both get through. He says he's got plenty for both Cal and me. If he doesn't live through it he's left a will which leaves enough to Cal and me to get us started after the war. He damn near had me crying. I can't leave him and Cal anything but I told them that if anything happened to me to help themselves to my stuff.

The farm idea sounds good to me. He wants to build a tennis court and a swimming pool and a landing field for a plane. He's going to build the pool so he can jump right out of the bedroom windows into it.

Cal is in the banking business, or rather was, and Springs says he thinks he owns a lot of stock in some bank and Cal can run it.

All that sounds fine but I don't guess there's much chance of all three of us getting through. And judging by the letters I've seen, I can imagine what his old man would say if we came down to live with him while he's doing his five years' penance in overalls. Besides that, I've got business to attend to myself after this scrap is over.

We were just about ready to jump out of the window into the pool when the Huns arrived in force and proceeded to drop thirty-two bombs just across the canal on the Handley-Page airdrome. That's the worst raid I've seen. They dropped a parachute flare first that lit up the ground like an arc light. Then they dropped a phosphorus bomb on a hangar and set fire to it. They dropped a big bomb on a dugout and killed forty officers and men. Fortunately, most of the Handleys were out on another raid themselves. The field was so full of holes that they couldn't land on it and either had to stay up all night or go over and land on the beach. Some splinters from one bomb hit one of the wheels and it rained nose-fuses.

I heard in Boulogne that Dick Mortimer has been killed.

Springs and I were sitting in the mess alone yesterday afternoon doing a little light drinking when in walked a man in naval officer's uniform. "Cheerio," says he.

"Chin-chin," say we, "have a drink."

"Thanks," says he, joining us and reclining on the back of his neck with us. He didn't seem like the naval officers we had met before and we gathered that he was just paying the flying corps a social visit and came over here after a Bronx, for which 85 is famous. He and Springs got into a heated literary argument. I held my fire until they got on my subject. Later on Capt. Baker told us who the bird was. It was Arnold Bennett, the writer, who is out here getting some local colour for a book.

June 8th

This morning I arose at three-thirty—two-thirty real time—and by six I was back for breakfast and the Huns had wasted a thousand pounds' worth of Archie shells on us. Our hands might have been a bit steadier as we raised a coffee cup, but a little exposure to the hate of the Hun does give you a wonderful appetite. This Archie gunner at Middlekerke is no amateur—his first burst almost made me loop! After that dodging was easy.

Before breakfast I went over to a farmhouse in a sidecar and got some cream for our cereal. Springs has taught the cook to make Eggs Benedict and we breakfast well.

As a matter of fact, we live well. We went down to Boulogne and got an ice cream freezer and we are the only outfit at the front that has ice cream for dinner every night. "In the midst of life we are in death." And in the midst of death we manage to have a hell of a lot of fun. Bronx cocktails, chicken livers *en brochette*, champagne, strawberry ice cream, and Napoleon brandy. That's the way we live. I don't think Bish is sorry he brought us along.

We had a lot of trouble getting that ice cream freezer. We went down to Boulogne to a department store and Springs opened fire with his drugstore French. They brought him an egg beater. He tried again and they insisted that what he really wanted was an ice pick. They brought him a dictionary but it wasn't in it. So he called for, "machinery to make cream hard." They brought him a churn and then a cream whipper. We gave it up and walked out. Then we saw one in the window and went back and got it.

Again at eleven I went out to do battle. We got into a dogfight over Ostend and had a merry little fracas.

I was up above the main formation to see that nothing dropped down out of the sun and a Pfaltz dove on me. He came right out of the sun but I've learned to put my thumb up and close one eye and unless they are at a dead angle, I can see them. I saw this one in time and just as he opened fire, I turned quickly and threw his sights off. His tracer was going a hundred feet behind my tail. The Hun went on by and half rolled onto my tail. I kept turning to keep his sights off me and he followed. We turned around and around—each manoeuvring to get into position to fire a burst at close range.

But I had learned my lesson well at Ayr and I could do perfect vertical banks and I began gaining on him. I was getting in position to open up when he half rolled to break away. I half rolled after him and was on his tail like a hawk after a chicken. I let him have both guns at close range.

My sights were dead on his cockpit and I must have got in about a hundred and fifty rounds. My Lewis jammed after fifty rounds but my

Vickers kept going. The Hun started to turn, then he flopped over on his back and went straight down. He was last seen headed towards his future home and breaking all records—hell bent for hades! I couldn't see him crash so I only got an "out of control." But I know I got him. At the speed he was diving he never could have pulled out. And I know now that I can fight as well as fly. It was quite evident that one of us had to die but I was cool as a cucumber and when we were turning around each other I could almost hear Nigger through the earphones from the front seat of an Avro telling me: "Little top rudder now. Easy. Keep your nose level. Pull your stick back. Take off a little aileron. Now cross your controls."

Our pink-cheeked little boy, commonly known as Lady Mary, decided it was high time he shot down a Hun so went up in search of one. The result has caused much merriment. He found plenty of Huns all right, enough to last him the rest of his life if taken singly. He ran into a school of them and didn't see them until they were right on top of him. As near as we can figure out the Huns must have gotten in each other's way getting to him or been laughing so hard they couldn't shoot straight. Anyway, he's back and is now a member of the "sadder-and-wiser-club" of which Springs is president. Maybe the Huns' wings pulled off when they tried to dive after him.

Trapp also qualified for membership in that august body. He met a couple of two-seaters and chased them twenty miles into Hunland. They saw their own airdrome and took courage and turned around and chased him all the way back.

Springs got in a fight and shot his own propeller to pieces and Cal had his tyre punctured by an energetic Hun.

Late every afternoon there is the most unearthly racket back of the mess on the tracks. Several thousand Chinese or rather Annamite *coolies* come back from where they work during the day. Their camp is about a mile below here on the canal. I hear that there are two hundred and fifty thousand of them in France. They were brought over to fill sand bags and dig reserve trenches behind the lines. There are trenches all the way back to the coast now. We can retreat twenty miles and still have prepared positions. But just think of bringing these Chinks all the way around the world. That just shows how scarce man-power really is in Europe. Why don't they go over and get two hundred and fifty thousand of our negroes? Probably because they know they'd never get any work out of them.

I talked to one of the officers in charge of the Chinks. He told me they were organised into military companies and regiments. Each one has an identification tag welded around his neck and they can speak a little pigeon English. He said they were fine workmen and give little trouble. They are scared to death when there's a bomb raid on and that's the only time he has any trouble with them. They have their own camp well sandbagged, I noticed.

This Dunkirk district certainly gets well straffed. Every clear night it gets bombed. The Huns pass over here on their way to London, Calais and Boulogne and use the harbour to set their sights on. If they don't reach their objective they let Dunkirk have their bombs on the way back, or if they have any left over they save them for us. I think they must send over all their new men to practice on Dunkirk. We don't get much sleep because they are over here all night. The only defence is Archie and these cable balloons. Both are worse than useless. They send up about a dozen balloons as soon as the last one of our machines is down and they are held by strong cables. The idea is that some Hun might run into one of them.

And every morning the long range gun at Ostend sends over four big shells addressed to the major of Dunkirk. This has been going on for four years and the civilian population seems to have gotten used to it. A shell hit a shoe store the other day and knocked the front of it down. We were in town that afternoon and business was going on as usual with the damaged boots out in front being sold at a discount.

The Germans certainly are methodical. They send over the same number of shells at exactly the same hour. Everybody knows when to take shelter and Mournful Mary, the siren, goes off automatically ten minutes before.

We have a fine place to swim though the water is pretty cold. There's a big moat around Ft. Mardick about twenty feet wide that has a canal running down to the ocean. Sometimes we go in the surf.

The French towns with their walls and moats are awfully pretty. There's a little town just below here named Gravelines that has walls shaped exactly like a star and the sun, sparkling on the moat, makes it look like a jewel. It's about a mile inland and has a canal running out to the ocean.

June 10th

Nigger let Thompson lead a patrol. We weren't too keen about it though he has been out to the front before. Cal, Springs, Inglis and I went along. We were supposed to patrol the coast between Ostend and Bruges to see that no high two-seaters came over to take photographs of the bomb hits last night. There were heavy clouds at ten thousand feet and we had trouble getting through them as Thompson flew a jerky pace. I didn't pay much attention to where we were but I thought it was funny that we weren't getting Archied. Boulogne, Calais, Dunkirk, Nieuport, Ostend and Bruges are all along the coast about twenty miles apart and they all look alike from fifteen thousand feet.

Thompson got Dunkirk and Boulogne mixed up and proceeded to do a very daring patrol over Fernes on our side of the lines, thinking he was up near Bruges. We figured out that he was doing about as much good there as anywhere and wandered off on our own. I went over and had a good look at Wipers. It made me sick. There's not a wall standing running north and south. And there's a stretch of country forty miles square that's as flat as a piece of paper,—no trees, no houses, nothing! I could see the flashes of the guns and see the smoke and dust where the shells burst. We hear firing twenty-four hours out of the day. And down on the ground it looks as if someone had drawn a lot of pencil marks in a row. That's the barbed wire! We were up over Holland the other day but we were too high to see the electric cable.

What a nightmare this war is! I'm beginning to understand the term "Anti-Christ." Both the Allies and the Germans pray to the same God for strength in their slaughter! What a joke it must seem to Him to see us puny insignificant mortals proclaiming that we are fighting for Him and that He is helping us. Think of praying to the God of Peace for help in War! The heavens must shake with divine mirth.

I can't kick. It's the best war I know anything about. It's been worth a lot to me so far. Sooner or later I'll join the company of the elect but I want to get a Hun first. I want to get one sure one,—a flamer or a loose-winged flop. I know how hard it is, but unless I get one, the government will simply be out all it cost to train me. If I get one, it'll be an even break. If I get two, I'll be a credit instead of a debit on the books.

Nigger is going to play the dive and zoom game. An S. E. will outzoom anything built and if we get above the Huns we can dive and fire and then zoom away. I understand a Fokker can outmanoeuvre an S. E. and if you dogfight with them they can outturn and outclimb you. A Fokker triplane can lick anything that has ever been built but they have a bad habit of falling to pieces in the air so the Huns are washing them out. I wonder how long it will be before we will have the Snipe and the Snark that we saw tested at Brooklands.

June 11th

We had a proper binge last night. We invited the C. O. and the flight commanders of 211 over for dinner to return their hospitality and a colonel from the A. S. C. who was a friend of MacDonald's in Saloniki. Everyone calls the C. O. Bobby. He is a great drinker and has the reputation of being able to drink the rest of the world under the table. We certainly gave him a good opportunity to exhibit his jewels. Springs and I were detailed as pacemakers and we mixed up a big bowl of punch and we all had a bottoms-up contest that was a classic. We had speeches from everyone after dinner and the colonel tried to get on the table to make his but it wasn't strong enough to hold him.

Then we had a football game in front of the mess. Cal and Bish collided head on in the dark at full speed and were both knocked cold. Bobby lived up to his reputation and won the contest easily. We had to carry the colonel out and put him in his car feet first. He came back today and wanted to know what was in that punch. When we told him what was in that innocent drink he nearly fainted. These Britishers will learn some day to respect our concoctions. They don't think a drink is strong unless it tastes bad.

Mac sure is funny when he dips into the flowing bowl. He's very much in love with a girl at home, or thinks he is, which is just as bad. She was only sixteen when he left and he hasn't seen her in four years. He still thinks she is young and innocent and sixteen. And every time he gets plastered he gets to worrying over the fact that she's such a sweet little thing and he's so tough. He says he isn't good enough for her and he's going to write and tell her so. He actually sheds tears over it. Then we get to kidding him and tell him that she probably has grown into the wildest thing in town and he'll be too tame for her when he gets home. That makes him cry out in agony and then he wants to fight. He bores everyone to death talking about her all the time. Then he gets one more drink and tells us about the little widow at Malta that he used to give a little dual to when he was stationed there.

Springs pretends to get the two mixed up and Mac spends the rest of the evening trying to straighten it out. Mac admits in all seriousness that the widow's morals were not what they might be, but claims that the climate of Malta is responsible and then he admits that he was a bit insistent. Living here together the way we do, it doesn't take long to exhaust all the topics of conversation and unless we are talking shop we all know what everybody else is going to say. When we have a binge everybody makes exactly the same speech that they made before, but as long as our guests laugh, so do we.

Cal is just like a nigger. He can wear anybody's clothes and does. He never worries about anything and hasn't a nerve in his body. He'd be happy in a shell hole on iron rations. All he wants is to be left alone. He's got no ideas or ambitions beyond the next meal. He plays the piano as if he'd never heard of a score and he never knows himself what he's going to play next. But he can rag a piano like no one else on earth. He can play classical stuff but doesn't very often. It's too much trouble. The gunnery officer plays according to Hoyle and Cal sits down beside him and jazzes the treble. He's the best natural pilot we have. Takes his flying just like his bridge. Nigger says he has the smoothest hand on the stick he ever saw. He's all right until he starts to figure. He and Springs argue for two hours after every patrol. We are all getting so we can see pretty well in the air now but at first we had to use our imaginations to keep up with Nigger and Mac.

Mac had all his teeth knocked out in a Pup crash last year and the other morning before the dawn patrol he lost his false teeth. Gosh, he was funny. He couldn't talk at all and he couldn't go on the patrol because he was afraid he'd get shot down without them.

Springs is just the opposite of Cal. He worries more over things at home than if he was there. He was almost in tears the other day because he found out his father had shown one of his letters about. He said he hated not to write to his father—he felt it was his duty—but his father would show the letters about and make a fool of him no matter what he wrote.

I told him he was the fool to worry over it. He might as well be worrying over his great-grandfather or great-grandchildren.

June 13th

We have a steady job now escorting the Nines over to Zeebrugge and Bruges every morning while they bomb the submarine bases. Bish leads the whole squadron and we are just spoiling for a good fight. The Nines take a half hour start and we meet them at twelve thousand feet out at sea. Then we climb together up to fifteen and come in over the Dutch border and shoot back across Belgium wide open. We stay up above them and they drop their bombs and one machine stays behind to take pictures of the hits. We get all the Archie that was intended for them. There were some Fokkers up yesterday but we were too strong for them and they wouldn't fight. We can see the ships that the British sunk in the harbours at Zeebrugge and Ostend. It doesn't look to me as if they are completely blocked. It was certainly a stout effort. We hear that they are going to do it again. They have dismantled some of the submarines and are taking them out overland from Bruges.

There is an American Naval squadron at Dunkirk flying French machines. We ran into a couple of the pilots and had lunch with them at the Chapeau Rouge. We seem to be the only Americans in Europe that are really enjoying this war. All the others I have met seem to be having to work or sleep without sheets or eat out of mess kits or do something unpleasant to spoil their holiday.

June 14th

You can't appreciate the R. F. C. until you see a squadron on the move. We came back from a dose of Archie without suffering from his hate about seven o'clock and after a good breakfast I got tired of baseball and decided I'd take a nap. About ten my batman shook me and said, "Orders has come, sir, that we are to move at twelve o'clock." At twelve o'clock our baggage, transport, equipment and dogs left and at four we flew down to our new airdrome at St. Omer. We thought we might as well pick up a Hun on the way so had a squadron show.

Bish led and we crossed the lines at Wipers and worked on down south to the Forest of Nieppe but we didn't see anything. It was the wrong time of day. Early in the morning or late in the evening is best. That's our new beat, from Wipers to Nieppe. At one place near Hazebrouck, the ground for about three square miles is dull yellow in colour. That's where there has been a gas attack.

Our airdrome is an old French one on a plateau about three miles from St. Omer. They are expecting a big battle down here.

Our new quarters are very comfortable. We are up on a beautiful wooded hill overlooking the field and there's a pretty sylvan glade on the other side where we can lie in peace and snooze in the breeze. Not bad at all but there's no place to swim.

After our transport left, we decided we'd go for a last swim and borrowed a tender from 211 to take us over to the beach by Ft. Mardick. Randy came along and when he undressed he was certainly a sight. There's hardly a spot on his body that isn't cut or shot. He ought to be in a museum. His back and chest look like he was tattooed by one of those futurist artists.

The R.F.C. at Work
Aerial action at an altitude of two and a quarter miles between four British machines and nine German

We were out in the surf when we heard a terrible explosion and saw the smoke the other side of the fort. Before we could get out of the water, there were about four more. Randy yelled that the long range gun was shelling the fort and to get out of the water on account of the concussion. We didn't know what to do. I never felt so naked in my life, standing there with shells bursting two hundred yards away and the debris flying up a hundred feet. We grabbed our clothes and ran for the tender which was nearly a mile away. We beat all existing records getting there and jumped into the tender and told the driver to drive like hell away from the fort. Then he told us what the trouble was. The French were exploding a lot of German mines that the mine sweepers had brought in. The joke was on us.

June 16th
My new motor is a dud. It chewed up a valve but I got back to the drome all right.

We're worried about Mac. When he was seen last we were going down on nine Huns about fifteen miles the other side of the lines. He got away from them all right, I think, but it's three hours since we got back and there's no word of him yet. I guess he had engine trouble for there wasn't much of a scrap. If he only gets back across the lines! We are all rather nervous.

My dog has fleas.

June 17th
Mac was all right. He shot his own prop off but he got back across the lines and landed about twenty miles from here all O. K. He came back on the truck that went after his plane and brought a cow back with him, so we have our own dairy now. Rosie has been trying to milk his goat without success.

I got a paper from home and read a column by "Biddy Bye." She gives a "Loyalty Menu" for loyal housewives to serve poor starved patriots. It read like an à *la carte* menu at the Ritz before the war. I'd like to find the lady and shove her menu down her throat. Hope our "Loyal Ones" aren't getting thin and wasting away. This is in a military zone and food and licker are scarce. We have to send to Dunkirk for extra supplies.

Springs had a letter from Kelly and he's ready to come out and Bish is going to arrange for him to come to us.

We have another one of the Oxford Cadets with us, Rorison, who is assigned to B flight. He's from Wilmington, N. C. He's a serious youth and can figure out anything on paper with a slide rule.

We have another patrol to do and then Bish and Nigger and the three of us are going over to their old squadron to dinner. As it is one of the best squadrons at the front, it ought to be a cheery evening. Bish and Nigger were both flight commanders there last year.

I had no idea there was so much to learn about this game. When you get to the front, you are just starting. There's something new to learn about your game every flight and then there're the idiosyncrasies of the Hun to be studied with your ear to the ground as well as the geographical and meteorological conditions.

For instance, there's a Hun balloon that's rather close to the lines. They always pull down the others when they see us coming but they leave this one up. It looked like easy pickings and Springs and I asked Nigger if we couldn't drop down and get it some time when the wind was with us strong. Nigger said he'd investigate and that we'd better leave balloons alone until we were sent after them because they were very dangerous toys.

He got word from the brigade that this balloon is a dummy and is there as a decoy. About four Archie batteries have it ranged and instead of having a passenger basket, it's loaded up with amatol and as soon as some sucker dives on it, the Huns will explode it and that will be the last heard of him. And you have to come through the Archie barrage to get to it. Archie has no bite at all—all bark—but it's hard on the nervous system. This is certainly a nice friendly little war. The Canadians originated that balloon trick.

June 18th

It was a good party. I think we won as when we left their C. O. was doing a Highland Fling with a couple of table knives for swords. Coming back, we just got inside the gates of St. Omer when the Huns began to bomb it. And they were after the town too, no mistaking it. You should have seen us getting out of it. Not a light showing anywhere and crooked narrow streets. Our chauffeur didn't know the town very well and we all five were yelling at him at the same time. A bomb burst about a block from us and we climbed the curb twice in our haste.

We were in bad shape for the early patrol. It was pretty dud looking when we got up at four-thirty. Nigger said he didn't think the fog would lift and there wasn't much use going out. He went back to bed and told Springs to take the two of us up and do a safety first patrol if it cleared up enough for us to get off. It cleared up about six and we took off and worked up towards Wipers. Springs led us about five miles over between Wipers and the Forest of Nieppe, but we didn't see anything as there was still a pretty heavy fog. We got a lot of Archie but that was all. We had about given it up as a wash-out when we spotted a two-seater on the other side of Estaires. Springs waggled his wings and pointed and we waggled back that we thought it was a Hun too and then we went down with our motors wide open.

I warmed up my guns on the way down and was all ready. When Springs was about four hundred yards away and a thousand feet above him, the Hun turned and the observer opened fire on him as he came in close. Springs got underneath him and Cal came down and cut him off from the other side and made him turn back. I came straight down from above and he was right in position for me and I put in a good burst from both guns right into his cockpit. We were all firing and I could see my tracer going right into his fuselage. I almost ran him down and just as I levelled off and pulled up, the Hun burst into flames and went down in a dive. The pilot must have fallen on his stick and I saw him go down like a comet. As he hit the ground a pillar of flames and smoke shot up.

We were so low by that time that the machine guns and pom-poms on the ground opened fire on us and I had the pleasure of watching a few tracers go through my wings. We were too low for Archie.

Nigger said he'd sent us out to do a safe and sane patrol and not to win the war before breakfast. He bawled Springs out and said that by the law of average we should all have been killed. We didn't pay any attention to him because our heads were all swelled up over getting a flamer.

There was no use all three of us claiming the Hun and we were going to just one of us take him. Cal and Springs were going to let me have him but Canning who saw the fight from a distance put in a claim too, because he said he was firing at him, so we all took one fourth each. If Canning had kept out one of us would have got credit for one whole Hun. Fractions don't mean anything. But as long as Canning was coming in any way we might as well all stay in. But I know I got that Hun. Springs and Cal were firing at him too but I could see my tracer going right into his fuselage.

Bish got one about noon and Lady Mary went out and bumped off another one.

MacDonald has been missing since yesterday.

June 19th

We have got to get up every morning at three from now on and go down to the hangars and stand by and be ready to leave the ground at five minutes' notice. That means we have to keep our motors running to keep them warmed up. The Hun is supposed to be going to start a push any moment and everything is ready for the counter attack. We have bomb racks fitted to our fuselage and we carry four twenty-pound copper bombs to use ground straffing. They think the Hun is going to push in front of Hazebrouck and try to pinch off the Salient. We aren't going to give an inch of ground but are going to start a counter attack and push back.

We had a squadron show and Thompson, Trapp, Lady Mary and myself had to go down and reconnoitre the road from Bailleul to Armentières at a couple of hundred feet looking for signs of troop movements. To protect us, were Nigger, Cal, Springs and Mac at one thousand feet and the rest of the squadron were at five thousand.

We flew down the road the whole way and back again but didn't see much except a lot of tracer bullets coming up at us. And I saw some flaming onions up close. They are nice little things—a lot of phosphorus balls that come up in front of you like a swarm of bees, and if you run into them, it's goodnight!

I saw Thompson get hit. He landed and turned over. I think he's alive as the machine certainly was under control. Trapp is missing but I didn't see him at all. Lady Mary found a balloon and shot it up and set fire to it on the ground. I got a few holes scattered about the plane but nothing serious. If the Huns are going to attack there, they are mighty quiet about it. I dropped my four little bombs on a truck train.

The top flight got into a dogfight and Bish dropped a Fokker. A flight lost a man.

June 20th

MacDonald is back. He got lost coming back from a patrol in the fog and landed a hundred miles from here. He made sure he wasn't in Germany all right. He was out of gas when he ceased to flee and it took two days to get a truck down there to him. A Frenchman entertained him royally at his *château* and Mac fell in love with his beautiful niece and kept the truck waiting an extra day. Moral: Always pick a good place to get lost. He brought a mangy looking cur back with him. Our menagerie is growing.

Heard that Joe Trees and Dick Reed have been killed.

A LURID END ABOVE THE CLOUDS

The colonel came over and congratulated us on our reconnaissance. He's a brother to one of the flight commanders at London Colney, Capt. Cairns, the fellow with one leg. He's with 74 now.

June 21st

Bish has been recalled to England to help organise the Canadian Flying Corps. Before he left he went up to have a final look at the war. He ran into five Hun scouts. He picked off the last one and the two in front collided when they did a climbing turn to get back of him. Then he got another one and on the way back he ran into a two-seater and got it. Pretty good morning. His score is now seventy-two! That's something for the boys to shoot at. Next to him is McCudden and then Mannock. We all went down to Boulogne to see him off and had a big champagne lunch.

An American Division was landing at Boulogne and these boys certainly have got funny ideas. They think they are crusaders and talk like headlines. They are full of catch-phrases and ideals. We talked to a bunch of them in the bar. They think they are on the way to a Sunday School picnic.

The Japanese think if they get killed in battle they will go to heaven. They've got nothing on these boys. They think they are going to get a golden harp just for enlisting.

One of the boys asked me where the Red Light district was. I told him that if God would paint the moon red, then Europe would be properly labelled.

There were two officers at the next table to us at lunch. One of them saw my R. F. C. wings and wanted to know why I was wearing a crown above my wings. I told him because I was a qualified R. F. C. pilot.

"Well," says he, "you can wear a crown if you want to. But as for me,—I can't get enough eagles on. I just want eagles all over me."

They had on funny belts. I said, "Where'd you get the funny Sam Browne belts?"

"Sam Browne belts?" said one of them. "These ain't Sam Browne belts. These is Liberty belts!!!"

That gave the squadron a laugh. They've been kidding us about it ever since. They call us the Liberty Boys and want to see our eagles.

We came back and had a patrol to do at five. Nigger took off down wind and we all followed him. Springs and Cal got to bouncing before they had flying-speed and smashed their undercarriages but they didn't go over on their backs. Springs nearly landed on top of Cal and just did bounce over him. Mac broke a bracing wire but came on with us.

June 22nd

I got up this morning feeling like a weekend in the city though I had no reason to. I drank too much coffee before going up and I'm as nervous as a kitten now. Must be getting the Woofits.

I had rather a surprise yesterday. I was some distance back of the patrol and saw a Hun two-seater about three miles across the lines so went for him. I expected about thirty seconds at close quarters under his tail and then to watch him go down in flames. It looked like cold meat. I started my final dive about one thousand feet above him and opened fire at one hundred yards.

Then I got a surprise. I picked the wrong Hun. Just as I opened fire, he turned sharply to the left and I was doing about two hundred so couldn't turn but had to overshoot and half roll back. As I half rolled on top of him, he half rolled too and when I did an Immelman, he turned to the right and forced me on the outside arc and gave his observer a good shot at me as I turned back the other way to cut him off from the other side. I fired a burst from my turn but my shots went wild so pulled up and half rolled on top of him again and opened fire from immediately above and behind. He stalled before I could get a burst in and side-slipped away from me but gave me a no-deflection shot at him when he straightened out. I didn't have to make any allowance for his speed or direction and his observer was shooting at me.

The observer dropped down in his cockpit so I suppose I killed him. But I couldn't get the pilot. He put the plane in a tight spiral and I couldn't seem to get in position properly. Cal and Tiny Dixon came in about that time and everybody was shooting at him from all angles. I know he didn't have any motor because he came down very slowly and didn't attempt to manoeuvre. We were firing from every conceivable angle but we couldn't seem to hit the tank or the pilot and every now and then he'd take a crack at me with his front gun when I'd try him head on.

He was a stout fellow, a good fighter and I hope he is still alive. If his observer had been any good I wouldn't be writing this now. He hit one of my front spars and that was all. I left him at one hundred feet as my engine was overheating and was sputtering and I've had enough machine gun fire from the ground to last me for a while and I don't like field guns from directly in the rear. Accidents will happen. So I started back and joined the patrol. Archie simply went mad.

The infantry reported the fight and said that the Hun was under control when he went down the other side of Kemmel Hill.

Then we all came down low over the trenches later and had a sham battle among ourselves. Nigger and I dove furiously on each other just back of No Man's Land and Springs and Cal and Mac rolled and looped desperately trying to get on one another's tails. The boys in the trenches must have enjoyed it. None of the Huns fired at us at all and even Archie the Avenger left us alone though we were within range. Then we spied some field sports four or five miles back of our lines and we started for them. They were very appreciative as they stopped the game to watch and wave at us. Must have been a Canadian Division for they had a baseball diamond. Mac ran his wheels on it.

We've gotten quite good at stunting in close formation. We fly very close together and can loop and roll in formation. Nigger signals and loops straight over. Mac and Cal loop with right rudder on and Springs and I loop with left rudder. That spreads us out and then we come back in close as we come out of the dive. Nigger puts his motor at half throttle so we can pick up our places. When we roll, Nigger and Cal and Mac roll to the right and Springs and I roll to the left.

A photographer with a movie camera came over last week and got some movies of us doing it. We fly up close enough to get our wings between the front man's wings and tail.

June 23rd

We were out on patrol this morning and just across the lines we saw a two-seater. Nigger was leading and signalled to us to follow and dove after him. It was a pretty silver L.V.G. and he turned and Nigger missed his first dive. The Hun circled and I overshot and half rolled to make sure of him. Springs missed too and Cal, who had turned higher up, came right down on his tail as Mac went under. Cal got him and the Hun turned over on his back and went down and crashed into the ruins of Sailly. Archie was right put out about it but was nowhere near us. The gunners are rotten down here.

We climbed up high and about a half an hour later saw about thirty machines in the sky at different levels. Six machines of ours were in the middle layer and we saw them dive on the lower ones. Then I saw one of the Huns from above dive vertically for three thousand feet and flatten out and open fire right on the tail of one of our machines. Most wonderful sight I ever saw. I wouldn't have believed it possible. That lad was good. But one of our machines jumped on his tail and while he was firing too long at the front machine, our plane got him and he went down in loose spin.

About that time, we reached the fight on a long dive and went in. There were plenty of Huns to go around and there were Huns diving and firing all about us. Worst dog fight I can imagine. Everybody was firing short bursts at everybody else. We had the advantage coming in on top and were having a fine time. Suddenly everybody pulled out and Archie opened up. A new bunch of ten Huns came up and we went back in again but there was too much confusion. Nigger and Springs went down on a black Pfaltz and got him. He went into a spin and crashed into a wood. The other S. E.s were from 74 and they got two Huns and lost one man.

The general came over and had tea with us and asked us who we wanted for C. O. He wanted to send us McCudden but we don't want him. He gets Huns himself but he doesn't give anybody else a chance at them. The rest of the squadron objected because he was once a Tommy and his father was a sergeant major in the old army. I couldn't see that that was anything against him but these English have great ideas of caste. We asked for Micky Mannock who is a flight commander in 74. He's got around sixty Huns and was at London Colney when we were in January. He wanted to take the three of us out with him in February but we weren't through at Turnberry. They say that he's the best patrol leader at the front—plans his squadron shows a day in advance and rehearses them on the ground. He plans every manoeuvre like a chess player and has every man at a certain place at a certain time to do a certain thing, and raises merry hell if any one falls down on his job.

74 is a stout outfit. We knew them all at London Colney where they mobilised. The other day, Grid Caldwell, the C. O. and Capt. Cairns collided in a fight. Cairns got down under control but the whole squadron saw Grid go spinning down. That night they had a wake and all got drunk and turned it into a celebration. About midnight Grid walked in. They thought they were seeing a ghost as he was all bloody and his clothes were torn to pieces. He had set his tail stabilizer and gotten out of his seat and crawled out on the wing and gotten the plane out of the spin. His aileron control was jammed and part of his wing tip was gone but he balanced it down and landed

it this side of the trenches by reaching in and pulling the stick back before he hit. The plane turned over and threw him into a clump of bushes. It had taken him ever since to get back as he crashed about thirty miles away. So he resumed command and took charge of the drinking and when the squadron went out for the dawn patrol, he led it. Then he went to the hospital.

Mannock trained Taffy Jones who was a pupil with us at London Colney. Taffy has eight Huns now and Mick says he's the best shot in the squadron. Mick has marvellous eyesight though he only has one eye. He's to get two weeks' leave and then come to us. In the meantime, Baker is in command.

June 24th

We found nine Hun scouts yesterday and dove on them but they wouldn't fight and ran for home. We chased them but couldn't catch them. Something funny about that. It must be a new type of plane and they were just practicing. They were fast whatever they were. My motor got to acting funny and the water began to boil. It cut out a few times and I just did get back and landed between Kemmel and Popheringhe in a big field that was mostly shell holes. There were some American troops up there of the 30th Division and they helped me to get some water and get going when it cooled off. It got me home but didn't run any too well. They have retimed it but unless it turns up better I am going to ask for a new one. These Hispano Vipers are fine when they are all right but the slightest trouble bawls them all up. Springs was messing around over by Messines and flushed a two-seater out of the clouds and got him. Tiny Dixon was firing at him too, so they halved him. Randall knocked down a high two-seater and Hall is missing.

We have a new pilot to take Thompson's place, Capt. Webster, a quiet, reserved fellow. He's not a captain in the flying corps but in his infantry regiment. When anyone transfers from their regiment to the flying corps they come in as second lieutenants but keep their honorary rank in their regiment and draw the pay of that rank. Then after they transfer, if they prove they're good and get a flight, then they become temporary captains and rank as captains in the flying corps and draw a captain's pay but keep their old regimental rank. We have seven captains now but only three of them rank as such and those are all lieutenants in their regiments. There's one man who is known in the gazette as, "Lieutenant, temporary brigadier general." He must

CHASING THE GERMAN SCOUTS

be good! That's the right system. In our army, if a major transfers to the aviation corps he comes in as a major and bosses men who have been flying for years and know more about it than he will ever know. I don't know who's going to do our fighting but I know who's going to get all the rank and all the medals.

June 25th

Springs and I flew up to Dunkirk to get some champagne yesterday. We landed at Petit Snythe and found an American squadron was being organised there, the 17th. Sam Eckert is C. O. and Tipton and Hamilton and Newhall are the flight commanders. They've got Le Rhone Camels and may the Lord make His face to smile upon them because they are going to need more than mortal guidance.

There was a brand new American major up there in a new Cadillac named Fowler. We turned our nose up at him but he insisted on being nice. His brother, who was killed at Issoudon, went to Princeton with Springs so they got to chewing the rag. He was so new the tags were still on his gold leaves and he didn't know how to salute,—saluted like an Englishman. When he heard why we'd come up he insisted on driving us into Dunkirk in his Cadillac. We got the champagne and he insisted on taking us into the Chapeau Rouge for a drink. We shot down a couple of bottles of champagne and he was all right, we thought, even for a new Kiwi. He kept on asking such simple questions. He wanted to know all about how our patrols were led and if we led any ourselves and how we got along with the British.

He acted awfully simple, just like an ordinary U. S. major, and we did the best we could to enlighten him as to the proper method of picking cold meat and bringing most of our men back. His ideas were all wrong and we concluded that he must have been reading some of the books by the boys at home. We got a snoutful and he brought us back to the field and we invited him down to dinner at 85 and then he left. We asked Sam what Fowler had done to get a gold leaf and he told us that Fowler had been out with the British since 1914 and had the Military Cross and had done about five hundred hours flying over the lines. The joke is certainly on us. But he ought to know better than to fill a pilot full of champagne and then ask him how good he is. To tell the truth I think we were very modest. And why doesn't he wear wings or his decorations? If I had the M. C. all the rules that Pershing can make couldn't keep it off my chest.

I heard up there that about fifteen of our boys have been killed.

Hooper and Douglas are among them.

We went down to have dinner with Nigger's brother at the 2nd A. D. They received us with open bottles. Those boys must have been in training for the event. That's the third of Nigger's brothers that has tried to uphold the family honour.

I heard a funny story down there. The Germans took Lille and the Allies held Armentières. For a long time, they continued to run the factories in Armentières on electricity that came from Lille. A Frenchman was kept to run the power plant by the Germans and he didn't cut Armentières off. It was several months before he was caught.

June 27th

Springs is missing. He and MacGregor and Inglis were out this morning on the dawn patrol. Mac was leading and spotted a two-seater over Armentières. They went after him and had to chase him a bit further. Mac got to him first and missed his dive. Springs got under him and stayed there. The Hun stalled up and the observer was shooting down at Springs when Mac got back in position and got him. That was the last seen of Springs. Inglis says he saw some smoke coming out of his fuselage when the observer was shooting at him. It's afternoon now and no word has come from him so I guess he's cooked. *Requiescat in pace*, as he would say! I've got to go on a balloon straff now.

June 29th

Springs is back. He brought back a school of pink porpoises and a couple of funny stories. His guns jammed when he went under the two-seater and he was trying to clear the stoppages when the observer hit his oil pipe. His motor didn't stop at once but brought him back a little way before the bearings melted. He glided back just across the lines and crashed down wind in a machine gun emplacement. His face is a mess where the butt of his Vickers gun knocked a hole in his chin and he got a crack on the top of his head and a pair of black eyes. One of the longerons tore his flying suit right up the back and just grazed his skin and removed his helmet. Some Tommies fished him out and sorted the ruins.

He says the first thing he thought of when he came to was his teeth on account of Mac. He ran his tongue around his mouth and couldn't find any front teeth. He let out a yell.

"What's the matter, sir?" a Tommy asked him.

"My teeth," sobs Springs, "they're all gone!"

"Oh, no they ain't, sir," says the obliging Tommy, "here they are, sir!" and with that he reaches down and pulls his lips off his teeth. His teeth were all right, they were just on the outside of his face.

There wasn't any anaesthetic up there but somebody brought a bottle of cognac. Every time he'd try to take a drink of it, it would all run out of the hole in his chin. So he spent the morning with his head tilted back and his mouth open while an Irish *padre* poured the cognac down his throat for him. He said after a little while the pain let up but they brought him another bottle so he kept up the treatment. He got back into the Forest of Nieppe and telephoned back to the wing that afternoon for a tender to come and get him. Then some doc up there gave him a shot of anti-tetanus serum.

The tender came up after him and they started back, stopping at every *estaminet* on the way. He didn't have on a uniform, just his pyjamas under his flying suit but had two or three hundred *francs* in his suit so they would stop and he'd buy champagne for the mechanics to pour down his throat. They got back here about dark, all of them tight as sausage skins. We had a celebration and made some strawberry julep to pour down his throat and we all managed to light up. Then someone noticed that his face needed a bit of hemstitching so we took him down to the Duchess of Sutherland's hospital in the woods below here. The doctor down there seemed to think the crack on his head was serious. We were in a hot room and none of us felt too good.

The doc told him to stand up and close his eyes and then open them. Of course he couldn't focus his eyes. I could have told the doc that. Then he told him to close them again and keep them closed. He swayed a couple of times and then keeled over on the floor and passed out of the picture.

"Ah, ha," says the doc, "I thought so! Concussion of the brain! We'll have to keep him in bed for a while." So they sewed up his face and he didn't know a thing about it next day. The doc says we can't see him for a few days as he must be kept absolutely quiet. I'd like to see them do it.

June 30th

We got into a dogfight this morning with the new brand of Fokkers and they certainly were good. They had big red stripes on the fuselage diagonally so they must be Richthofen's old circus. There were five of us and we ran into five Fokkers at fifteen thousand feet. We both started climbing, of course. And they outclimbed us. We climbed up to twenty thousand five hundred and couldn't get any higher. We were practically stalled and these Fokkers went right over our heads and got between us and the lines. They didn't want to dogfight but tried to pick off our rear men. Inglis and Cal were getting a pretty good thrill when we turned back and caught one Hun napping. He half rolled slowly and we got on his tail. Gosh, it's unpleasant fighting at that altitude. The slightest movement exhausts you, your engine has no pep and splutters; it's hard to keep a decent formation, and you lose five hundred feet on a turn.

The other Huns came in from above and it didn't take us long to fight down to twelve thousand. We put up the best fight of our lives but these Huns were just too good for us. Cal got a shot in his radiator and went down and Webster had his tail plane shot to bits and his elevator control shot away. He managed to land with his stabilizer wheel but cracked up. I don't know what would have happened if some Dolphins from 84 hadn't come up and the Huns beat it. I think we got one that went down in a spin while Cal was shooting at it but we couldn't see it crash.

I got to circling with one Hun, just he and I, and it didn't take me long to find out that I wasn't going to climb above this one. He began to gain on me and then he did something I've never heard of before. He'd be circling with me and he'd pull around and point his nose at me and open fire and just hang there on his prop and follow me around with his tracer. All I could do was to keep on turning the best I could. If I'd straightened out he'd have had me cold as he already had his sights on me. If I had tried to hang on my prop that way, I'd have gone right into a spin. But this fellow just hung right there and sprayed me with lead like he had a hose. They have speeded up guns too. All I could do was to watch his tracer and kick my rudder from one side to the other to throw his aim off. This war isn't what it used to be. Nigger has noted the improvement in the Huns and is awful thoughtful.

We went to see Springs this afternoon and he seems to be doing all right. He's got lips like a nigger minstrel's and a mouthful of thread and a couple of black eyes. We took him a couple of bottles of champagne but he didn't need it as they serve it to him there. Things have been sort of quiet at the front lately in this sector and there were only three of them in there. One is a brigadier general who had been wounded seven times before this last shot in his leg. He and Springs were full of champagne and have a bar rigged up in a tent outside. The third is a Chink from a labour battalion who has been parted from his appendix forcibly.

There are about eighteen nurses there and it is the custom for all the nurses from the Duchess down to walk by and ask each patient how he feels each morning. The general says if they just had short skirts on and would whistle he'd applaud and join the chorus. Springs's face is going to be all right because they sewed it up from the inside.

Mac made a date to call on a pretty little nurse. That boy is a fast worker. I'll bet he gets sick in a few days.

July 1st

I hear that Mathews is now a member of the sadder-but-wiser club. He dove straight down on a two-seater and the observer didn't do a thing but shoot the front end of his plane full of holes. He got back to the lines but cracked up and lit on his neck. These boys will learn some day that one two-seater can lick one scout any time unless the scout can stick under his blind spot. But these Hun two-seaters haven't got any blind spot. The long ones have a hole in the bottom of the fuselage and they can shoot down at you and these new ones have a double tail and are so short that the observer can stand up and fire right down at you while the pilot simply pulls up in a stall.

And you can't take them from a front angle because the observer can traverse his guns over the top of the upper wing. Of course, if there're two of you, that is another story, but it takes two scouts to lick a good two-seater. These Bristol pilots say they can lick two scouts. They fight them like scouts and the observer simply guards the tail. If you want to go to heaven, the easiest way I know is to dive on a two-seater. We all do it and take a chance but the percentage of gentlemen who get cured of it is mounting.

July 2nd

Springs came back last night. He walked back in red silk pyjamas and a pair of fur flying boots. The doctor decided he was nutty and wanted to send him back to England. They took his clothes away from him so he lit out like he was. The reason the doc was so sure he was crazy was that he overheard a telephone conversation. Major Fowler's adjutant called up to tell him that he'd been made a flight commander in the new American squadron up at Dunkirk. Springs said he didn't want to be a flight commander and he didn't want to go to any American squadron. He told the adjutant to give the job to someone else quick. The doc overheard him refusing promotion and was sure he was cuckoo. The doc came over after him but we persuaded him that

Springs wasn't nutty and after we filled him full of julep he finally said he could stay but that he mustn't fly for a week. We got hold of Col. Cairns and he said he'd arrange for him to stay here and report him unfit for duty. But G. H. Q. called up later and said that he had to go anyway so he's to go up to Dunkirk tomorrow. It's either that or back to the hospital and the doc will sure send him home. But he isn't in any shape to take charge of anything.

July 5th
Cal and I flew up to Petit Snythe yesterday for a baseball game between the mechanics of the 17th and the 148th U. S. squadrons. We couldn't stay long as we had to get back for a patrol.

Mort Newhall is C. O. of the 148th and Bim Oliver and Henry Clay are the other flight commanders besides Springs. Springs made some horrible punch that knocked out everybody that got a smell of it. He wants Cal and me to join his flight and Fowler said he'd arrange it but we said nothing doing. I don't want to fly Camels and certainly not Clerget Camels. I told him I'd crown him eternally if he got me put on those little popping firecrackers. My neck isn't worth much but I want an even break.

Bobby was there and kept in the limelight by getting hit by a foul ball. They say that his latest stunt was a bear. His squadron had been working pretty hard and the colonel gave them a holiday to rest up. Instead of letting his squadron rest, he decided that they ought to practice moving. So he made them pack up everything on the place and load it on the lorries and move it down the road ten miles. Then he drove up magnificently in the squadron car and inspected them and gave orders to them to move back again and unpack. They were so mad they wanted to kill him. Imagine a practice move!

He was a colonel once but he got demoted for one of his celebrated stunts! When the Hun broke through on the Somme in March, the infantry retreated so fast that the mechanics on the airdrome didn't have time to get away and joined the infantry and fought with them. At one place they weren't able to save the planes because of a fog. Bobby was in command of a wing, and he decided that he ought to prepare for such an emergency and ought to train his mechanics as infantrymen. So he got rifles for them and had regular drill. That part was all right and met with the approval of the brigadier. But he decided that he ought to have a sham battle as well. He had two squadrons entrenched along the canal at the far side of the airdrome, and then he had two other squadrons representing Huns to attack them. He was to be the hero of the occasion. About that time some inspecting general happened by and saw Bobby, with sword waving, tight as a tick, dashing madly across the airdrome at the head of the charge. He won the battle but lost his job. At least that's the story I heard. I'll say this for him. If licker was ammunition he'd be a field marshal.

There's quite a few of the old Oxford gang up there. Clay, Oliver, Curtis, Fulford, Forster, Whiting, Ziztell, Kindley, Clements, Knox, Hamilton, Campbell, Dixon, Goodnow, Dorsey, Avery and Desson. Stew Welch is over at 211 with Bonnalie.

July 7th

The new Fokkers are giving us hell. A flight lost two men yesterday and Webster got all shot up again. He doesn't consider the day well spent unless his mechanics have a few holes to patch.

Capt. Baker, who is acting C. O. until Mannock gets here, put Springs in for a decoration, the D. F. C. which is the Royal Air Force's Military Cross. The colonel sent the citation back. He said he was a good fellow but he'd only gotten four Huns and that wasn't worth a decoration. But just think what would have happened if he'd been down on the French front with an American squadron! He'd have gotten a D. S. C. and a *Croix de Guerre* for each Hun.

I flew up to see him yesterday and he sure was a funny sight. He's all swollen up like a poisoned pup and is red as a beet and broken out all over—inside as well. The anti-tetanus serum was sour and it has poisoned him.

John Goad is dead. He was shot down in flames flying a Bristol Fighter. When the flames got too hot he turned the machine upside down and jumped.

July 10th

Springs and Oliver came down for dinner the other night. Gosh, they were funny telling about their Camels. They had a Crossley car with a general's veil on it to keep the wind off the back seat and were certainly hot. The squadron has both British and American transport so Mort has a Cadillac and the flight commanders have the Crossley and all the rest have sidecars. Springs is a wreck. He's blind in one eye and the other one isn't much good. He's got haemorrhage of the retina, whatever that is, but the doc says it will clear up in a little while. He's also got cirrhosis of the liver from that serum. He'll be a fine flight commander. Between all that and the stiff neck he ought

Shot down in flames after duel with large German bi-plane

to be one of their best assets. Bim says they are the tin woodman and the scarecrow from the land of Oz and they are looking for Dorothy to put them together again. They kept us laughing all evening and everybody got plastered.

Mannock has arrived to take charge all rigged out as a major with some new barnacles on his ribbons, and he certainly is keen. He got us all together in the office and outlined his plans and told each one what he expected of them. He's going to lead one flight and act as a decoy. Nigger and Randy are going to lead the other two. We ought to be able to pay back these Fokkers a little we owe them.

I hear that Deetjen is gone. They're going so fast now that I can't keep track of who's dead and who's alive. I guess I'll find out before long though. I heard in Boulogne that Alan Winslow is missing.

July 11th
One of our dashing young airmen, who, according to his own story had done innumerable deeds of valour but had never been caught in that act, changed his tune yesterday. He landed after he'd been out alone and his plane had about fifty holes in it. His altimeter and Aldis sight were both hit. He was as limp as a rag and had to be assisted to his quarters. There he remained as sick as a dog for two days. When questioned about what happened to him he would get hysterical and sick at his stomach again. The wing doctor came over to see him and sent him to hospital though there's nothing wrong with him except he's badly frightened. That's the last of his illustrious career. He'll go home and write a book on the war now. I always did think he was yellow.

What I believe happened to him is this. He's been telling so many lies about what he's been doing that he believed some of them himself and decided he'd go out and really have a look at a Hun. The first ones he saw shot him up and his constitution couldn't stand the fright. One thing about this game out here: those that are good are awfully good, and those that are bad are awfully sour. Thank God the Huns have the same trouble. Six real good determined pilots could shoot down twenty of this kind that have business to attend to after the war.

July 18th
Mannock led a show yesterday and gave us all heart failure. He was leading the bottom flight with three men and found ten Fokkers and played them for fifteen minutes. At any moment it looked as if we were all going to get shot down but Mannock knew what he was

about and kept the top flight up in the sun. He sucked the Huns into where he wanted them and went right under them. They knew there was a flight above up in the sun so only five of them came down. Then Randy and three men came down on them just as they got to Mannock, and instead of their top five getting the cold meat as they expected, Nigger, Mac, Cal, Inglis and myself leapt on them so that our eight below had a picnic with the bottom five Huns. They got two of the bottom ones and Mac got one of the top ones that tried to get down to join the fight below.

MacDonald got his wish and got hit in the arm and is now in the Duchess's hospital with the world in his lap. Lucky dog. I'm willing to compromise with the Lord on an arm or leg any time. I'll spot Him one and shoot Him for the other. We are certainly getting away with some good patrols. Mick is master. He has taken Cal with him and is going to train him as deputy leader. If the Huns would just figure with Cal instead of fighting with him he'd argue himself to Berlin. He takes his fighting just like he takes his bridge. By the time he and Mick are ready to go into a fight they know what the Huns had for breakfast.

Tiny Dixon and Canning have both been promoted and sent to other squadrons as flight commanders. Dixon ought to make a good one.

July 20th

Mannock is dead, the greatest pilot of the war. But his death was worthy of him. Inglis had been doing a lot of fighting but had never gotten a Hun. But he tried hard and Mannock told him that he would take him out alone and get him a Hun. So just the two of them went out late in the afternoon. Mannock picked up a two-seater over Estaires and went down after him. Mannock has a special method of attacking a two-seater. He takes them from the front at an angle and then goes under them if he misses his first burst. It is very hard to do but is unquestionably the best method. Instead of going under and getting him for himself, he held his fire and turned the Hun and held him for Inglis. Inglis got him and they started back but they were down low. Mannock got hit by machine gun fire from the ground just like Richthofen and dove right on into the ground. Inglis went back and flew right down to the ground and saw the wreck and is sure he's dead.

Mannock is the only man I've known who really hates the Hun and he certainly does. He wants to kill every man that was born in Germany. He was a member of Parliament from Ireland before the war and quite a politician. He seems to hold the Germans responsible for the yellow cowardly contemptible part that Ireland has played in the war. He certainly did cuss the Germans and their Irish sympathizers. He told us if we ever let a German get away alive that we could have killed, he'd shoot us himself. He was also the most accomplished after dinner speaker I ever heard.

We've had the two finest C. O.'s that the flying corps had and the general came over and asked us who we wanted next. We are going to get Billy Crowe. He's not so much of a pilot but he ought to fit in with this outfit. A couple of weeks ago the wing had a party in Dieppe. There were three majors down there in one car, Crowe, Atkinson, and Foggin. Coming home, Crowe insisted on driving the car and he hit a tree going too fast in the dark. Atkinson and Foggin were killed. Crowe was court-martialled and found guilty of driving a car against orders and reduced to a captain for a month. As additional punishment they are going to send him to us. We must have a swell reputation.

Tubby Ralston had a dud bus and they wouldn't give him a new one so he decided he'd crash it deliberately. He picked out a good place to do it and went down and pancaked. He crashed it all right and nearly killed himself doing it.

Loghran has been killed. He was at Hounslow when we first went there.

July 23rd

I have learned many things, especially that *discretion is the better part of valour*. And in this game, not only the better part, but about ninety-nine *per cent* of it. When there are more than two Huns above you and your immediate vicinity is full of lead, well, my boy, it is high time to go home. Never mind trying to shoot down any of them. Go home and try again tomorrow. How do you go home? You are far in Hunland and you are lonesome. If you put your nose down and run for home, you will never live to tell it. All the Huns will take turn about shooting at you until you look like a sieve. These new Fokkers can dive as fast as we can.

First you must turn, bank ninety degrees and keep turning. They can't keep their sights on you. Watch the sun for direction. Now there's one on your right—shoot at him. Don't try to hit him—just spray him—for if you try to hold your sight on him you'll have to fly straight and give the others a crack at you. But you put the wind up him anyway and he turns. Quick, turn in the opposite direction. He's out of it for a moment. Now there's another one near you. Try it on him—it works! Turn again, you are between them and the lines. Now go for it, engine full on, nose down!

Two of them are still after you—tracer getting near again. Pull up, zoom and sideslip and if necessary, turn and spray them again. Now make another dive for home and repeat when necessary. If your wings don't fall off and you are gaining on them, pull up a little. Ah, there's Archie, that means they are behind you—*woof*—that one was close—you now have another grey hair—they've been watching you—better zigzag a bit. You can laugh at Archie, he's a joke compared to machine guns. You dodge him carefully and roll in derision as you cross the lines and hasten home for tea—that is if you know where it is. That is discretion—many a man has gotten one out of a fight only to lose to the others who have nothing to do but shoot him down at leisure.

July 28th
McCudden the great has been killed. He was taking off in an S. E. and he hit a tree. He'd just gotten back from England and had been flying with a light load over there. He forgot that he had four bombs on now and a full load of ammunition and he pulled up too steep. I guess he deserves a lot of credit. His brother was shot and is a prisoner.

I can't write much these days. I'm too nervous. I can hardly hold a pen. I'm all right in the air, as calm as a cucumber, but on the ground I'm a wreck and I get panicky. Nobody in the squadron can get a glass to his mouth with one hand after one of these decoy patrols except Cal and he's got no nerve,—he's made of cheese. But some nights we both have nightmares at the same time and Mac has to get up and find his teeth and quiet us. We don't sleep much at night. But we get tired and sleep all afternoon when there's nothing to do.

I got shot up by a damn two-seater yesterday and then got dived on by a couple of ambitious Fokkers. My tail plane looked like a Swiss cheese. This war gets more dangerous every day. And now this colonel has gotten bloodthirsty and wants some balloons. He's welcome to them. It means in addition to other things that we will carry flatnosed buckingham to set the balloons on fire and if we get shot down in Hunland they will shoot us at once on the ground if they find any of it in our guns. It's dirty stuff and the phosphorus in it burns you so that the wound will never heal. But the Huns use it all the time so I don't see why we shouldn't too. Cal picked one of them out of his spar the other day and there's no question as to what it was because it kept burning and you could smell the phosphorus and see by the hole it made that it was flatnosed. It's not softnosed—that's dum-dum and is barred by the Hague treaty. I don't think either side has ever used any of that. I understand that the British have an enormous quantity of it and are ready to use it if the Huns ever start. I carry a belt arranged with one round of tracer and one round of buckingham and one round plain when I am expecting to go down on a balloon. Then I am ready for anything. Since I set fire to that two-seater with plain tracer I am perfectly content with it but I guess buckingham is surer.

July 31st

We saved Springs's bacon today. He and four little Camels were over by Roulers at nine thousand feet. Some Fokkers chased away his top patrol—they can't get above fifteen thousand with these Clergets; and then took their time to finish him off. The five Fokkers were above just ready to attack and in spite of that he went down on a balloon. The Fokkers went down on the Camels and we came up just at that point and leapt on them. We had a merry little dogfight. Imagine these poor benighted Camels wandering about Hunland and going down on a balloon with no top protection! Can you beat that! Why you can't even tie it! It turned out to be another dummy and they got a regular bath in Archie and pom-poms. 17 and 148 may be awfully good, I guess they are, but they can't get away with that sort of stuff. Springs called up later to thank us and confirmed a Hun for Nigger. He said it was his twenty-second birthday today but his next would be his thirty-third as he had aged ten years today. I talked to him and asked him what sort of a bloody fool had he turned out to be. He said he wasn't leading that patrol. His deputy flight commander was leading it and was trying to show him a good time. I told him he'd better lead himself even if he was blind in both eyes. At least he's got a head.

Poor old 74 took an awful beating yesterday. Cairns was killed and two others. He had a wing shot off.

We don't get a chance to scrap on this side of the lines often or even within ten miles of the lines but one of these new Fokkers came over after a balloon and A flight nailed him after he got two and was trying to get back. We went up to see it. They have the new motor in them—the B. M. W., I think it's called. It's a lot better than the old Mercedes. I know that without seeing one on the ground. It's a beautiful plane,—has a fuselage made of welded steel tubing and has an extra lifting surface on the undercarriage.

August 8th

Springs flew down this afternoon for tea. He's still all shot to pieces but has been leading patrols right along and got a Fokker the other day over Ostend. He said it was pure self-defence. The doc thinks he's got ulcer of the stomach and he's on a licker allowance. He claims he can drink all right but he can't eat. That's a new disease. They must have a great outfit in 148. They are all first lieutenants and every one bawls everybody else out to suit themselves. And they have about six different bosses and get orders from all over the world. And they all hate Camels except Clay who wants to do like Tipton and win the war before breakfast. Springs got a couple of cases of port from His Lordship's wine-merchant and he brought down a couple of bottles to us. Longton took his Camel up and did things with it that I didn't know any machine would do. Longton has been decorated with the A. F. C. for developing a two-seater Camel last year. What I can't see is why he didn't come out on Camels if he's so good on them. His prize pupil didn't last long.

Jerry Pentland was over the other night for dinner. He's a flight commander in 84. He was on crutches as a two-seater hit him in the foot. We called him Achilles and kidded the life out of him about going through Gallipoli and then coming to France and getting hit by a two-seater. Jerry swears that he was at twenty-two thousand. No wonder we can't get up to these high Rumplers. But a Dolphin will go higher than that if you don't freeze first.

24 squadron got caught out by a bunch of these new Fokkers and got shot up badly. They had to have some men with experience so we sent over Capt. Caruthers and Rorison.

August 11th

Again I've got that feeling, gee, it's great to be alive! The last three days have been particularly strenuous and eventful. Ordinarily I wouldn't be able to sleep at all, but I'm so tired that I slept like a baby last night. And I'm getting so bored at being shot at that I don't bother to dodge any more. I sat up in the middle of Archie bursts yesterday for five minutes, yawned and refused to turn until they knocked me about a hundred feet. I used to be scared to death of Archie and gunfire from the ground. Now it almost fails to excite even my curiosity.

Day before yesterday we had four dogfights. In the morning we attacked five Huns. I paired off with a Fokker on my level and we manoeuvred for a couple of minutes trying to get on each other's tail. I finally got inside of him, put one hundred rounds into him and he went down out of control. Another one was after me by that time and we had quite a scrap but he made the fatal blunder of reversing his bank and I got on his tail and pumped about two hundred rounds into him. I couldn't see what happened to him as another one was coming down on me from above. This one should have gotten me but he didn't. He had every advantage and one of my guns jammed. I was down on the carpet by that time and had to come back low for five miles with this Hun picking at me while I was trying to clear the stoppage and do a little serious dodging.

Yesterday we did ground straffing down south. That's my idea of a rotten way to pass the time. Orders came through after dinner and all night I felt just like I did that night before the operation. I shivered and sweated all night. I took off with four little twenty-pound bombs strung under my fuselage; then we flew over about four miles across the lines at three thousand feet. Nigger gave the signal when he saw what we were after which was Hun transport and we split up and went down on the carpet.

All the machine guns on the ground opened up and sprayed us with tracer and a few field guns took a crack at us but we got through somehow and dropped our messages with pretty good effect and shot up everything we could see on the ground. I saw what looked like a battery and emptied my guns into it and then chased home zigzagging furiously. As soon as we got back, they told us to get ready to go out and do it again. So over we went and this time I saw a road packed with gun limbers. I dropped my bombs on them and then started raking the road with my guns. My bombs hit right on the side of the road and everything scattered. Two planes were shot up pretty badly and A flight lost a man. Don't know what happened to him.

Then we did a high patrol with A flight. They got after a two-seater and there were some Fokkers up above them that didn't see us on account of the clouds. We went down after them and three of them pulled up to fight us. Inglis and I took them on and the rest went on down. I got into a regular duel with one of them and we fought down from eight thousand to about fifteen hundred. He did a half roll and I did a stall turn above him and dropped right onto his tail. I'd have gotten him if the other one hadn't come on down after me. Then it was my turn to half roll and I was careful to do a good one and not lose any altitude. He half rolled with me a couple of times but the dogfight

Trench Strafing: co-operating with low-flying British scouts in an infantry attack on the Western Front

was working down and he decided to postpone the engagement and dove for home.

Zellers and Dietz and Paskill have been killed.

August 14th

We have moved south for the Battle of Amiens and have an airdrome at Bertangles four miles from Amiens. 17 and 148 are down in this region somewhere.

I heard that Walter Chalaire got shot in the leg on a D. H. Four.

August 17th

I'm not feeling very well today. I fought Huns all night in my sleep and after two hours of real fighting today, I feel all washed out. Yesterday produced the worst scrap that I have yet had the honour to indulge in. It lasted about twenty minutes and the participants were nine little Fokkers and myself. I say participants because each Hun fired at me at least once and I fired at each one of them several times, collectively and individually. We went down on a two-seater and I stuck with him and fought him on down after the others pulled up. It was one of these new Hannoveranners and he licked me properly. They just haven't got any blind spot at all and the pilot was using his front gun on me most of the time. On my way back I spotted a flock of Fokkers about three thousand feet above me.

I didn't know what was going on, but it looked to me as if the thing to do was to suck those Fokkers down on me and then there would be plenty of our machines up above to come down on them and get some easy picking. I knew I was a good way over but I thought sure there would be a squadron of Dolphins about in addition to the S. E.s, so I climbed for all I was worth and waited for the Huns to see me and come down. Archie put up a burst as a signal and I didn't have long to wait. I turned towards the lines and two of them came down. I put my nose down and waited for them to catch up. As soon as one of them opened fire I pulled up in a long zoom and turned.

One Hun overshot and I found myself level with the other one. He half rolled and I did a skid turn and opened up on him. He wasn't much of a pilot because I got about a hundred and fifty rounds into him. He went into a dive. But that first lad was all that could be expected. He got a burst in my right wing on his first crack and now he was stalling up under me and the first thing I knew about it was when I saw his tracer going by. I half rolled and sprayed a few rounds at him and went on down out of it too.

THE DECISIVE FACTOR?

I was getting worried about where the rest of the boys were and couldn't see any signs of an S. E. Three Huns came down on me from above and played their new game. They try to fight in threes. They have some prearranged method of attack by which one sits on your tail while the other two take time about shooting from angles. They were all three firing and all I could do was to stay in a tight bank and pray. I thought I was gone. One of them pulled up and then came straight down to finish me off. I turned towards him and forced him to pull up to keep from overshooting. As soon as I saw his nose go by, I put mine down for I saw it was time to think more about rescuing the decoy than holding any bag for the rest of them.

One Hun was on my tail in a flash and we were both doing about two hundred and fifty. I turned around to see what he was doing and as soon as his tracer showed up close, I pulled straight up. He tried to pull up but overshot and went on by, about fifty feet from me. I was close enough to see his goggles and note all the details of his plane, which was black and white checked with a white nose. I waved to him and I think he waved back, though I'm not sure. I tried to turn my guns on him but he went up like an elevator and tried to turn back to get on my tail.

I put my nose down again and we more or less repeated. The rest of his crew didn't seem to be in a fighting mood and only picked at me from a distance so I got away. I had to come back on the carpet and I shot up some infantry on the ground but it was too hot for me and I zigzagged on home. I felt fine then but before I got back I was shivering so I could hardly land. And I haven't been feeling right since. My heart seems to be trying to stunt all the time.

These present quarters aren't much and the food down here is terrible. Bully beef, boiled potatoes and Brussels sprouts. I've never been able to understand those people who go out into the woods with a tent and a frying pan and have such a wonderful time. And now that I am actually in possession of a tent and a frying pan, I understand that form of exercise much less. Bring back, oh, bring back, my shower and breakfast in bed! True I can't really call this roughing it, with a valet to bring me hot water when there is any water, and a good chef to cook for me when there is anything to cook, and a bartender to shake up a drink when there is anything to shake; but this is closer to nature than my table of organization calls for. Don't bother about my liberty, give me a suite!

A general came over to see us the other day. I was down at the hangars and he walked up unannounced and we started conversing. I didn't know who he was as his insignia wasn't showing on his flying suit and he spoke so familiarly of various matters that I thought he was a captain and we had quite a little argument about these new Hun planes. It turned out that he was the general in London who fixed it up for us to come out with Bish. These British great moguls are the finest in the world. They make Lord Chesterfield appear like a truck driver for polish. He invited me over to his *chateau* for dinner next week.

I hear Cheston has gone West. He was shot down in flames on D. H. Nines.

I was over at a Nine squadron the other day and saw Clayton Knight. He showed me some sketches he had made of planes and fights. They were very good. That boy will be an artist someday if he lives through it.

August 19th

We got permission from the colonel to put on a joint decoy stunt with Springs's flight. Cal and Springs worked out the details. The point of the story was that the Hun was supposed to be surprised. Nigger led and the five of us flew over to 148's drome and rendezvoused at five thousand feet at five yesterday afternoon. We both climbed on the way to the lines and they crossed at about thirteen thousand. We stayed back and climbed up to seventeen thousand and had four planes from A flight up above us. We stayed between Springs and the sun and kept about five miles from him so that Huns wouldn't see us. He worked on over about twelve miles getting some Archie.

Then six Fokkers came up to see what was going on and the Archie ceased. It looked like cold meat to the Huns but they wanted to make sure of it and took their time. They came down to about a thousand feet above Springs and he dove back towards us to get them in proper position for a thorough slaughtering.

Everything was working beautifully and we were waiting for the Huns to start their dive. The trap was all ready to be sprung when the Hun Archie opened up. They didn't fire at us or at Springs but at the Huns. The Huns got the signal and must have seen us as we started down for they put their noses down and beat it back for all they were worth. We didn't get within two miles of them.

But we'll pull our little stunt again and when we do, the slaughter will be terrific. I don't know which will get me first, a bullet or the nervous strain. This decoy game is about the most dangerous thing in the world. I know I'll never be able to shoot at a bird again. I know too well how they must feel. I also sympathize with the nigger who dodges baseballs with his head through a hole.

Cal is prostrated. His family passed one of his letters around and it got in the papers. Needless to say he is going to write nothing more about the war. I saw a letter from his father. It was a peach. He was trying to cheer Cal up instead of making him gloomy with a lot of bum advice. I should like to meet him some day. He certainly has a sense of humour. I don't think he will take me off to one side and ask me if Cal took anything to drink during the war. I imagine he will get on well with any of Cal's friends.

We are going to form a new society,—"The Society for the Extermination of Amateur Aerial Authors," the purpose of which will be to protect the public from a flood of bunk. "Sergeant Pilot Wright" is to be our first Honorary Member. With each fresh paper from home we get a list of new victims. One writer who signs himself the "Terror of the Huns" writes in his article that he opened fire "violently." Wonder he didn't break the trigger! He's proud because he got his Hun right over his own airdrome. Lord, I wish I could catch one within five miles of the lines much less across it. We have to go over to their airdromes after them.

Which reminds me that this volume is getting to be quite a book. I've written three whole books full of it. I am a bit worried about what to do with it. I guess someone will take care of it if anything happens to me. Springs asked me to leave it to him, but he's on Camels and it wouldn't be safe with him. Cal will look after it as long as he is here. It will never do to let the people at home find out the truth about this war. They've been fed on bunk until they'd never believe anything that didn't sound like a monk's story of the Crusades.

Every time I get a paper from home I either break into a loud laugh or get mad. I'm as bad as Springs. I see where all the patriotic women are studying public speaking and bird life. I can't see the why of either.

The Women's Committee of the Council of National Defence is certainly taking a step in the right direction. They have issued special rules about Service Stars regulating how people may proclaim to the world at large that a member of their family is a hero. A man is killed in action—certainly somebody ought to be able to swank about and get his glory! But I don't think they go far enough. Why not benefit the living as well as swank for the dead? Why not help out those that live through it? Let the *bona-fide* wives of dead heroes wear a gold star with an edging of mourning. Let the war brides of lucky cannon fodder wear two gold stars and mourning. Let the would-be wives of eager and successful belligerents wear a single plain gold star and black stockings. Let the anxious and unsuccessful ones wear a gold star and coloured stockings. Thus every woman could swank, mourn, and advertise all at the same time, and the itinerant doughboy would be saved much curiosity and vain labour.

Yes, the Women's Committee is certainly on the job when it comes to winning the war. The American attitude towards soldiers is without parallel or equal and beyond the imaginative concept of even Jules Verne. Every day I hear something new which makes me glad I am in France.

If it were the lower classes who indulged in the rotten, cheap, maudlin sentimentality that even the French peasants scorn, I could understand it. But no, in America our best people have proved the contention of democracy that all are equal by showing how poor democracy's best are, and stooping to a level that aristocracy's servants scorn. Of course, American people are proud that their men are fighting for what they think is right, but at the same time they must go about proclaiming it to the world, taking credit for it, boasting of it, advertising it and endeavouring to transfer the pride in the soldier to selfish egotism. Will American families wear the decorations, wound stripes and service chevrons of their beloved ones also? Why not?

One thing I will say: America's attitude has turned out a fine army of fighters. When they go into battle they fight to the finish because the people at home have shown them just how valuable life is. A British staff colonel told me in Boulogne that the division of U. S. troops that have been with them was the finest body of fighting men that he'd ever seen. He was very flattering but he didn't think much of their higher officers. He said they'd all be killed if they were turned loose with American staff work.

The French are willing to let us have their share of the war cheap. They admit cheerfully that we saved Paris and they are perfectly confident that we are going to win the war without any further argument. We get great news from the South. I hope it's all true. But everybody thought the Cambrai show last Fall was the beginning of the end. Then the Huns turned around and chased us back the whole way and absolutely wiped out the cavalry.

My eyes are so sore that it's getting hard to write. You can't wear goggles when you are out hunting and the wind blows your eyelids when you sideslip or skid. And our ears are ruined forever. The sudden changes of altitude play hell with them. Going up in an elevator a few hundred feet used to affect mine. Now I dive five thousand at a crack and they ache all night.

August 20th

We're doing ground straffing and go out in pairs or alone and make three or four trips a day.

I was out yesterday afternoon and had a busy hour. And I got a chance to see a battle from a grandstand seat. There were heavy clouds at two thousand so I crossed over under them and looked for a target. As I crossed the lines I saw about forty white puffs of smoke in a line, about twenty feet apart. That was a barrage and as the puffs would die away, more would take their places. Nothing could be seen on the ground at all. Further over was a village and high explosive shells were rapidly obliterating it. I would see several buildings rise about twenty feet in a mass, then disintegrate, muck fly about, and then as it settled, I would hear a dull thud and my machine would wobble from the concussion.

Two miles farther I saw some Hun artillery on a road and went down on the carpet. I dropped my bombs and then saw some troops just off the road and put about five hundred rounds into them. Machine gun fire from the ground was pretty hot and then I heard a crack, crack, crack, pitched in a higher key. I looked around and coming down out of the clouds were five Fokkers. Two of them were firing and I could see their tracer coming towards me. I twisted and turned and tried to work back. I was right on the carpet and over a little ruined village. I kept zigzagging and eventually reached a point that I knew was occupied by our troops.

Then I drew the first breath in three minutes. Shells were bursting everywhere—shrapnel in the open spaces with its white puffs and high explosive with its cloud of dust and debris on the trench parapets. Here and there were tanks, some belching lead and some a mass of flames or a misshapen wreck, hit by field guns. I was down right on the ground but saw very few dead bodies but any number of dead horses. The ground was all pockmarked and what little vegetation remained was a light straw in colour from the gas. Further down I saw the Huns using gas, a thin layer of brownish green stuff was drifting slowly along the ground from a trench about three hundred yards long. But no men were to be seen anywhere. Only dead horses and tanks.

The Fokkers were hovering about in the clouds waiting on me to come back or for some other cold meat. I looked my plane over carefully and couldn't see any holes so started back. I was right over our reserve lines and our artillery was banging away and the concussion was making me bob about so I was nearly seasick. I got an idea. The Huns were up in the clouds. Why not beat them at their own game? So I climbed up into the clouds and headed towards where I thought they would be. The clouds were intermittent so I had to climb up to nine thousand before I got high enough to see any distance. I saw my Huns, seven of them now, and worked into position between them and the sun. They went into a cloud and I lost them. Then I got myself lost. I found out where I was and found my Huns again, four of them this time. But before I could get into position I lost them in the clouds.

I went down through a gap and deposited the rest of my ammunition in the Hun trenches and along the roads and went on a personally conducted tour of the battlefield. I saw everything,—advanced trenches, reserve trenches, tanks, reserve tanks, armoured cars, artillery in action, support going up, demolished towns, cuts that once were railroad beds, thousands of yards of barbed wire,—in fact the whole rotten business.

The British seem to be going after the control of the air. So far neither side has ever had the control of the air. First one side and then the other has had the supremacy of the air depending on superiority of planes and pilots but neither side has ever been able to do its air work unmolested or keep the other side from doing theirs. Both sides have accomplished certain things and had to fight constantly to do it. But the British seem to be planning to drive the Huns out of the air by carrying the aerial warfare back to their airdromes. I understand that the Huns have a decided supremacy over the French and Americans. I'd like to get down on the American Front with a British squadron and get some cold meat. I'm tired of having to go so far over. Makes the odds too high against you.

If I was running the war the first thing I would do would be to get control of the air no matter what it cost. That's what's saved England all these centuries—control of the seas. And her fleet is big enough to keep control without fighting. The Air Force would do the same thing.

August 21st

More rumours of more battles. We were in the Folkestone in Boulogne and Henry told us that there is going to be a big push shortly. Push? What's a push to us? That's for the Poor Bloody Infantry to worry over. We push twice a day, seven days in the week. We go over the top between each meal. Oh, yes, the flying corps is the safe place for little Willy,—that is as long as he doesn't have to go near the front!

Nigger and I flew up for tea with Springs. He was not too good. He and Bim have had tombstones made for themselves. They are hollow and if they go down on the Hun side, they are to be filled with high explosive and dropped over, if they are killed on this side, they are to be filled with cognac so it will leak on them.

Mac is back with a new version of the widow of Malta.

Hilary Rex has been killed. He was in a fight with a Fokker and his machine was disabled and he had to land. He landed all right and got out of his plane. The Hun dove on him and shot him as he was standing by his plane.

Armstrong is in the hospital with an explosive bullet in his back.

August 23rd

The colonel has decided that we are to pull a daylight raid on a Hun airdrome. That's a good idea! The 5th. group pulled one off up at Varssenaere but there are not so many Fokkers up there. We'd never get away with it down here. That was a fine show up North though. One of the American Camel squadrons, the 17th, did the dirty work and went down on the carpet. Here's the official report I got out of *Comic Cuts*:

> A raid was carried out by No. 17 American Squadron on Varssenaere Aerodrome, in conjunction with Squadrons of the 5th. Group. After the first two Squadrons had dropped their bombs from a low height, machines of No. 17 American Squadron dived to within 200 feet of the ground and released their bombs, then proceeded to shoot at hangars and huts on the aerodrome, and a *chateau* on the N. E. corner of the aerodrome was also attacked with machine gun fire. The following damage was observed to be caused by this combined operation: a dump of petrol and oil was set on fire, which appeared to set fire to an ammunition dump; six Fokker biplanes were set on fire on the ground, and two destroyed by direct hits from bombs; one

large Gotha hangar was set on fire and another half demolished; a living hut was set on fire and several hangars were seen to be smouldering as the result of phosphorus bombs having fallen on them. In spite of most of the machines taking part being hit at one time or another, all returned safely, favourable ground targets being attacked on the way home.

August 25th
Cal was missing all day and gave me an awful sinking spell. It just made me sick at my stomach to think of him gone. He came back late in the afternoon with a beautiful package. He had a spar in his bottom wing shot through in a dogfight and it broke in two and he side-slipped back and landed in the support trenches. He wiped off the undercarriage but didn't hurt himself. He spent the day with an Archie battery. It was a naval outfit and so had plenty of issue rum. The British Navy seems to do everything but get wet. Cal spent the day swilling rum with the C. O. They let him fire the guns occasionally and he saw a couple of fights through the glasses and brought back a couple of shells to be made into cocktail shakers. He says that the Archie gunners don't expect to hit anything, they just fire for the moral effect.

August 27th
Many things have happened. I hear that Bobby got shot down up at Dunkirk and is no more. Tommy Herbert has been shot in the rear with a phosphorus bullet. Leach has been shot through the shoulder and isn't expected to pull through. Explosive bullet. Read is dead and so is Molly Shaw.

Alex Mathews is dead. He was walking across the airdrome after a movie show over at 48 and a Hun bomber saw the light when the door was opened and dropped a two hundred and twelve-pound bomb on him. They dropped about thirty bombs on the airdrome and killed about forty of 48's men and set fire to the hangars. They broke all the bottles in our bar. Cal and Nigger and I were further ahead and threw ourselves into a ditch. Nothing hit us but we sure were uncomfortable. The night flying Camels brought down one of the Huns, it had five engines and a crew of six men. It came down in flames and lit up the whole place.

Barksdale got shot down in an S. E. and landed in German territory but set fire to his plane and got in a shell hole and covered himself up with dirt. The next morning the British attacked and took that sector. Barksdale said the Scotsman who pulled him out couldn't speak English any better than the Germans and he thought he was a prisoner at first.

One of our noblest he-men, a regular fire-eater to hear him tell it, has turned yellow at the front. He was quite an athlete and always admitted he was very hot stuff. He was ordered up on a bomb raid and refused to go. The British sent him back to American Headquarters with the recommendation that he be court-martialled for cowardice. He would have been too, if his brother hadn't have been high up on the A. E. F. staff. He pulled some bluff about the machines being unsafe and they finally sent him home as an instructor and promoted him. He may strut around back home but I'll bet he never can look a real man in the eye again.

Springs had a wheel shot off in the air last week. Ralston came back and took up a wheel to show him and everybody ran about the airdrome firing Very pistols and holding up wheels for him to see. He understood and side-slipped down all right without killing himself. He said he saw a Dolphin pilot kill himself several weeks ago landing with a wheel gone. The Dolphin pilot didn't know it was off and the plane turned over on him.

Bonnalie was never considered much of a pilot. He was an aeroplane designer before he enlisted and knew a lot of theory but he took a long time to learn to fly and no one thought he would ever be much good. He put on one of the best shows on record and has been decorated with the D. S. O. His citation appeared in *The Gazette*. Here it is:

> On the 13th of August, this officer led two other machines on a long photographic reconnaissance. Bonnalie, in spite of the presence of numerous enemy aircraft, succeeded in taking all the required photographs and was returning to our lines; they were intercepted by six Fokker biplanes which dived to the attack. In the ensuing combat Lt. Bonnalie perceived one of our planes making its way to the lines with an Enemy Aircraft on its tail. This officer at once broke off combat with the remaining E. A. and dived to the assistance of the machine in trouble. He drove off the E. A. regardless of the bullets which were ripping up his own machine from attacking E. A.
> Eventually half of Lt. Bonnalie's tail plane was shot away and the elevator wire shot through and the machine began to fall out of control in stalling sideslips. Lt. Bonnalie managed to keep

the machine facing towards our lines by means of the rudder control while the observer and the third machine drove off the E. A. which were attacking. Eventually with the aid of his observer who, as the machine was tail heavy, left his cockpit and lay along the cowling in front of the pilot, Lt. Bonnalie re-crossed the trenches at a low altitude and managed to right the machine sufficiently to avoid a fatal crash. The machine crashed within four miles of the lines. Lt. Bonnalie's machine was riddled with bullets.

Now that's what I call a good show. Who would have thought it? There's an R. F. C. officer over at 20 Squadron on Bristols, from New York, named Paul Iaccaci, who has the D. F. C. and is quite a pilot.

17 and 148 have been having a hard time. 17 has lost Campbell, Hamilton, Glenn, Spidle, Gracie, Case, Shearman, Shoemaker, Roberts, Bittinger, Jackson, Todd, Wise, Thomas, Frost, Wicks, Tillinghast and a couple of others. Hamilton and Tipton were the two best Camel pilots we had. And they have about six others in the hospital too. Wicks and Shoemaker collided in a fight.

148 has lost Curtis, Forster, Siebald, Frobisher, Mandell, Kenyon and Jenkinson; and Dorsey and Wiley and Zistell are in the hospital. Jenkinson, Forster and Siebald went down in flames. Frobisher was shot through the stomach and died later.

Of course that's not a bad showing when you consider that they have shot down a lot of Huns and done a lot of ground straffing and have been flying Camels which were all the British could spare them. The British have washed out the Camels and are refitting their own squadrons with Snipes. A Camel can't fight a Fokker and the British know it.

But we've lost a lot of good men. It's only a question of time until we all get it. I'm all shot to pieces. I only hope I can stick it. I don't want to quit. My nerves are all gone and I can't stop. I've lived beyond my time already.

It's not the fear of death that's done it. I'm still not afraid to die. It's this eternal flinching from it that's doing it and has made a coward out of me. Few men live to know what real fear is. It's something that grows on you, day by day, that eats into your constitution and undermines your sanity. I have never been serious about anything in my life and now I know that I'll never be otherwise again. But my seriousness will be a burlesque for no one will recognize it. Here I am, twenty-four years old. I look forty and I feel ninety. I've lost all interest in life beyond the next patrol. No one Hun will ever get me and I'll never fall into a trap, but sooner or later I'll be forced to fight against odds that are too long or perhaps a stray shot from the ground will be lucky and I will have gone in vain. Or my motor will cut out when we are trench straffing or a wing will pull off in a dive. Oh, for a parachute! The Huns are using them now. I haven't a chance. I know, and it's this eternal waiting around that's killing me. I've even lost my taste for licker. It doesn't seem to do me any good now. I guess I'm stale.

Last week I actually got frightened in the air and lost my head. Then I found ten Huns and took them all on and I got one of them down out of control. I got my nerve back by that time and came back home and slept like a baby for the first time in two months. What a blessing sleep is! I know now why men go out and take such long chances and pull off such wild stunts. No discipline in the world could make them do what they do of their own accord. I know now what a brave man is. I know now how men laugh at death and welcome it. I know now why Ball went over and sat above a Hun airdrome and dared them to come up and fight with him. It takes a brave man to even experience real fear. A coward couldn't last long enough at the job to get to that stage. What price salvation now?

No date
War is a horrible thing, a grotesque comedy. And it is so useless. This war won't prove anything. All we'll do when we win is to substitute one sort of Dictator for another. In the meantime, we have destroyed our best resources. Human life, the most precious thing in the world, has become the cheapest. After we've won this war by drowning the Hun in our own blood, in five years' time the sentimental fools at home will be taking up a collection for these same Huns that are killing us now and our fool politicians will be cooking up another good war. Why shouldn't they? They have to keep the public stirred up to keep their jobs and they don't have to fight and they can get soft berths for their sons and their friends' sons. To me the most contemptible cur in the world is the man who lets political influence be used to keep him away from the front. For he lets another man die in his place.

The worst thing about this war is that it takes the best. If it lasts long enough the world will be populated by cowards and weaklings and their children. And the whole thing is so useless, so unnecessary, so terrible! Even those that live through it will never be fit for anything else. Look at what the Civil War did for the South. It wasn't the defeat that wrecked us. It was the loss of half our manhood and the demoralisation of the other half. After the war the survivors scattered to the four corners of the earth; they roamed the West; they fought the battles of foreign nations; they became freebooters, politicians, prospectors, gamblers, and those who got over it, good citizens. My great-uncle was a captain in the Confederate Army and served throughout the war. He became a banker, a merchant, a farmer and a good citizen, but he was always a little different from other men and now I know where the difference lay.

At the age of seventy he hadn't gotten over those four years of misery and spiritual damnation. My father used to explain to me that he wasn't himself. But he was himself, that was just the trouble with him. The rest were just out of step. My father used to always warn me about licker by telling me that uncle learned to drink in the army and it finally killed him. I always used to think myself that as long as it took forty years to do it, he shouldn't speak disrespectfully of uncle's little weakness. And as the old gentleman picked up stomach trouble from bad food in the campaign of '62, I always had a hunch that perhaps the licker had an unfair advantage of him.

The devastation of the country is too horrible to describe. It looks from the air as if the gods had made a gigantic steam roller, forty miles wide and run it from the coast to Switzerland, leaving its spike holes behind as it went.

I'm sick. At night when the colonel calls up to give us our orders, my ears are afire until I hear what we are to do the next morning. Then I can't sleep for thinking about it all night. And while I'm waiting around all day for the afternoon patrol, I think I am going crazy. I keep watching the clock and figuring how long I have to live. Then I go out to test out my engine and guns and walk around and have a drink and try to write a little and try not to think. And I move my arms and legs around and think that perhaps tomorrow I won't be able to.

Sometimes I think I am getting the same disease that Springs has when I get sick at my stomach. He always flies with a bottle of milk of magnesia in one pocket and a flask of gin in the other. If one doesn't help him he tries the other. It gives me a dizzy feeling every time I hear of the men that are gone. And they have gone so fast I can't keep track of them; every time two pilots meet it is only to swap news of who's killed. When a person takes sick, lingers in bed a few days, dies

and is buried on the third day, it all seems regular and they pass on into the great beyond in an orderly manner and you accept their departure as an accomplished fact. But when you lunch with a man, talk to him, see him go out and get in his plane in the prime of his youth and the next day someone tells you that he is dead—it just doesn't sink in and you can't believe it.

And the oftener it happens the harder it is to believe. I've lost over a hundred friends, so they tell me,—I've seen only seven or eight killed—but to me they aren't dead yet. They are just around the corner, I think, and I'm still expecting to run into them any time. I dream about them at night when I do sleep a little and sometimes I dream that someone is killed who really isn't. Then I don't know who is and who isn't. I saw a man in Boulogne the other day that I had dreamed I saw killed and I thought I was seeing a ghost. I can't realise that any of them are gone. Surely human life is not a candle to be snuffed out. The English have all turned spiritualistic since the war. I used to think that was sort of farfetched but now it's hard for me to believe that a man ever becomes even a ghost. I have sort of a feeling that he stays just as he is and simply jumps behind a cloud or steps through a mirror. Springs keeps talking about Purgatory and Hades and the Elysian Fields. Well, we sure are close to something.

When I go out to get in my plane my feet are like lead—I am just barely able to drag them after me. But as soon as I take off I am all right again. That is, I feel all right, though I know I am too reckless. Last week I actually tried to ram a Hun. I was in a tight place and it was the only thing I could do. He didn't have the nerve to stand the gaff and turned and I got him. I poured both guns into him with fiendish glee and stuck to him though three of them were on my tail. I laughed at them. I ran into an old Harry Tate over the lines the other day where he had no business to be. He waved to me and I waved back to him and we went after a balloon. Imagine it! An R. E. Eight out balloon straffing! I was glad to find someone else as crazy as I was.

And yet if I had received orders to do it the night before, I wouldn't have slept a wink and would have chewed up a good pair of boots or gotten drunk. We didn't get the balloon—they pulled it down before we got to it, but it was a lot of fun. That lad deserves the V. C. And he got all the Archie in the world on the way back. So did I, for I stayed with him. He had a high speed of about eighty and was a sitting shot for a good gunner but I don't think he got hit. I didn't.

I only hope I can stick it out and not turn yellow. I've heard of men landing in Germany when they didn't have to. They'd be better off dead because they've got to live with themselves the rest of their lives. I wouldn't mind being shot down; I've got no taste for glory and I'm no more good, but I've got to keep on until I can quit honourably. All I'm fighting for now is my own self-respect.

17 and 148 seem to get a lot of Huns these days. That's one thing about a Camel; you've got to shoot down all the Huns to get home yourself. There's not a chance to run for it. Clay, Springs and Vaughn are all piling up big scores. But their scores won't be anything to those piled up on the American and French fronts. Down there if six of them jump on one Hun and get him, all six of them get credit for one Hun apiece. On the British front each one of them would get credit for one sixth of a Hun. Of course, what happens up here is that the man who was nearest him and did most of the shooting gets credit for one Hun and the others withdraw their claims. Either that or the C. O. decides who should get credit for it and tears up the other combat reports.

Cal has five or six now and I've got four to my credit. Springs and Clay have been decorated by the king with the D. F. C. Hamilton and Campbell got it posthumously and Kindley and Vaughn have been put in for it. Cal is going to get it too. Springs tells me that Clay is the finest patrol leader at the front. He's certainly gotten away with some good work from all reports. And on Clerget Camels too! These boys are lucky if they just get back.

I heard unofficially that Clay and Springs are going to get squadrons of their own and that Cal and I are to take their flights. Not if we can help it! Tubby Ralston is down there in Springs's flight now and he reports hell on roller skates.

I hear that Tipton and Curtis and Tillinghast are prisoners. I'm glad they aren't done in for good.

Clay and Springs got separated from their men after a dogfight the other day and decided they'd have a look at Hunland by themselves. They found a formation of ten Hannoveranners and jumped on them. These Hannoveranners have been licking us all so regularly that they wanted to make sure of getting one so they both leapt on the rear plane to make sure of it and one took him from above and the other from below. The rest of them mixed in and they had trouble getting out of it. They kidded each other all day about what rotten shots they were and that afternoon Rainor of 56 flew over to tell them that he was down below and saw their Hannoveranner crash. They thought he was kidding them at first but he gave them the pinpoints and they flew over there again and sure enough there was the crash.

Our infantry pushed the next day and they went up in a tender and got up to the crash. They were stripping it when the Hun artillery opened up on them and all they brought back was the black crosses off the fuselage and the machine guns. The pilot's seat looked like a sieve where Clay had got a burst in from below and the cowling was full of holes from above where Springs was decorating the observer. That's some shooting. They said the way the plane hit it looked like one of them must have still been alive as it wasn't smashed up badly. It had one of the new Opal motors in it. That's the hardest plane to fight on the front.

Everybody in 17 and 148 are still 1st. lieutenants. Yet all the regulars and politicians' sons stay at home and get their promotions automatically.

I heard that Ed Cronin was killed on D. H. Fours down South. He was sent out late in the afternoon and had to land in the dark when he came back and cracked up. Jake Stanley was shot down on Bristols and is in a German hospital. Anderson, Roberts, Fred Shoemaker, Wells, Leyson and Bill Mooney are all missing. Touchstone is a prisoner of war and wounded and so is Clayton Knight with a bullet in his leg. Knight got into a fight with a bunch of Fokkers and they shot his machine all to pieces. He was flying a D. H. Nine and his observer was wounded early in the fight so all he had was his front gun. They thought he went down in flames but got a postcard from him later that he was alive. Frank Sidler has been killed and so has Ritter and Perkins and Suiter and Tommy Evans and Earl Adams.

I saw Springs the other day in Boulogne. He said his girl at home sent him a pair of these Ninette and Rintintin luck charms. Since then he's lost five men, been shot down twice himself, lost all his money at blackjack and only gotten one Hun. He says he judges from that that she is unfaithful to him. So he has discarded them and says he is looking for a new charm and that the best one is a garter taken from the left leg of a virgin in the dark of the moon. I know they are lucky but I'd be afraid to risk one. Something might happen to her and then you'd be killed sure. A stocking to tie over my nose and a Columbian half dollar and that last sixpence and a piece of my first crash seem to take care of me all right, though I am not superstitious.

(Original) Editor's Note

Here the diary ends due to the death of its author in aerial combat. He was shot down by a German plane twenty miles behind the German lines. He was given a decent burial by the Germans and his grave was later found by the Red Cross.

ALSO FROM LEONAUR
AVAILABLE IN SOFTCOVER OR HARDCOVER WITH DUST JACKET

WINGED WARFARE *by William A. Bishop*—The Experiences of a Canadian 'Ace' of the R.F.C. During the First World War.

THE STORY OF THE LAFAYETTE ESCADRILLE *by George Thenault*—A famous fighter squadron in the First World War by its commander..

R.F.C.H.Q. *by Maurice Baring*—The command & organisation of the British Air Force during the First World War in Europe.

SIXTY SQUADRON R.A.F. *by A. J. L. Scott*—On the Western Front During the First World War.

THE STRUGGLE IN THE AIR *by Charles C. Turner*—The Air War Over Europe During the First World War.

WITH THE FLYING SQUADRON *by H. Rosher*—Letters of a Pilot of the Royal Naval Air Service During the First World War.

OVER THE WEST FRONT *by "Spin" & "Contact"* —Two Accounts of British Pilots During the First World War in Europe, Short Flights With the Cloud Cavalry by "Spin" and Cavalry of the Clouds by "Contact".

SKYFIGHTERS OF FRANCE *by Henry Farré*—An account of the French War in the Air during the First World War.

THE HIGH ACES *by Laurence la Tourette Driggs*—French, American, British, Italian & Belgian pilots of the First World War 1914-18.

PLANE TALES OF THE SKIES *by Wilfred Theodore Blake*—The experiences of pilots over the Western Front during the Great War.

IN THE CLOUDS ABOVE BAGHDAD *by J. E. Tennant*—Recollections of the R. F. C. in Mesopotamia during the First World War against the Turks.

THE SPIDER WEB *by P. I. X. (Theodore Douglas Hallam)*—Royal Navy Air Service Flying Boat Operations During the First World War by a Flight Commander

EAGLES OVER THE TRENCHES *by James R. McConnell & William B. Perry*—Two First Hand Accounts of the American Escadrille at War in the Air During World War 1-Flying For France: With the American Escadrille at Verdun and Our Pilots in the Air

KNIGHTS OF THE AIR *by Bennett A. Molter*—An American Pilot's View of the Aerial War of the French Squadrons During the First World War.

AVAILABLE ONLINE AT **www.leonaur.com**
AND FROM ALL GOOD BOOK STORES

ALSO FROM LEONAUR
AVAILABLE IN SOFTCOVER OR HARDCOVER WITH DUST JACKET

OFFICERS & GENTLEMEN *by Peter Hawker & William Graham*—Two Accounts of British Officers During the Peninsula War: Officer of Light Dragoons by Peter Hawker & Campaign in Portugal and Spain by William Graham.

THE WALCHEREN EXPEDITION *by Anonymous*—The Experiences of a British Officer of the 81st Regt. During the Campaign in the Low Countries of 1809.

LADIES OF WATERLOO *by Charlotte A. Eaton, Magdalene de Lancey & Juana Smith*—The Experiences of Three Women During the Campaign of 1815: Waterloo Days by Charlotte A. Eaton, A Week at Waterloo by Magdalene de Lancey & Juana's Story by Juana Smith.

JOURNAL OF AN OFFICER IN THE KING'S GERMAN LEGION *by John Frederick Hering*—Recollections of Campaigning During the Napoleonic Wars.

JOURNAL OF AN ARMY SURGEON IN THE PENINSULAR WAR *by Charles Boutflower*—The Recollections of a British Army Medical Man on Campaign During the Napoleonic Wars.

ON CAMPAIGN WITH MOORE AND WELLINGTON *by Anthony Hamilton*—The Experiences of a Soldier of the 43rd Regiment During the Peninsular War.

THE ROAD TO AUSTERLITZ *by R. G. Burton*—Napoleon's Campaign of 1805.

SOLDIERS OF NAPOLEON *by A. J. Doisy De Villargennes & Arthur Chuquet*—The Experiences of the Men of the French First Empire: Under the Eagles by A. J. Doisy De Villargennes & Voices of 1812 by Arthur Chuquet.

INVASION OF FRANCE, 1814 *by F. W. O. Maycock*—The Final Battles of the Napoleonic First Empire.

LEIPZIG—A CONFLICT OF TITANS *by Frederic Shoberl*—A Personal Experience of the 'Battle of the Nations' During the Napoleonic Wars, October 14th-19th, 1813.

SLASHERS *by Charles Cadell*—The Campaigns of the 28th Regiment of Foot During the Napoleonic Wars by a Serving Officer.

BATTLE IMPERIAL *by Charles William Vane*—The Campaigns in Germany & France for the Defeat of Napoleon 1813-1814.

SWIFT & BOLD *by Gibbes Rigaud*—The 60th Rifles During the Peninsula War.

AVAILABLE ONLINE AT **www.leonaur.com**
AND FROM ALL GOOD BOOK STORES

www.ingramcontent.com/pod-product-compliance
Lightning Source LLC
Chambersburg PA
CBHW031617160426
43196CB00006B/167